Anatomy of IoT Botnets and Detection Methods

The book *Anatomy of IoT Botnets and Detection Methods* delves into the evolving landscape of cybersecurity threats associated with the Internet of Things (IoT), specifically focusing on the anatomy, behavior, and detection of IoT-based botnets. As IoT devices proliferate in both consumer and industrial settings, their inherent vulnerabilities—such as weak authentication, limited processing power, and lack of regular updates—make them prime targets for attackers. The book begins by exploring how IoT botnets are formed, highlighting key attack vectors such as malware propagation, command and control (C&C) mechanisms, and commonly exploited protocols such as Telnet and UPnP. Notable case studies, including the Mirai and Mozi botnets, illustrate real-world impacts, emphasizing the scale and damage these threats can inflict. The core of the book then transitions into detection methodologies, covering both traditional and AI-driven approaches. Techniques such as signature-based detection, anomaly detection using machine learning, network traffic analysis, and honeypot deployment are thoroughly examined. The authors also address the challenges in detecting IoT botnets, including encrypted traffic, device heterogeneity, and low visibility in resource-constrained devices. Furthermore, the book emphasizes the importance of proactive defense strategies, such as firmware hardening, secure boot mechanisms, and real-time behavioral analytics. It underscores the role of collaborative intelligence sharing among stakeholders to enhance detection capabilities. By integrating theoretical concepts with practical insights and current research trends, the book provides a comprehensive guide for researchers, cybersecurity professionals, and IoT developers aiming to understand and counteract botnet threats. Ultimately, *Anatomy of IoT Botnet and Detection Methods* serves as a crucial resource for strengthening the cybersecurity posture of IoT ecosystems through informed detection and mitigation practices. The content of the book is categorized into the following sub-sections:

- **Introduction to IoT and Botnets:** An overview of IoT technology, its adoption, and the rising threat of botnets.

- **IoT Device Vulnerabilities:** Analysis of common security weaknesses in IoT devices that cybercriminals exploit.
- **Botnet Architecture:** Detailed examination of how IoT botnets are structured, including command and control mechanisms.
- **Infection and Propagation:** Methods used by attackers to spread malware across IoT networks.
- **Detection Techniques:** Overview of current detection methods, including anomaly detection, signature-based approaches, and machine learning.
- **Mitigation Strategies:** Practical advice on how to secure IoT devices, including best practices for manufacturers and users.
- **Case Studies:** Real-world examples of IoT botnet attacks and their impact.

The book concludes with a discussion on the future of IoT security, emphasizing the need for continuous innovation in detection and prevention methods.

Anatomy of IoT Botnets and Detection Methods

Umang Garg
Neha Gupta
Rajesh Singh
Anita Gehlot
Ankur Dumka

CRC Press
Taylor & Francis Group
Boca Raton London New York

CRC Press is an imprint of the
Taylor & Francis Group, an **informa** business

Designed cover image: Shutterstock Image ID 2490430935

First edition published 2026
by CRC Press
2385 NW Executive Center Drive, Suite 320, Boca Raton FL 33431

and by CRC Press
4 Park Square, Milton Park, Abingdon, Oxon, OX14 4RN

CRC Press is an imprint of Taylor & Francis Group, LLC

© 2026 Umang Garg, Neha Gupta, Rajesh Singh, Anita Gehlot and Ankur Dumka

ISBN: 978-1-041-05022-3 (hbk)
ISBN: 978-1-041-05135-0 (pbk)
ISBN: 978-1-003-63146-0 (ebk)

DOI: 10.1201/9781003631460

Typeset in Sabon
by SPi Technologies India Pvt Ltd (Straive)

This work is dedicated to the countless cybersecurity researchers, engineers, and ethical hackers who work tirelessly to protect our digital world, and to my family, whose unwavering support made this journey possible.

Contents

Foreword   viii
Preface   ix
Acknowledgments   xiii
Author biographies   xiv
List of abbreviations   xvi

1 Introduction   1

2 IoT device vulnerabilities   21

3 Understanding IoT botnets   47

4 Real-world IoT botnet case studies   87

5 Detection techniques for IoT botnets   101

6 Mitigation and prevention strategies   121

7 The role of IoT manufacturers and developers   137

8 Global perspectives on IoT security   159

9 Future trends in IoT botnets and security   172

Summary   200
Bibliography   204
Index   206

Foreword

The rapid proliferation of IoT devices has transformed the way we live, work, and interact with technology. From smart homes and connected vehicles to industrial control systems, IoT has become deeply integrated into modern infrastructure. However, this growth has also introduced unprecedented security challenges, particularly in the form of IoT botnets—malicious networks of compromised devices orchestrated to launch large-scale cyberattacks.

Anatomy of IoT Botnets and Detection Methods arrives at a critical juncture in our digital evolution. This book offers a timely and thorough examination of how IoT botnets are structured, deployed, and leveraged by cybercriminals. It combines real-world case studies, technical insights, and advanced detection techniques to equip readers with both the foundational knowledge and practical tools needed to defend against these threats. The author skillfully bridges the gap between theoretical research and applied cybersecurity, making this work valuable not only for academics and students but also for practitioners on the front lines of digital defense. As cyber threats become more complex and distributed, the ability to understand and detect botnet activity at the IoT level is no longer optional—it is essential. I commend the authors for tackling such a multifaceted subject with clarity and precision. This book is not only a contribution to cybersecurity literature but also a call to action for stronger, smarter, and more collaborative efforts in securing our connected future.

Thank you

Preface

The widespread adoption of IoT devices has deeply embedded smart technology into everyday life, revolutionizing sectors from home automation to critical infrastructure. Particularly within Industry 4.0, IoT, along with cloud computing and data analytics, has transformed domains such as smart manufacturing, energy systems, biomedical applications, and healthcare through automation, real-time monitoring, and data-driven decision-making. However, this technological advancement brings significant cybersecurity concerns. Integrating IoT into legacy systems—often built on outdated protocols and weak access controls—creates vulnerabilities that cybercriminals can exploit. Recent statistics underscore the growing threat; for instance, Fortinet reported that 55% of smart manufacturing firms in India experienced more than six cyber intrusions in 2023, up dramatically from 11% the previous year. Similarly, Bitdefender highlighted that consumer IoT devices such as smart TVs, plugs, and routers contribute heavily to system vulnerabilities, with smart TVs alone accounting for 34%. The increasing connectivity of these devices fosters malicious activities such as DoS attacks, replay attacks, crypto-jacking, and spoofing, all of which compromise system integrity and privacy. A notable incident in 2024 involved the breach of over 576,000 fake accounts, illustrating how consumer-level IoT devices are susceptible to mass-scale attacks. These events not only endanger personal information but also pose serious risks to public safety and national security. The heterogeneous nature of IoT systems, combined with inconsistent security practices and device limitations, further complicates defense mechanisms. Implementing robust, end-to-end security frameworks and access controls is vital to ensure that only authorized users can operate connected devices. Given these challenges, a strong foundational understanding of IoT security is essential. This book addresses these urgent issues by presenting a comprehensive coverage of modern IoT security practices. Featuring expert contributions from around the world, each chapter functions as a standalone section that offers insights, tools, and methodologies to build resilient and secure IoT ecosystems.

The **first chapter** "Introduction" provides a foundational understanding of the IoT, outlining its evolution, applications, and growing relevance in modern digital ecosystems. It introduces the concept of IoT, highlighting how interconnected devices enable seamless automation and data exchange across various sectors. Section 1.2 explores the key challenges in IoT, such as device heterogeneity, scalability, and integration with legacy systems. In Section 1.3, the focus shifts to critical security issues, including weak authentication, data breaches, and limited device-level protection. Section 1.4 discusses the emergence and rapid growth of IoT botnets, emphasizing how vulnerable devices are exploited for malicious purposes. Section 1.5 outlines the primary objectives and scope of the book, detailing the importance of detecting and mitigating IoT botnets. Finally, Section 1.6 concludes the chapter by reinforcing the urgency of addressing IoT security challenges and sets the stage for the subsequent in-depth exploration of detection methods and mitigation strategies.

The **second chapter** delves into the various vulnerabilities that make IoT devices susceptible to cyber threats. It begins in Section 2.1 with an overview of IoT architecture, key communication protocols, and the underlying technologies that form the foundation of IoT systems. Section 2.2 identifies common security weaknesses, such as insecure default settings, outdated software, and lack of regular updates. Section 2.3 focuses on firmware and software vulnerabilities, which often expose devices to remote exploitation. Section 2.4 highlights issues related to weak or missing authentication and authorization mechanisms, enabling unauthorized access. Section 2.5 addresses insufficient data protection and privacy, where sensitive information is left unencrypted or poorly secured. Section 2.6 emphasizes the critical role manufacturers play in ensuring device security through secure development practices, timely patches, and transparency. The chapter concludes in Section 2.7 by summarizing the major threats and reinforcing the importance of addressing these vulnerabilities to build secure IoT ecosystems.

The **third chapter** provides an in-depth analysis of IoT botnets, detailing their structure, evolution, and impact on cybersecurity. Section 3.1 introduces the anatomy of a botnet, explaining how compromised devices, or "bots," are controlled by a central entity. Section 3.2 traces the development of botnets from traditional PC-based networks to modern IoT botnets, which exploit vulnerable smart devices. Section 3.3 outlines the most common attacks launched by botnets, including DDoS, spam campaigns, and data theft. Section 3.4 explores the C&C infrastructure, the backbone of botnet operations that enables remote coordination and execution of malicious tasks. Section 3.5 discusses how botnets spread through various infection vectors and propagation techniques. Section 3.6 examines how they maintain persistence and evade detection through obfuscation and stealth tactics. The chapter concludes in Section 3.7, emphasizing the complexity and growing threat of IoT botnets and setting the stage for detection and mitigation strategies.

The **fourth chapter** explores prominent real-world IoT botnet attacks to provide insight into their structure, behavior, and impact. Section 4.1 focuses on the Mirai botnet, which gained global attention by hijacking IoT devices through weak default credentials and launching large-scale DDoS attacks. Section 4.2 examines the Hajime botnet, notable for its peer-to-peer architecture and attempts to secure devices post-infection, raising questions about intent and ethical hacking. Section 4.3 highlights the Reaper botnet, which differs from Mirai by exploiting known software vulnerabilities to propagate more intelligently and aggressively. Section 4.4 provides an analysis of recent IoT botnet attacks, showcasing emerging trends and techniques used by attackers. Section 4.5 summarizes key research findings from these case studies, identifying common vulnerabilities, attack patterns, and lessons learned. These case studies underscore the evolving threat landscape and emphasize the urgent need for enhanced security practices across IoT networks to mitigate future botnet threats effectively.

The **fifth chapter** explores various techniques used to detect IoT botnets, focusing on both traditional and advanced methods. Section 5.1 introduces signature-based detection, which relies on known patterns of malicious activity but struggles against new or evolving threats. Section 5.2 delves into anomaly and behavior-based detection, with 5.2.1 covering self-intelligence-based behavior models that adapt to changing environments, and 5.2.2 explaining programmed behavior-based approaches using predefined rules. Section 5.3 discusses DNS-based analysis, a technique that monitors domain name queries to identify suspicious activities linked to botnet command-and-control servers. Section 5.4 highlights Explainable AI (XAI)-based approaches, which enhance the transparency and trustworthiness of AI-driven detection models. Section 5.5 focuses on network traffic analysis and behavioral monitoring to uncover irregular patterns indicative of botnet activity. Finally, Section 5.6 outlines the major challenges in IoT botnet detection, such as device heterogeneity, encrypted traffic, and limited processing resources, emphasizing the need for adaptive and scalable solutions.

The **sixth chapter** focuses on practical strategies to mitigate and prevent IoT botnet threats by strengthening device and network security. Section 6.1 outlines best practices for securing IoT devices, including disabling unused services, changing default credentials, and enabling security features by default. Section 6.2 emphasizes the importance of regular firmware updates and patch management to fix known vulnerabilities and protect against evolving threats. Section 6.3 discusses the implementation of strong encryption protocols and robust authentication techniques to ensure secure communication and user validation. Section 6.4 highlights network isolation and segmentation as effective ways to contain breaches by limiting device-to-device communication within networks. Section 6.5 explores incident response and recovery mechanisms, such as early detection, automated containment, and system restoration, to minimize damage and downtime during attacks. The chapter concludes in Section 6.6 by reinforcing the need for a layered, proactive defense strategy to build resilient IoT environments against future botnet threats.

The **seventh chapter** emphasizes the critical responsibility of IoT manufacturers and developers in building secure devices and ecosystems. Section 7.1 introduces the Secure Software Development Life Cycle (SDLC) tailored for IoT, highlighting the need to integrate security practices at every stage—from design to deployment. Section 7.2 explores the concept of Security by Design, where security is embedded as a foundational element rather than added later, focusing on secure coding, hardware integrity, and risk assessments. Section 7.3 underscores the importance of user education and awareness, as many vulnerabilities stem from user misconfigurations or lack of knowledge. Section 7.4 reviews industry standards and certifications, such as ISO/IEC and NIST guidelines, which help establish trust and consistency in IoT security practices. The chapter concludes in Section 7.5 by stressing the collective responsibility of developers, manufacturers, and users to prioritize security and build resilient, trustworthy IoT systems from the ground up.

The **eighth chapter** presents a global overview of efforts to enhance IoT security through collaboration, regulation, and standardization. Section 8.1 discusses international standards and frameworks, such as those developed by ISO, ITU, and NIST, which provide guidelines for securing IoT systems and promoting interoperability across borders. Section 8.2 explores the role of governments and regulatory bodies in enforcing compliance, establishing cybersecurity mandates, and supporting secure innovation through legislation and public policy. Section 8.3 highlights collaborative efforts among nations, industries, and research institutions to combat IoT botnets through information sharing, coordinated response, and public-private partnerships. Section 8.4 examines the future of global IoT security, focusing on the growing importance of unified strategies, AI-driven defense mechanisms, and resilient infrastructure in an increasingly connected world. The chapter concludes in Section 8.5 by emphasizing that securing the global IoT landscape requires coordinated, forward-thinking approaches to stay ahead of evolving threats.

The **ninth chapter** explores the evolving landscape of IoT botnets and the future of cybersecurity in increasingly connected environments. Section 9.1 identifies emerging threats in IoT ecosystems, such as more sophisticated botnet architectures and the exploitation of newer device categories such as wearables and autonomous systems. Section 9.2 examines the role of artificial intelligence and machine learning in future botnets, where intelligent malware may adapt in real-time, making detection and defense more difficult. Section 9.3 focuses on strategies for predicting and preparing for the next wave of attacks by analyzing threat patterns and adopting proactive security frameworks. Section 9.4 presents innovations in detection and prevention technologies, including AI-powered threat hunting, blockchain-based integrity checks, and edge computing for real-time protection. The chapter concludes in Section 9.5 by emphasizing the need for continuous research, collaboration, and innovation to stay ahead of rapidly advancing threats and secure the future of IoT.

Acknowledgments

We extend our sincere gratitude to Prof. R.C. Joshi, Hon'ble advisor of Graphic Era Deemed to be University, Dehradun for his invaluable support and encouragement. We sincerely appreciate the chapter contributors across different countries for their expertise and dedication, which have significantly enriched this handbook. Their research and insights have made it a valuable resource for the cybersecurity community. We also thank the reviewers for their meticulous evaluations and constructive feedback. Their critical insights have been instrumental in enhancing the clarity and quality of each chapter.

We thank the management, Pro-VC sir, head of the department, and faculty members of the Department of Computer Science and Engineering, MIT ADT University, Pune, India, for affording their valuable support and inspiration. The book has been inspired by the domain expertise of the editors in the area of cybersecurity, reflecting their extensive research, academic contributions, and practical insights in this evolving field. Their deep understanding of emerging threats, security frameworks, and cutting-edge technologies has played a crucial role in shaping the themes and content of this authored volume.

We would also like to extend our sincere gratitude to the Taylor and Francis publishing team, particularly Ms. Gabriella Williams, Commissioning Editor, and her dedicated team. Their constant encouragement, continuous assistance, and unwavering support have been instrumental in bringing this handbook to completion. We wholeheartedly thank our family for being the source of continuous love, unconditional support, and prayers not only for this work but throughout our life.

Last but far from least, we express our heartfelt thanks to the Almighty for bestowing over us the courage to face the complexities of life and complete this work.

Author biographies

Umang Garg, PhD, is working as an Associate professor in the School of Computer Science and Engineering, IILM University, Gurugram, Haryana, India. He is committed to advance both research and teaching in the field of security. He has a combined research and teaching experience of over 14 years and done a significant contribution toward the research community working in IoT security using machine learning. Dr. Garg has done PhD (IoT Security), MTech (CSE), and BTech (CSE), demonstrating his strong academic background. He has published more than 40 research articles in reputed journals and highly indexed conferences. He is a member of Computer Society of India (CSI) and Institute of Electrical and Electronics Engineers (IEEE).

Neha Gupta, PhD, is working as an Assistant Professor in the School of Computer Science and Engineering, IILM University, Gurugram, Haryana, India. She is committed to advance both research and teaching in the field of IoT and healthcare applications. She has a combined research and teaching experience of over 12 years and done a significant contribution toward the research community working in IoT healthcare applications. Dr. Gupta has done PhD (5G-IoT in Healthcare), MTech, and BTech, demonstrating her strong academic background.

Rajesh Singh, PhD, is associated with Uttaranchal University as Professor and Director (Research & Innovation) with more than 20 years of experience in academics and research. His areas of expertise include embedded systems, robotics, wireless sensor networks, Internet of Things, and machine learning. He has been honored as a keynote speaker and session chair at various international and national conferences, faculty development programs, workshops, and webinars. He has filed more than 500 IPR, including 100+ Indian and International patents, and five PCT, and has published more than 439 research papers in SCI and Scopus journals. He has authored and edited 43 books in the area of Embedded Systems and Internet of Things with reputed publishers such as CRC/Taylor & Francis, Springer, Narosa, NIPA, River Publishers, Bentham Science, IGI Global, NOVA Science, etc. He has been featured in Indian and International media for the smart systems and devices he has designed including—OBDAS, E-Parirakshak, Kawach, 20Sec4Life, Ally, Alithis, CT scan Diagnosis, among which five are designed to prevent COVID-19 as per WHO guidelines.

Anita Gehlot, PhD, is associated with Uttaranchal University as Professor and Head—Research & Innovation with more than 16 years of experience. Her area of expertise includes embedded systems, wireless sensor networks, Internet of Things, Artificial Intelligence, and Automation. She has been featured among top ten inventors for ten years 2010–2020, by Clarivate Analytics in "India's Innovation Synopsis" in March 2021. She has filed more than 500 patents including more than 100 Indian and International patent grants, five PCT and has published more than 350 research papers in SCI and Scopus journals. Five scholars have been awarded with PhD under her supervision.

Ankur Dumka, PhD, has been working as an Associate Professor for the past six years and has held various administrative positions. He was the coordinator and member of the Smart City Dehradun team responsible for drafting the proposal. He has published more than 140 research papers, including more than 60 in SCI and Scopus journals and more than 120 papers in Scopus. He has authored 8 books published by reputed international publishers, contributed 15 book chapters, and holds 8 patents granted under his name and 7 published.

Abbreviations

6LOWPAN	IPv6 over Low-power Wireless Personal Area Networks
ABAC	Attribute-based Access Control
ACL	Access Control List
AES	Advanced Encryption Standard
AI	Artificial Intelligence
AMQP	Advanced Message Queuing Protocol
APEC	Asia-Pacific Economic Cooperation
API	Application Programming Interface
AR/VR	Augment Reality/Virtual Reality
ASLR	Address Space Layout Randomization
BAAS	Botnets-as-a-Service
BCP	Business Continuity Plans
BLE	Bluetooth Low Energy
C&C	Command and Control
CASB	Cloud Access Security Broker
CCPA	California Consumer Privacy Act
CCPA	Central Consumer Protection Authority
CMMC	Cybersecurity Maturity Model Certification
COAP	Constrained Application Protocol
COBIT	Control Objectives for Information and Related Technologies
CSS	Chirp Spectrum
CTA	Cyber Threat Alliance
D2C	Device-to-Cloud
DAG	Directed Acyclic Graph
DAST	Dynamic Application Security Testing
DDOS	Distributed Denial of Service
DEP	Data Execution Prevention
DGAS	Domain Generation Algorithms
DLLS	Dynamic Link Libraries
DOH	DNS over HTTPS
DOS	Denial of Service
DPI	Deep Packet Inspection

DRP	Disaster Recovery Plans
DTL	Datagram Transport Layer
DTLS	Datagram Transport Layer Security
E2EE	End-to-end Encryption
EDR	Endpoint Detection and Response
EDRX	Extended Discontinuous Reception
ENISA	European Union Agency for Cybersecurity
EPP	Endpoint Protection Platform
FWAAS	Firewall-as-a-Service
GCA	Global Cyber Alliance
GDPR	General Data Protection Regulation
GFCE	Global Forum on Cyber Expertise
GCNN	Graphical Convolutional Neural Network
GRC	Governance, Risk, and Compliance
HF	High Frequency
HIPAA	Health Insurance Portability and Accountability Act
HSM	Hardware Security Module
HTTP	Hypertext Transfer Protocol
ID-CVAE	Intrusion Detection Conditional Variational Autoencoder
IDBN	Improved Deep Belief Network
IDS	Intrusion Detection System
IETF	Internet Engineering Task Force
IOC	Indicators of Compromise
IOT	Internet of Things
IPSEC	Internet Protocol Security
IRT	Incident Response Team
ISAC	Information Sharing and Analysis Center
ITIL	Information Technology Infrastructure Library
LORAWAN	Long Range Wide Area Network
LTE	Long-Term Evolution
LWM2M	Lightweight M2M
MFA	Multi-factor Authentication
MITM	Man-in-the-Middle
MQTT	Message Queuing Telemetry Transport
NB-IOT	Narrowband Internet of Things
NFC	Near-Field Communication
NIST	National Institute of Standards and Technology
NTA	Network Traffic Analysis
OMA	Open Mobile Alliance
OSINT	Open-Source Intelligence
OTA	Over-the-Air
P2P	Peer-to-Peer
PASTA	Process for Attack Simulation and Threat Analysis
PCI DSS	Payment Card Industry Data Security Standard

PII	Personally Identifiable Information
PKCS	Public Key Cryptography Standards
PKI	Public Key Infrastructure
PPP	Public-Private Partnerships
PQC	Post-Quantum Cryptography
PSM	Power Saving Mode
QOS	Quality of Services
RAAS	Ransomware-as-a-Service
RAT	Remote Administration Tools
RBAC	Role-based Access Control
RDP	Remote Desktop Protocol
ROHS	Restriction of Hazardous Substances
ROI	Return on Investment
RPL	Routing Protocol for Low-Power and Lossy Networks
S/MIME	Secure/Multipurpose Internet Mail Extensions
SASE	Secure Access Service Edge
SDLC	Secure Software Development Life Cycle
SDN	Software-Defined Networking
SIEM	Security Information and Event Management
SLA	Service-level Agreements
SME	Small and Medium-sized Enterprises
SOC	Security Operations Center
STRIDE	Spoofing, Tampering, Repudiation, Information Disclosure, Denial of Service, Elevation of Privilege
SWG	Secure Web Gateway
TCN	Temporal Convolution Network
TPM	Trusted Platform Modules
UPNP	Universal Plug and Play
URI	Uniform Resource Identifier
VLAN	Virtual LAN
VPN	Virtual Private Network
WEEE	Waste Electrical and Electronic Equipment
WMI	Windows Management Instrumentation
XAI	Explainable Artificial Intelligence
XSS	Cross-Site Scripting
ZKP	Zero-knowledge Proofs
ZTA	Zero Trust Architecture

Chapter 1

Introduction

1.1 OVERVIEW OF THE INTERNET OF THINGS

The network of physical devices that are equipped with sensors, software, and other technologies to communicate and share data with other devices over the Internet is called the Internet of Things (IoT). These gadgets, which differ from industrial sensors to intelligent home appliances, use real-time data to provide the knowledge that can be used. Given its development over the last ten years, IoT has now been a key part of numerous top solutions in industries, including industrial automation, intelligent cities, healthcare, and agriculture. IoT is changing how many organizations function, how we engage with technology, and how data is used for decision-making by linking billions of devices worldwide. The IoT is considered to have distinct components, such as the following:

- Sensors: That are used to collect information.
- Identifiers: That can identify the data sources.
- Internet connectivity: That can communicate and notify.
- Software: That can analyze data.

All things considered, the IoT is a network of objects with different element identifications, software intelligence, sensors, and a ubiquitous Internet connection. To communicate data across networks without problems, the IoT depends on communication protocols. By considering elements such as speed, security, and energy efficiency, these protocols—which include MQTT (telemetric transport report), HTTP, COAP (limited application protocol), and Bluetooth—are produced to suit different cases of use. Protocols like MQTT, for instance, are ideal for battery-operated devices in remote locations because they can withstand low bandwidth conditions. The interoperability and scalability of IoT systems depend on an understanding of the main protocols, which allow devices from various platforms and manufacturers to cooperate.

Figure 1.1 shows a complex ecosystem composed of various interrelated components that work together to collect, transmit, process, and act upon data from the physical world. Sensors are devices that detect and measure

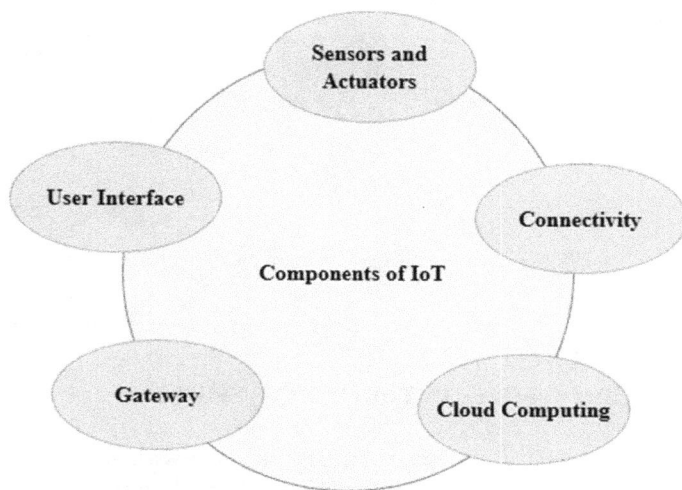

Figure 1.1 IoT components.

physical phenomena such as temperature, motion, humidity, or light, converting them into digital signals. Actuators receive control signals and act upon the environment by triggering a physical response, such as opening a valve or adjusting a thermostat. These devices form the edge of the IoT network and serve as the primary interface between the digital and physical worlds. Once data is captured by sensors, it is transmitted through various connectivity technologies such as Wi-Fi, Bluetooth, Zigbee, LoRaWAN, or cellular networks. Connectivity ensures seamless communication between IoT devices and central systems, allowing real-time data exchange. The gateway serves as an intermediate bridge that aggregates data from multiple sensors, performs local processing or filtering, and securely transmits the data to the cloud. It often translates different communication protocols and enhances security and efficiency by reducing the volume of data sent to the cloud. Once data reaches the cloud computing infrastructure, it is stored, analyzed, and processed using advanced analytics and machine learning algorithms. The cloud provides scalable resources and computing power, enabling complex computations and data storage without the need for on-premise servers. This processed information is then made accessible through a user interface, which can be a mobile app, web dashboard, or desktop application. The user interface enables end-users to monitor device status, visualize data insights, configure settings, and control devices remotely. It plays a crucial role in making IoT systems user-friendly and interactive. Together, these components form an integrated framework that transforms raw sensor data into actionable intelligence, enabling automation, predictive maintenance, real-time monitoring, and smarter decision-making across industries such as healthcare, agriculture, manufacturing, and smart homes.

IoT system architectures typically follow a multilayered approach to manage data flow and functionality. At the base layer, there are the physical devices that collect data. This data is transmitted through communication networks through a gateway that serves as an intermediary between devices and cloud systems. The cloud layer then processes, analyzes, and stores a huge amount of data generated by IoT devices, while the application layer allows users to interact with this data through web or mobile platforms. This architecture helps optimize data flow and ensure efficient communication and management of the device. Since the attack surface of potential cyber products decreases with the number of connected devices, security is probably the most important factor. IoT protocols are therefore necessary for secure data transfer between devices and cloud platforms to guarantee the confidentiality, integrity, and verification of transmitted data. While some, such as DTLs (Datagram Transport Layers), ensure that even limited devices can connect safely, others, such as HTTPS, have fully integrated communication routes. To avoid any illegal access, security breaches, or compromise of user privacy, a comprehensive IoT security architecture should be developed.

Scalability is another important IoT challenge, in addition to security. The system must be able to manage the rise in data traffic and guarantee smooth functioning when more devices are connected to a network. Large-scale deployments are supported by IoT architectures. Additionally, cloud platforms have scalable processing and storage capacities. Processing data closer to its source is known as edge computing. To manage real-time data analysis and lower latency, this technology has also become a supplementary one. Scalability must therefore be given top priority in the architecture and protocols selected for IoT systems to facilitate future expansion and advancement. Scalability, data management, interoperability, energy consumption, and security vulnerabilities are some of the issues that the IoT faces. The proposed techniques address different security limitations, but each solution comes with its own set of difficulties. Each technique is described in the following list, along with a discussion about its relative strengths and weaknesses.

The absence of proper security measures stands as a significant IoT problem because many devices experience frequent integration. Multiple secure practices, including encryption methods, together with authentication techniques and intrusion detection systems, are now widespread in the market. The transmission of sensitive information remains secure through AES and RSA encryption methods that produce an additional hurdle to unauthorized access of data. Devices need authentication by OAuth and JWT authentication protocols for identification purposes before they receive network and service authorization. Network activities remain under constant IDS surveillance to detect any potential intrusion attempts by monitoring patterns of activity. Security enhancement occurs from these methods, yet multiple procedures result in elevated latency and increased power usage that produce unwanted effects on resource-limited devices.

The ability to scale poses a difficult problem because this end requires the management of thousands of IoT devices. The battle against this challenge uses three technological solutions: cloud computing, edge computing, and fog computing. Resource scaling becomes effortless through cloud computing because it provides a centralized system for data processing and storage. Edge computing accepts data processing tasks directly at their source points to provide better latency and bandwidth performance while streamlining decisions. The framework called fog computing enhances cloud network capabilities by extending them to the edge while delivering a distributed architecture that unites cloud and edge resources. These architectures improve the scalability of IoT systems with possible trade-offs regarding added complexity and resource management.

Data Management Techniques: A considerable amount of data is produced by IoT devices, and there is a need to strategize the management of data. This is done through data aggregation, data analytics, and even machine learning to manage that data. Data aggregation reduces the size of data as it aggregates data at the edge or local devices, saving bandwidth. Data analytics tools process and analyze the aggregated data to extract actionable insights, which are useful in predictive maintenance or operational optimization. Machine learning algorithms also improve data analysis by identifying patterns and trends, thus enhancing the decision-making quality. However, these techniques require much computational power, which could be limited in some IoT environments.

Interoperability Solutions: Interoperability is one of the major challenges in IoT, since devices manufactured from various sources rarely intercommunicate. Standardization techniques, middleware solutions, and APIs help address this issue. Efforts for standardization, such as MQTT and CoAP, ensure common protocols across various platforms. Middleware solutions act as a cross-pointer between various devices and applications. They translate protocols and data formats for compatibility. APIs enable more applications that are more integrated with, and interact better with, devices and services on a variety of different networks. However, a significant disadvantage of these approaches is the difficulty in achieving industry consensus.

Energy-Management Technologies: IoT devices, especially those running on batteries, need to be power conscious. Typical technologies used to consume less power within an IoT device include energy harvesting, low-power communication protocols, and modes for sleep. Energy harvesting technologies such as solar panels and piezoelectric generators enable devices to be self-powered, thereby increasing the battery longevity. Low-power communication protocols or technologies such as ZigBee and LoRa are among those that reduce the amount of energy needed to transmit data, yet do not weaken the connection. Sleep modes allow devices to go into low power whenever they are not in use, thus conserving energy in reserve until it is needed again.

Such techniques play a crucial role in prolonging the operation time of the IoT devices, but at the cost of performance that may relate to responsiveness, as well as data transmission rates.

1.2 CHALLENGES IN IoT

The IoT is a game-changing technology that links systems, sensors, and gadgets to improve efficiency, simplify procedures, and raise people's quality of life. A number of obstacles prevent IoT from being widely adopted and fully implemented, despite its enormous potential. The success of the IoT ecosystem depends on finding strong solutions to these problems, which have societal, economic, and technical aspects. Although the IoT revolution holds unmatched potential, overcoming its obstacles is essential to achieving its full potential. Innovative solutions are needed to address security and privacy concerns, scalability and interoperability challenges, energy efficiency demands, and regulatory complications. To build an inclusive and sustainable IoT ecosystem, cooperation between governments, businesses, and academic institutions is crucial. IoT can continue to revolutionize industries, improve people's quality of life, and open the door to a smarter, more connected future by addressing these challenges. Figure 1.2 shows the distinct IoT challenges.

Security and Privacy: One of the most important challenges in IoT is to ensure security and privacy. IoT devices collect a huge amount of data, often sensitive, such as personal health metrics, location information, and financial transactions. Without robust security measures, this data is vulnerable

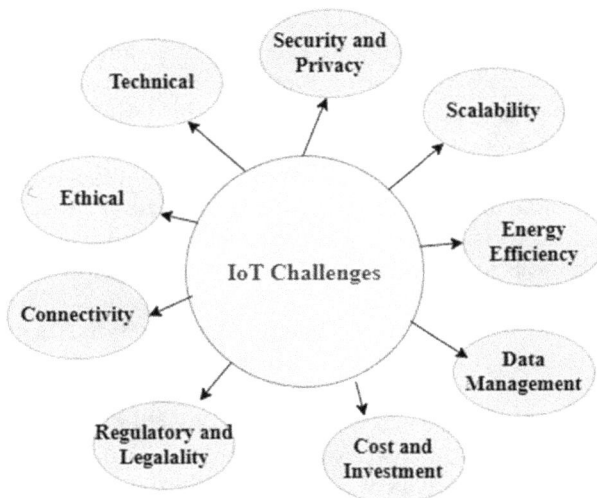

Figure 1.2 IoT challenges.

to cyberattacks, including data disruption, ransomware, and Denial of Service (DoS). Implementation of complex safety mechanisms is demanding because many IoT devices have low processing power. In addition, because the IoT is connected, one compromised device has the potential to compromise the entire network. Users often do not have say about how their data is collected, stored, and distributed. The lack of uniform personal data protection laws in many jurisdictions and sectors deteriorates this situation by exposing the use of their information to consumers. In the IoT ecosystem, security and privacy are essential concerns that represent the main obstacles to its expansion and use. IoT devices are the main goals for cyberattacks because they collect, process, and send huge volumes of sensitive data, such as financial, operational, and personal data.

Due to low processing power, hardware limitations, or a lack of focus on secure design, many IoT devices lack strong security features. Unauthorized access, data breaches, and device exploitation for malevolent intent, including initiating Distributed Denial of Service (DDoS) assaults, are frequently caused by this vulnerability. IoT's interconnectedness makes the issue worse because a single compromised device can compromise a whole network. Furthermore, IoT systems' widespread data collecting methods, which are frequently carried out without the express knowledge or consent of users, give rise to privacy problems. Users of smart homes, wearable technology, and industrial systems may be subject to profiling, surveillance, or unlawful data use if precise behavioral patterns are revealed by the data. The problem is made more difficult by the absence of uniform privacy laws and security procedures across geographies and sectors. There is a better chance of data violation and abuse, as many IoT implementations depend on third-party systems for data processing and storage. In addition, the distrust of users increases if there is no transparency regarding the storage, sharing, and analysis of data. Strong encryption, safe verification methods, frequent software upgrades, and the use of privacy principles according to the design are essential components of a comprehensive strategy to protect IoT systems. Policymakers, manufacturers, and users must collaborate to establish comprehensive regulations, standardized security practices, and user-centric privacy controls. Without addressing these pressing security and privacy challenges, the promise of IoT may be overshadowed by risks that undermine user confidence and system reliability.

Scalability and Interoperability: The rapid growth of IoT devices presents significant scalability challenges. By 2030, it is estimated that over 50 billion IoT devices will be in use globally, requiring networks capable of handling massive data traffic and device management. Existing network infrastructures, such as 4G LTE, may not suffice, necessitating the adoption of advanced technologies such as 5G. Interoperability is another critical issue. IoT devices often come from diverse manufacturers, each employing proprietary communication protocols and standards. This lack of uniformity creates silos, preventing seamless communication and integration among devices. Achieving true interoperability requires the development and adoption of universal standards, which is challenging given the competitive nature of the industry. Scalability and interoperability are key challenges in the rapidly expanding IoT ecosystem, which affects its efficiency and global adoption.

The scalability concerns the IoT system to adapt to the growing number of devices, users, and data volume without endangering performance. Since it is assumed that the number of IoT devices will exceed 50 billion by 2030, networks face increasing pressure on efficient control of massive data streams and equipment interactions. The current infrastructure, including traditional 4G LTE networks, seeks to meet these requirements and requires adopting advanced technologies such as 5G, Edge Computing, and SDN Software (SDN). However, scaling IoT systems is not just about network capacity; it also requires robust frameworks for device management, resource allocation, and fault tolerance to maintain system reliability and responsiveness. On the other hand, interoperability pertains to the seamless interaction and communication between IoT devices from different manufacturers, often using proprietary technologies and protocols. This lack of uniformity creates isolated "silos," hindering device integration and limiting the ecosystem's functionality. For example, smart home devices from different brands may not work together efficiently, requiring users to rely on multiple apps or interfaces. Achieving interoperability demands the establishment of universal communication standards and protocols, such as MQTT, CoAP, and Bluetooth Low Energy (BLE), to ensure cross-platform compatibility. Furthermore, middleware solutions and open-source frameworks are being explored to bridge compatibility gaps, enabling diverse devices and systems to operate cohesively. The lack of scalability and interoperability not only affects performance but also discourages innovation, increases costs, and slows down the adoption of IoT solutions. As devices proliferate, ensuring that systems can scale and interact effectively without significant reconfiguration or investment becomes critical. Collaboration between industry stakeholders, standardization bodies, and policymakers is essential to address these challenges. By fostering the development of scalable architectures and interoperable frameworks, the IoT ecosystem can unlock its full potential, delivering seamless connectivity and transformative benefits across industries and applications.

Energy Efficiency: Energy consumption is the main problem of IoT, especially those that are still controlled or deployed in remote locations. Ensuring a long battery life while maintaining functionality is a complicated challenge. Equipment such as sensors and drivers must balance energy efficiency with power to remain viable. Energy efficiency is a critical challenge in the IoT ecosystem because billions of connected devices rely on the efficient operation of limited energy sources. Many IoT devices, such as sensors, action members, and wearable technologies, are controlled or deployed at distant locations where the maintenance or battery replacement is impractical. This creates a pressing need to optimize energy consumption without compromising performance, reliability, or functionality. The constant data exchange, processing, and communication required in IoT systems can rapidly drain device batteries, particularly when high-frequency sensing or real-time operations are involved. Additionally, the cumulative energy demands of millions of IoT devices place a significant strain on power grids, raising environmental concerns about the sustainability of IoT deployment.

To address this, advancements in low-power communication protocols such as Zigbee, LoRaWAN, and BLE are helping to minimize energy consumption during data transmission. Moreover, energy harvesting technologies, such as solar, thermal, or kinetic energy capture, are gaining traction as sustainable power sources for IoT devices, reducing dependency on traditional batteries. Hardware optimization is another critical area, with ultra-low-power microcontrollers and energy-efficient semiconductor designs enabling IoT devices to perform complex tasks with minimal energy use. Similarly, software strategies, including adaptive duty cycling, data compression, and edge computing, allow devices to conserve energy by reducing processing loads and limiting unnecessary communication with cloud servers. Despite these advancements, achieving widespread energy efficiency remains a challenge due to the diversity of IoT applications and environments, each requiring tailored solutions. Collaboration between device manufacturers, researchers, and policymakers is essential to develop standardized energy-efficient practices and promote the adoption of green IoT technologies. By prioritizing energy efficiency, the IoT ecosystem can not only extend the operational life of devices and reduce operational costs but also contribute to environmental sustainability, paving the way for a more resilient and eco-friendly future.

Data Management and Analytics: The IoT ecosystem presents significant issues in data management and analytics due to the vast amount, diversity, and speed of data produced by billions of linked devices. The vast volumes of data that IoT systems routinely gather from sensors, actuators, and other devices create a flood of data that must be effectively processed, stored, and analyzed. Latency, inconsistency, and system bottlenecks are some of the problems that arise when traditional data processing and storage techniques are unable to handle the volume and complexity of IoT data. Furthermore, efficient data handling is made more difficult by the variety of IoT data formats and structures, which range from unstructured multimedia information to structured numerical readings. Ensuring data quality, integrity, and security across a distributed IoT network is equally challenging, particularly when devices operate in diverse environments and may have limited computational capabilities. On the analytics front, deriving actionable insights from raw IoT data requires advanced techniques, including real-time processing, machine learning, and AI.

These tools can detect formulas, predict trends, and optimize operations in various industries such as healthcare, transport, and production. However, the implementation of these technologies requires considerable computing resources and expertise that may be inaccessible to smaller organizations. Edge computing has proved to be a promising solution, allowing data processing closer to the source to reduce the use of latency and bandwidth while increasing real-time analytical capabilities. Despite these advancements, privacy and compliance concerns loom large, as IoT data often involves sensitive information that must be handled under stringent regulatory frameworks such as GDPR and CCPA. Balancing data accessibility with privacy protection requires robust encryption, secure data-sharing protocols, and anonymization techniques. The problems of data governance, such as ownership, accountability, and ethical use, also increase with the size of IoT ecosystems. To fully utilize IoT data, organizations need to invest in scalable data architectures, cloud-integrated systems, and qualified staff. To create standardized procedures and frameworks that facilitate effective data management and analytics, cooperation between business, academics, and legislators is essential. The IoT ecosystem can open up revolutionary possibilities by tackling these issues, enabling companies to improve operational effectiveness, make data-driven decisions, and provide creative solutions for a variety of uses.

Cost and Investment: Cost and investment are significant barriers to the widespread adoption and implementation of IoT solutions, particularly for small and medium-sized enterprises (SMEs) and emerging economies. Deploying IoT systems involves substantial upfront expenses, including purchasing sensors, devices, gateways, and network infrastructure. Beyond hardware, organizations must invest in software development, cloud services, and integration with existing systems, which can be complex and resource-intensive. Additionally, ongoing operational costs such as device maintenance, firmware updates, energy consumption, and data storage can further strain budgets. For SMEs, the financial burden is often compounded by the lack of clear and immediate return on investment (ROI), as the benefits of IoT—such as improved efficiency, predictive maintenance, and enhanced customer experiences—may take time to materialize. Customization costs also add to the challenge, as IoT solutions often require tailoring to specific use cases, industries, or environments, driving up implementation expenses. Furthermore, the lack of standardized pricing models and transparency in service offerings from IoT vendors can create confusion, making it difficult for organizations to plan and allocate budgets effectively.

In developing regions, where access to advanced infrastructure such as 5G and edge computing is limited, the cost of building or upgrading networks for IoT compatibility presents an additional obstacle. Governments and private sector stakeholders must explore innovative funding mechanisms to address these financial challenges, including public–private partnerships, subsidies, and flexible financing models. Shared infrastructure initiatives, such as IoT-as-a-Service platforms, can help reduce costs by allowing multiple users to share resources and spread expenses. Open-source tools and frameworks also offer cost-effective alternatives for developing and deploying IoT applications. Moreover, businesses can prioritize cost optimization by adopting energy-efficient devices, leveraging scalable cloud solutions, and implementing predictive analytics to minimize resource wastage. To drive investment, organizations must build compelling business cases that highlight the long-term value of IoT in terms of cost savings, revenue generation, and competitive advantage. Policymakers can further incentivize investment by offering tax breaks, grants, and regulatory support for IoT initiatives. Addressing cost and investment barriers is crucial to ensuring that IoT solutions are accessible, scalable, and sustainable across diverse sectors and regions, unlocking their transformative potential and driving global innovation.

Regulatory and Legal Issues: Regulatory and legal issues pose significant challenges to the growth and adoption of the IoT ecosystem, as the technology often outpaces the development of comprehensive laws and policies. One of the primary concerns lies in the lack of standardized global regulations, resulting in fragmented legal frameworks that vary across countries and industries. This disparity creates uncertainty for businesses, particularly those operating in multiple regions, as they must navigate a maze of overlapping or conflicting compliance requirements. Key areas of regulatory concern include data privacy, security, and liability. IoT devices frequently collect and process sensitive user data, raising critical questions about consent, ownership, and usage rights. Privacy regulations, such as the General Data Protection Regulation (GDPR) in the European Union and the California Consumer Privacy Act (CCPA) in the United States, aim to safeguard user data but are not universally applicable, leaving gaps in protection and enforcement. Security regulations for IoT devices are similarly inconsistent, often failing to mandate basic protections such as encryption, secure authentication, or regular software updates, leaving devices vulnerable to cyberattacks.

Liability issues further complicate the legal landscape, particularly in cases of device malfunction, data breaches, or harm caused by autonomous IoT systems. Determining accountability among manufacturers, service providers, and users is often ambiguous, leading to prolonged legal disputes. Additionally, ethical concerns surrounding IoT usage, such as surveillance, data monetization, and potential misuse of collected data, require robust legal oversight to protect individual rights and public trust. Emerging IoT applications, including autonomous vehicles and smart cities, introduce new regulatory challenges related to safety standards, data governance, and cross-jurisdictional coordination. Policymakers must address these issues through the development of clear, adaptable, and technology-neutral legal frameworks that encourage innovation while safeguarding users. Industry stakeholders, including manufacturers, developers, and advocacy groups, should collaborate with regulators to establish best practices and voluntary compliance standards to bridge gaps in existing legislation. Governments can further promote compliance by offering incentives for adopting secure and privacy-centric IoT designs, such as tax breaks or certification programs. International cooperation is essential to harmonize regulations, enabling the seamless operation of IoT systems across borders. By addressing these regulatory and legal challenges, the IoT ecosystem can foster trust, mitigate risks, and unlock its full potential to deliver transformative benefits across industries and societies.

Connectivity and Infrastructure: Connectivity and infrastructure are foundational to the success of the IoT ecosystem, but they also present critical challenges that must be addressed to realize its full potential. Reliable and efficient connectivity is essential for IoT devices to communicate, exchange data, and function seamlessly, yet many regions lack the necessary infrastructure to support widespread IoT deployment. Urban areas typically benefit from advanced networks such as 5G, fiber-optic broadband, and dense cellular coverage, enabling high-speed, low-latency communication. However, rural and underserved regions often face significant connectivity gaps due to limited network availability, high costs, and inadequate investment in infrastructure. These disparities hinder the adoption of IoT solutions in agriculture, healthcare, and remote industrial operations, where they could have the most transformative impact. Additionally, existing networks such as 4G LTE or Wi-Fi may struggle to handle the exponential growth in IoT devices, which are projected to exceed 50 billion by 2030, leading to congestion, latency, and reduced performance.

Infrastructure challenges extend beyond connectivity to include power supply, edge computing facilities, and data storage systems, all of which must scale to meet the demands of a growing IoT ecosystem. For example, deploying edge computing nodes closer to IoT devices can reduce latency and bandwidth usage, but it requires significant investment in local data centers and supporting technologies. Moreover, diverse IoT applications, from smart homes to industrial automation, have varying connectivity requirements, necessitating a mix of technologies such as LoRaWAN, NB-IoT, and satellite networks to address their specific needs. Building resilient and scalable infrastructure demands collaboration among governments, private enterprises, and telecommunication providers to invest in advanced technologies and expand network coverage to underserved areas. Innovations such as satellite-based Internet services, mesh networks, and hybrid connectivity models are helping bridge gaps, but their adoption is often limited by cost and technical complexity. Policymakers must prioritize infrastructure development by offering subsidies, fostering public–private partnerships, and implementing regulatory frameworks that incentivize investment. By addressing these connectivity and infrastructure challenges, the IoT ecosystem can enable seamless integration across industries, ensuring equitable access to its benefits while supporting a future of ubiquitous, reliable, and efficient connected systems.

Ethical and Societal Concerns: Ethical and societal concerns are pivotal challenges in the adoption and implementation of the IoT, as its pervasive nature raises profound questions about privacy, security, equity, and human autonomy. IoT systems collect, process, and analyze a huge amount of personal and behavioral data, often without explicit consent of the user or full understanding, leading to ethical dilemmas on data ownership, use, and monetization. This data can be used for supervision, profiling, or targeted advertising, arouse concerns about manipulating the user, loss of privacy, and the potential of abuse by corporations and governments. Furthermore, the IoT ecosystem risks exacerbating societal inequities, as access to advanced IoT technologies may be limited to wealthier populations or urban areas, leaving rural and underserved communities further behind. The digital divide not only restricts equitable access to IoT benefits but also deepens socio-economic disparities, particularly in education, healthcare, and economic opportunities.

Additionally, the ethical implications of automation in IoT systems, such as smart cities or autonomous vehicles, challenge the balance between efficiency and human oversight. For instance, decision-making algorithms can perpetuate bias if not designed or monitored carefully, leading to unfair treatment or outcomes in critical areas such as law enforcement, healthcare allocation, or employment screening. IoT systems can also erode human autonomy by fostering over-reliance on automated processes, reducing individual control over decision-making. Security vulnerabilities in IoT devices pose further ethical concerns, as compromised systems can lead to significant harm, including data breaches, physical danger, or the disruption of essential services. Ethical dilemma also arises in terms of environmental impact, because the spread of IoT equipment contributes to electronic waste and energy and raises questions about sustainability and social responsibility. The solution to these concerns requires the approach of more participating parties, including cooperation between the creators of politicians, technologies, ethics, and civil society. Political creators must set up robust regulatory frameworks to protect user rights, ensure data transparency, and uphold ethical standards when designing and deploying IoT. Meanwhile, businesses must prioritize ethical considerations by adopting privacy-by-design principles, promoting inclusivity, and ensuring accountability in IoT operations. Public education and awareness are equally vital to empower users with knowledge about their rights and the implications of IoT adoption. By addressing ethical and societal concerns, the IoT ecosystem can build trust, foster responsible innovation, and ensure that its transformative benefits are equitably distributed across all segments of society.

Technical Challenges: Technical challenges are an important obstacle for trouble-free deployment and operation of IoT, as its ecosystem includes a complex interplay of equipment, network, and platforms. One of the primary challenges is the heterogeneity of the device, with IoT devices being very different in terms of hardware capabilities, operating systems, communication protocols, and data formats. This diversity complicates interoperability and integration, often requiring adapted solutions that increase costs and complexity. Scalability is another pressing issue, as the exponential growth of IoT devices demands robust architectures capable of handling massive data volumes, maintaining low latency, and ensuring system reliability. Many existing networks, particularly legacy infrastructures, struggle to support the demands of large-scale IoT deployments. Power management presents another critical technical challenge, as many IoT devices are battery-operated and deployed in remote or hard-to-reach locations. Optimizing energy efficiency while maintaining functionality and connectivity is essential for prolonged device operation.

Additionally, IoT systems are inherently vulnerable to cyberattacks due to limited computational resources, insecure communication protocols, and the absence of standardized security measures. Ensuring robust security, including secure authentication, encryption, and regular updates, is technically challenging but crucial to safeguarding devices and data. Data management is equally complex, as IoT generates vast amounts of structured and unstructured data that require efficient storage, processing, and analysis. Real-time analytics demands high-performance computing resources, while privacy concerns necessitate the use of advanced data anonymization and encryption techniques. Edge computing offers potential solutions by reducing the need for cloud dependency, but its implementation requires significant investment in localized infrastructure. Network reliability is another critical factor, as uninterrupted connectivity is essential for IoT applications in healthcare, industrial automation, and transportation. However, network outages, congestion, or latency can disrupt system performance, compromising the reliability of IoT solutions. Furthermore, designing IoT systems to adapt to dynamic and often unpredictable environments poses additional technical hurdles, requiring flexibility and resilience. In order to resolve these challenges, ongoing research and development, together with the adoption of standardized frames and protocols, is necessary. Cooperation between the parties, academic communities, and governments can speed up the development of innovative solutions and ensure that the IoT ecosystem is robust, scalable, and safe. Overcoming these technical challenges will unlock the full potential of IoT, allowing its transformative impact across industries and companies.

1.3 SECURITY ISSUES IN IoT

IoT security is a major concern, as the growing number of connected devices introduces serious vulnerabilities that can compromise system dependability, data integrity, and user privacy. Due to financial limitations, a lack of emphasis on cybersecurity throughout the design process, or insufficient computational capabilities, IoT devices—from smart household appliances to industrial sensors—frequently function with few security measures. Because they are commonly used with obsolete software, poor security methods, and default passwords, these devices are prime targets for hackers. One of the biggest security risks in the IoT is unauthorized access, in which hackers take advantage of flaws to take over devices and maybe inflict bodily harm or interfere with necessary functions. An example would be the manipulation of a hacked smart thermostat to waste energy, and assaults on industrial IoT systems could lead to safety issues or malfunctioning gear. Because IoT devices frequently gather and communicate sensitive data, including location information, financial transactions, and personal health information, data breaches are another significant problem. This data can be intercepted or stolen by malicious actors in the absence of appropriate encryption or secure communication protocols, which could result in fraud, identity theft, or illegal spying. Due to the size of IoT networks, fraudsters have a large attack surface to exploit, increasing the danger. DDoS attacks are another prevalent threat, with attackers leveraging botnets of compromised IoT devices to overwhelm and disrupt targeted networks or services. Such attacks, such as the infamous Mirai botnet incident, highlight how poorly secured IoT devices can be weaponized on a global scale.

The multiplicity of devices, platforms, and communication protocols exacerbates IoT security issues and makes it more difficult to apply conventional security measures. Furthermore, it is challenging to efficiently monitor and secure every endpoint due to the decentralized nature of IoT devices. There is a greater chance of theft or tampering because many IoT devices are placed in hostile or isolated locations with little physical security. The issue is made worse by firmware flaws and irregular upgrades, which leave devices vulnerable to known exploits for lengthy periods of time. Furthermore, there are worries about possible cyberattacks that might have serious repercussions for national security and public safety because of the integration of IoT devices with vital infrastructure, including power grids, transit networks, and medical facilities.

It takes cooperation from manufacturers, users, legislators, and cybersecurity specialists to address IoT security concerns. Strong authentication, secure boot procedures, and end-to-end encryption must be implemented by manufacturers as a top priority when designing and developing IoT devices. Regular firmware updates and patch management should be mandatory to address emerging threats. Policymakers need to establish and enforce regulations that mandate minimum security standards for IoT devices, incentivizing manufacturers to adopt best practices. Public awareness campaigns can educate users about the importance of securing their IoT devices, such as changing default credentials, applying updates, and isolating IoT devices from critical networks. On the technical front, advancements in AI and machine learning can enhance threat detection and response capabilities, enabling the identification of anomalies and potential attacks in real time. Network segmentation and intrusion detection systems can further bolster

IoT security by limiting the spread of attacks and ensuring prompt action against suspicious activities. A unified effort to address these security challenges is essential to fostering a safe and resilient IoT ecosystem. By prioritizing security at every level, the IoT industry can build trust among users and stakeholders, enabling the continued growth and innovation of connected technologies while safeguarding against emerging threats.

1.4 RISE OF IoT BOTNETS

A major threat to the security and stability of the IoT ecosystem is the emergence of IoT botnets, which are fueled by the proliferation of IoT devices with inadequate protection and the growing sophistication of cybercriminals. Networks of hacked IoT devices, including wearables, routers, smart cameras, and thermostats, are known as IoT botnets. These devices are taken over and managed remotely by attackers to carry out coordinated destructive actions. These botnets frequently take advantage of flaws in IoT devices, such as unpatched software, weak default passwords, and unsecured communication protocols, to obtain illegal access and take over. With billions of connected devices, the IoT environment is an enormous target pool that gives attackers the ability to build botnets of previously unheard-of size and strength. The Mirai botnet is among the most notorious instances; it used the default credentials of IoT devices to launch huge DDoS assaults, momentarily taking down important websites and services. These assaults reveal the vulnerability of IoT systems to coordinated cyberthreats in addition to disrupting essential infrastructure and companies. Figure 1.3 illustrates the rise in IoT botnet malware in recent years.

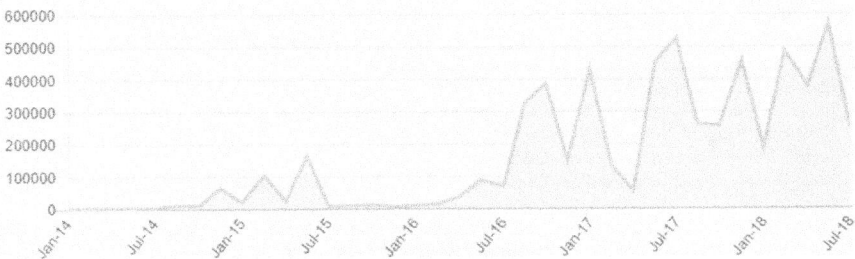

Figure 1.3 IoT botnet growth.

https://www.verdict.co.uk/rise-of-the-iot-botnet/.

The rise of IoT botnets is supported by several factors, including the rapid acceptance of IoT technology, the lack of standardized safety measures, and relatively easy use of IoT equipment. Many manufacturers prefer functionality and costs over security, resulting in equipment with minimal guarantees against unauthorized access. In addition to that, users generally ignore to change in the default username and password that may increase the vulnerability of IoT devices. The decentralized nature of IoT networks also complicates the detection and alleviation of botnets, as compromised devices are often distributed in various places and networks. After being threatened, these devices can be used to perform several harmful activities, including DDoS attacks, stealing credentials, and data theft. In some cases, attackers monetize IoT botnets by offering them as services to other criminals, fueling a thriving underground economy, and lowering the barrier to entry for cybercrime. Table 1.1 shows the recent incidents related to IoT botnet activities.

Table 1.1 Recent IoT botnet incidents

Botnet	Date	Description
Mirai[a]	October 12, 2016	Searched large Internet blocks for available Telnet ports. Shutdown of major websites, including Twitter, Netflix, and other online services.
Espoo finland[b]	December 4, 2018	Used Malicious software to attack IoT devices.
Netscout[c]	October 28, 2019	Hack home routers and IP-enabled video cameras.
Emotet[d]	February 5, 2020	Most widespread botnet currently.
Dark Nexus[e]	April 14, 2020	A new botnet is launching a variety of DDoS attacks against millions of IoT devices.
Mozi as CenturyLink[f]	September 17, 2020	Built into an IoT botnet with the ability to execute payloads, conduct DDoS attacks, and exfiltrate data.
Meris[g]	November 9, 2021	About 250,000 devices were infected with malware, which causes the majority of DDoS attacks.
KV Botnet[h]	December 5, 2023	This botnet hijacks SOHO (small office home office) routers and VPN devices.

[a] https://www.cloudflare.com/learning/ddos/glossary/mirai-botnet/.
[b] https://www.nokia.com/about-us/news/releases/2023/06/07/nokia-threat-intelligence-report-finds-malicious-iot-botnet-activity-has-sharply-increased/.
[c] https://www.netscout.com/ddos-attack-map.
[d] https://www.hhs.gov/sites/default/files/emotet-the-enduring-and-persistent-threat-to-the-hph-tlpclear.pdf.
[e] https://securityaffairs.com/101264/malware/dark-nexus-iotbotnet.html#:~:text=Cybersecurity%20researchers%20discovered%20a%20new,used%20to%20launch%20DDoS%20attacks.
[f] https://blog.centurylink.com/new-mozi-malware-family-quietly-amasses-iot-bots/.
[g] https://blog.cloudflare.com/meris-botnet.
[h] https://www.bleepingcomputer.com/news/security/stealthy-kv-botnet-hijacks-soho-routers-and-vpn-devices/amp/.

A multifaceted strategy combining manufacturers, users, legislators, and cybersecurity specialists is needed to mitigate the threat posed by IoT botnets. When designing and developing IoT devices, manufacturers must put security first by including features such as secure firmware upgrades, robust authentication methods, and encrypted communication protocols. To ensure that manufacturers follow best practices, policymakers should create standards and laws requiring IoT devices to meet minimum security criteria. Campaigns for public awareness can inform users of the value of protecting their IoT devices, including how to employ network segmentation to reduce the potential harm caused by compromised devices, change default passwords, and apply updates. On the technical front, progress in network monitoring, detection of anomalies, and intelligence threats can help identify and neutralize IoT botnets before they cause considerable damage. The cooperation between the parties involved is essential for the development of a durable IoT ecosystem capable of resisting the growing threat of botnets. The rise of IoT botnets underlines the urgent need for proactive measures to solve the security problems of the IoT landscape. Since IoT continues to expand to critical sectors such as healthcare, transport, and intelligent cities, the potential consequences of attacks on botnets become even more serious and threaten not only financial losses but also public security and national security. By solving vulnerability, which enables IoT botnets and supports the culture of development and use of security, the ecosystem of IoT can develop in a safer and more reliable environment for innovation and connection.

1.5 OBJECTIVES AND SCOPE OF THE IoT BOTNET

The objectives and scope of IoT botnets are intricately tied to the malicious intent of their creators, with far-reaching implications for cybersecurity, data integrity, and critical infrastructure. IoT botnets are networks of compromised IoT devices, such as smart home gadgets, industrial controllers, and connected vehicles, that have been hijacked and controlled remotely by attackers. The primary objective of an IoT botnet is to harness the collective computational power and connectivity of these devices to execute coordinated attacks on a scale that would be impossible with a single device. These botnets are primarily used for DDoS attacks, overwhelming targeted networks or services with traffic to render them inaccessible. High-profile incidents, such as the Mirai botnet attack, have demonstrated the devastating potential of IoT botnets in disrupting major websites, online services, and critical infrastructure, highlighting their ability to exploit the inherent vulnerabilities of IoT devices. Beyond DDoS attacks, IoT botnets are increasingly being used for sophisticated cybercrimes, including data theft, ransomware deployment, and cryptocurrency mining. In these scenarios, attackers leverage the processing power of compromised devices to mine digital currencies, steal sensitive data for financial or strategic gain, or lock critical systems in exchange for ransom payments.

The scope of IoT botnets is vast, spanning multiple industries, geographies, and use cases, due to the ubiquitous nature of IoT devices and their often lax security standards. In industrial settings, IoT botnets can target operational technology systems to disrupt manufacturing processes, energy grids, or transportation networks, with the potential to cause economic damage and threaten public safety. In consumer environments, compromised smart home devices can be exploited to violate user privacy, monitor activities, or launch further attacks. The proliferation of IoT in critical sectors, such as healthcare and defense, has expanded the scope of botnet operations to include high-stakes targets, where the consequences of successful attacks can be catastrophic. Attackers can also use IoT botnets to create cascading effects, where the compromise of one network or system leads to vulnerabilities in interconnected systems, amplifying the impact of their actions.

The objectives of IoT botnets also extend to enabling the underground economy of cybercrime, as attackers often monetize these networks by renting them out for malicious purposes. Botnets-as-a-Service (BaaS) has become a lucrative model, allowing even less-skilled attackers to execute large-scale attacks by purchasing access to a ready-made botnet. This commercialization of IoT botnets lowers the barrier to entry for cybercriminals and fuels a growing ecosystem of illegal activities. Furthermore, IoT botnets have been used for espionage and geopolitical objectives, as state-sponsored attackers exploit them to gather intelligence, disrupt rival nations, or stage attacks with plausible deniability. In such cases, IoT botnets are weaponized as tools of cyber warfare, targeting critical infrastructure, communication networks, or sensitive data repositories to gain strategic advantages.

The widespread vulnerability of IoT devices amplifies the threat posed by botnets. Many devices lack robust security measures, such as strong authentication protocols, encrypted communications, and regular firmware updates, making them easy prey for attackers. Default passwords, hardcoded credentials, and outdated software are common entry points for botnet creators. The decentralized and heterogeneous nature of IoT networks further complicates detection and mitigation efforts, as compromised devices are often distributed across different locations and network environments. The ease with which attackers can scan the Internet for vulnerable IoT devices and compromise them highlights the pressing need for better security practices at every level, from device manufacturers to end-users.

Relieving the threat of IoT botnets requires a comprehensive approach that addresses their goals and scope. Manufacturers must adopt the principles of security according to the design and from the beginning to insert robust safety features into the IoT device, including strong authentication mechanisms, secure processes of firmware updating, and hardened communication protocols. Standardization of safety measures across the IoT ecosystem can help reduce the surface of the attack and improve the resistance of the device against the threat of botnets. End-users must also play a proactive role by changing the initial login data, using software updates, and implementing network segmentation to reduce the dissemination of attacks. Governments and politicians play a decisive role in determining and enforcing regulations that set minimal safety standards for IoT equipment and motivate compliance with regulations. Efforts to cooperate between the parties involved cybersecurity experts, and international organizations are essential for the development of intelligence frames, knowledge sharing, and responding effectively to the evolving tactics of botnets.

In addition, advances in artificial intelligence (AI) and machine learning can increase the detection and alleviation of IoT botnets by identifying formulas, anomalies, and real-time threats. Network tracking tools, disruption detection systems, and automated response mechanisms can provide another layer of defense against botnet operations. Public awareness campaigns can also educate users about the risks of IoT botnets and promote proven procedures for ensuring their equipment. The Community of cybersecurity can alleviate the risks associated with these threats and protect the integrity and reliability of the IoT ecosystem, which allows it to deal with vulnerabilities that allow IoT botnets and promote a shared responsibility culture. As IoT continues to expand and integrate into critical aspects of modern life, addressing the objectives and scope of botnets is crucial to ensuring a secure and resilient future for connected technologies.

1.6 CONCLUSION

The conclusion of this chapter underscores the critical importance of addressing the multifaceted challenges associated with the IoT to ensure its secure, efficient, and equitable development. As the IoT continues to revolutionize industries and reshape daily life through unparalleled connectivity and data-driven insights, it simultaneously introduces significant technical, ethical, and security challenges that demand comprehensive and proactive solutions. From the rise of IoT botnets exploiting device vulnerabilities to the broader issues of privacy, scalability, interoperability, and energy efficiency, each aspect of the IoT ecosystem presents unique risks and opportunities. The chapter highlights the need for collaborative efforts among stakeholders—including manufacturers, users, policymakers, and cybersecurity experts—to design and implement robust frameworks that address these challenges holistically. Manufacturers must prioritize security and energy efficiency in device design while adhering to global standards for interoperability and data protection. Policymakers should enforce regulations that mandate baseline security measures, promote ethical IoT practices, and bridge the digital divide to ensure equitable access to IoT technologies. Meanwhile, users must be educated about the importance of securing their devices and adopting best practices to mitigate risks. Advances in artificial intelligence, machine learning, and edge computing offer promising avenues to enhance IoT security, scalability, and data management, but these technologies must be integrated thoughtfully to avoid introducing new vulnerabilities or ethical concerns. By fostering a culture of innovation, transparency, and accountability, the IoT ecosystem can evolve into a secure, efficient, and inclusive infrastructure that benefits society at large. Ultimately, this chapter calls for a shared vision and concerted action to overcome the IoT's challenges, enabling its transformative potential to be realized responsibly and sustainably across industries and communities worldwide.

Chapter 2

IoT device vulnerabilities

2.1 IoT ARCHITECTURE, PROTOCOL, AND TECHNOLOGY

The architecture, protocols, and technologies of the Internet of Things (IoT) form the backbone of its functionality, enabling seamless connectivity, data exchange, and intelligent operations across diverse environments. These elements work in harmony to create an ecosystem where devices, networks, and platforms interconnect to deliver value across various applications.

2.1.1 IoT architecture

The IoT architecture typically follows a multilayered model that encompasses four main layers: perception layer, network layer, middleware layer, and application layer. Figure 2.1 shows the IoT architecture with distinct protocols, components, functions, and attacks at each layer.

Perception Layer: The perception layer consists of sensors, actuators, computational software, and mechanisms for addressing and identifying the things. It is mainly responsible for perceiving the data from the real-time environment. This layer includes the physical IoT devices and sensors that collect data from the environment. Devices such as temperature sensors, cameras, RFID tags, and actuators detect physical parameters and convert them into digital signals. This layer is the foundation of the IoT as it bridges the physical and digital worlds. Rather than sensing, it also has some other functions such as encryption–decryption, modulation–demodulation, frequency selection, reception, and transmission of data. Some malicious activities that can be performed at this layer are as follows (line A).

Eavesdropping: IoT sensors are generally designed for low-energy-consuming hardware. Due to their limited capabilities, highly complex encryption techniques cannot be applied to tiny devices such as sensors. Eavesdropping can target the confidentiality of the IoT system by passively listening to the data when the sender does not get any feedback. Hackers can install similar devices and sniff the wireless traffic to extract the vulnerable information.

DOI: 10.1201/9781003631460-2

Application Layer			
Business Sublayer	Profit Model	CoAP, MQTT, XMPP, AMQP	
Semantic Sublayer	Map reduce, HDFS	- Decision Making - Smart object tracking - Application Interface	
Session Sublayer	Enable Interface		

D → - Disclosure of Sensitive data
- SQL Injections
- Software Modification Attack
- Cross-Site Scripting
- Brute-Force Attack

Middleware Layer			
Data Abstraction Sublayer	Normalization, Indexing	DLS, DTLS	
Support Sublayer	Third Party vendor	- Stores, Process, and Analyse data - Diverse set of services to lower layers - Storage for huge data	
Cloud Sublayer	Remote Storage		

C → - Improper Queries
- Account Hijacking
- Malicious Node Injection
- Message Fabrication
- Data Breach

Network Layer/ Adoption Layer			
Edge Computing Sublayer	Signal analysis	6LoWPAN, IPv4/IPv6 IEEE 802.15.4	
Gateway	Internet	- Communication at device level - Communication between components - Transmission of information to next level	
Short Range Communication	WSN, LAN		

B → - DoS Attack
- Fragmentation Attack
- Network Intrusion
- Reconnaissance Attack
- Spoofing, Flood, or Replay Attack

Perception Layer			
Identification & Addressing	EPC, RFID	LTE-A, EPC Global, IEEE 802.15.4, Z-Wave	
Software	OS, Android, tinyOS	- Data Sensing and Collection - Modulation and De-modulation - Identification and Addressing	
Hardware Component	Sensors, Actuators		

A → - Eavesdropping
- Hardware Failure
- Disclosure of Critical Information
- Cloning of Nodes
- Invasive Intrusion

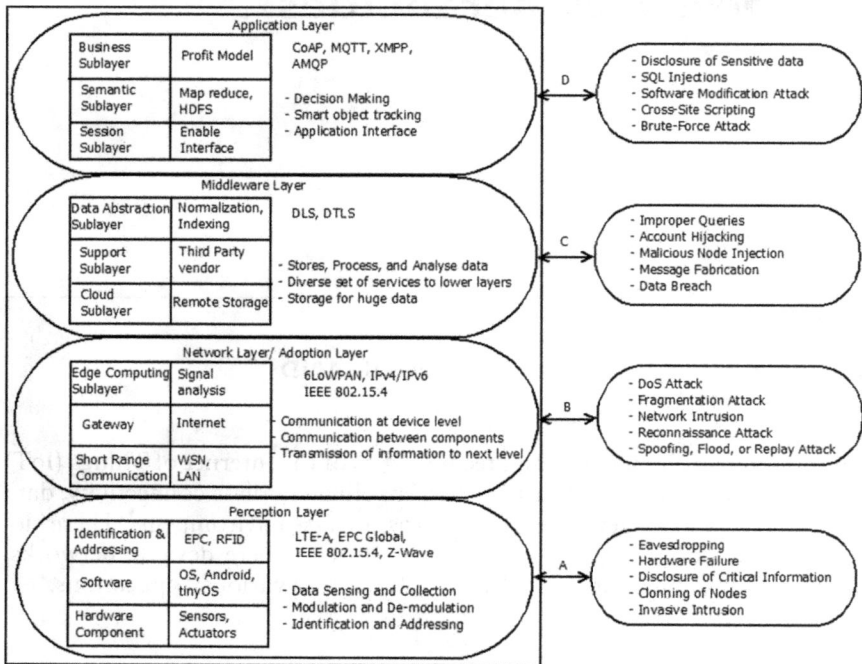

Figure 2.1 IoT architecture.

Hardware Failure: Hardware failure can occur due to manufacturing faults or as a result of an attack that can lead to physical damage or modification of functionality. If hardware tampering is done by an attacker, it may result in sending incorrect data to the network. Another drawback that may arise during the manufacturing process of any device is that it can have the same parameters for distinct devices, even when they were manufactured in the same company.

Disclosure of Critical Information: Critical information could be shared among the sensors through a wireless network. A malicious attacker may be able to continuously monitor the wireless network and try to exploit it or access the information in an unauthorized way even when the data is in encrypted form. Exposure of critical information can reveal the design of a new product or send some incorrect information to the authorized user.

Cloning of Nodes: There is no common standard for designing a new IoT device, which may result in the development of hardware which is not tamper-proof. Therefore, such devices can easily be forged or replicated in unauthorized ways. Node cloning can be done during two phases—the manufacturing phase and the operational phase.

Invasive Intrusion: These attacks are serious threats due to small or BGA packaging of devices, as boot sequence relies on the trusted on-chip assets.

Invasive attacks can reveal the valuable information stored on chips and may compromise the device even if it is secured with an Advanced Encryption Standard (AES) key. An attacker can decapsulate the information using a manual method with fuming nitric acid and acetone at 60 degrees or, automatically, using a mixture of HNO_3 and H_2SO_4.

Network/Adoption Layer: The network or adoptive layer is mainly responsible for providing communication between devices and middleware components using IEEE 802.15.4, IPv4/IPv6, or 6LoWPAN. This layer enables the transfer of data collected by a layer of perception to other parts of the system, such as a gateway, cloud servers, or local processing units. It uses communication technologies such as Wi-Fi, Bluetooth, ZigBee, LoRaWAN, Cellular (3G/4G/5G), and satellites to ensure data transfer across different networks. This layer aggregates data from several devices and provides routes via the gate. This layer, most vulnerable due to its global range, is considered one of the possible attacks (line B).

DoS Attack: The rejection of a service occurs when the targeted devices or servers deny any request generated by the client due to excessive flooding of data in the channel. It can happen due to various flaws in the medium access control and communication protocols. These include collision attacks, battery exhaustion attacks, identity conflicts, and channel congestion attacks.

Fragmentation Attack: An IP fragmentation attack is a type of DoS attack through which a bad actor can exploit the datagram fragmentation mechanism. In the process of IP fragmentation, IP datagrams are broken into small packets, transmitted through the network channel, and then reassembled at the receiver side. A bad actor can exploit this vulnerability and involve the transmission of fraudulent UDP or ICMP packets.

Network Intrusion: It refers to an unauthorized activity in an IoT network during the transmission of data. In the network intrusion, a bad actor can steal some valuable information or modify it for the incorrect behavior of the devices. Multirouting, buffer overwriting, protocol specific attacks, or flooding are some common attacks that are possible during the network intrusion.

Reconnaissance Attack: There are several possible attacks that are used to gather important information about targets such as a network, open port, etc. There are several open-source tools available such as Nmap, Nipper, or Saint to scan the vulnerable ports. After the collection of all important information, threat actors can exploit the network using tools such as Metasploitable or Netsparker.

Spoofing, Flood, or Replay Attack: Spoofing is when the unauthorized device can access the user device by falsifying its address as a legitimate user. This kind of attack can be the reason for DDoS attacks against IoT infrastructure, such as man-in-the-middle (MITM) attacks and sybil attacks. These attacks may take the benefits of weak authentication mechanism and anti-replay attacks.

Middleware Layer: IoT devices can generate an unrivalled amount of data every second from sensors, which can cause a huge load for the Internet infrastructure. The network layer data is processed in this layer, which includes both computer devices and cloud platforms. EDGE processes data locally, reduces the use of the bandwidth and bandwidth, while cloud processes extensive data storage, analytics, and management. This layer is responsible for converting the raw data into actionable information. Therefore, there is a requirement for more storage and generate more complex data from heterogeneous devices. Thus, the integration of cloud and the IoT can provide more storage, services on request, and scalable network services. Although the middleware layer provides several functionalities, it also has some vulnerabilities through which attackers can perform some attacks at this layer (Line C).

Improper Queries: A malicious actor can generate some error messages to gain full access to the data, which may contain tables with their structure. The main motive of this attack is to gather information about the database by using a legitimate user's credentials. After getting guidance, an attacker can damage the system or mislead it. A PREPARE statement in SQL has some pre-defined templates that can provide all the details about the databases.

Account Hijacking: Account or service hijacking is one of the serious attacks at the middleware. Account hijacking occurs if an attacker can access the account of some legitimate user using compromised credentials. Once the attacker has stolen the credentials, they can exploit the information, manipulate data, or eavesdrop. This attack may lead to several other attacks such as insufficient input validation, patching, or unauthenticated data.

Malicious Node Injection: In this attack, a bad actor can insert some malicious code into the SQL server, which results in the malfunctioning of the application. If the server does not have sufficient code checkpoints, it can lead to several malfunctions or misbehavior of the application. Some security checks, like checkpoints or firewall techniques, can prevent malicious node injection.

Message Fabrication: In this kind of attack, an attacker tries to alter or delete the messages. Once a smart device sends any message to the network, it may be encrypted by using the hash value of the message with the private key of the sender. A receiving unit can verify the integrity of the message using the public key. If the fabrication of the message can be done by an attacker with the stolen public key of the receiver, then it may delete or alter the message.

Data Breach: A data breach incident can happen, which can steal sensitive information and use it in an unauthorized way. It can damage the company's reputation or break the trust of clients. A data breach can be done using a customer's credentials in an unauthorized manner and may generate some financial losses. Since cloud services are provided by third-party vendors, there may be some malicious insiders who can breach the data.

Application Layer: Service delivery and efficiency are two major factors that application providers focus on. Application layer security does not come under the preference of the providers due to the rapid growth of the

IoT devices in the market and pressure to launch the product. This layer is where the users interact with IoT systems through applications and services. It includes user interfaces and dashboards, where processed data is presented in a meaningful way, enabling users to monitor, control, and make decisions. Examples include smart home apps, industrial control systems, and healthcare monitoring platforms. As a result, the applications can be compromised by attackers, and data security could be breached. There are several attacks possible at the application layer (Line D).

Disclosure of Sensitive Information: Sensitive information can be exposed due to insecure web applications. The vulnerable web API can exploit the confidentiality and privacy of the data which may collected by the smart devices. The data exchange occurs through HTTP between application and the ethernet-enabled bridge. The proper inclusion of the cryptographic algorithm can ensure the disclosure of sensitive information.

SQL Injection: An IoT device can provide its services with the help of an Android app or a website remotely. To provide the services, it must have some credentials to provide the authenticated services to the end-user. A bad actor can find an SQL injection in the Android app to bypass the authentication or encryption services. This kind of SQL injection can generate some other attacks such as a DoS attack, a root-level access attack, or firmware updates.

Software Modification Attack: The software modification attack can take advantage of the weak application security and lack of authentication mechanisms. An attacker can modify the software code using some JavaScript code or module to change the functionality of the software that results in the misbehavior of the application or the device. The exploitation can also be done through code substitution, code extension, or binary patching.

Cross-site Scripting: Cross-site scripting is a web-based application attack that can exploit the vulnerability of a website. The vulnerability of the cross-site scripting can be exploited by using some JavaScript code in the victim's browser. It may lead to account hijacking or the theft of private data. These JavaScript codes come from a trusted source, can access any cookies, sensitive information, or session tokens.

Brute-Force Attack: Brute force attack or dictionary-based attack is one of the most dangerous attacks that can be performed on IoT devices due to the large number of IoT devices launched in the market with default usernames and passwords. An example of this is the Mirai attack, which happened in 2016, that used a list of 84 pre-defined usernames and passwords. It affects hardware devices such as DVRs and CCTV cameras to exploit the vulnerability and gain full control over the devices.

2.1.2 IoT protocols

The IoT relies on a variety of protocols to enable communication between devices, gateways, and cloud systems. These protocols operate across different layers of the networking stack, including physical, data link, network, transport, and application layers. Each protocol is designed to address specific requirements of the IoT, such as low power consumption, high scalability, security, and interoperability. The IoT relies on a wide range of protocols to ensure efficient communication across its ecosystem.

Figure 2.2 shows the IoT protocol stack. Key protocols include the following.

ZigBee: ZigBee is a wireless communication protocol with a low-performance system based on IEEE 802.15.4, designed for applications requiring reliable, low-data communication over short to medium distances. It is generally used in intelligent houses, industrial automation, healthcare, and environmental monitoring. ZigBee supports the topology of the network, Star and Tree, thus making it very scalable and durable. The key advantage of ZigBee is its energy efficiency, which has been followed in small batteries for many years. Its network capacity increases reliability by allowing the device to direct data through medium nodes and ensure communication, even if some nodes fail. ZigBee operates in the 2.4 GHz ISM band around the world with other regional frequencies and offers data speeds up to 250 kbps. The protocol uses strong security features, including AES-128 encryption, which ensures the confidentiality and integrity of data. ZigBee also supports interoperability through the ZigBee Alliance certification program and allows equipment from various manufacturers to work smoothly. Despite its advantages, ZigBee has limitations such as a relatively short range (10–100 m indoors) and lower data speed when compared to Wi-Fi. However, its cost efficiency, low energy

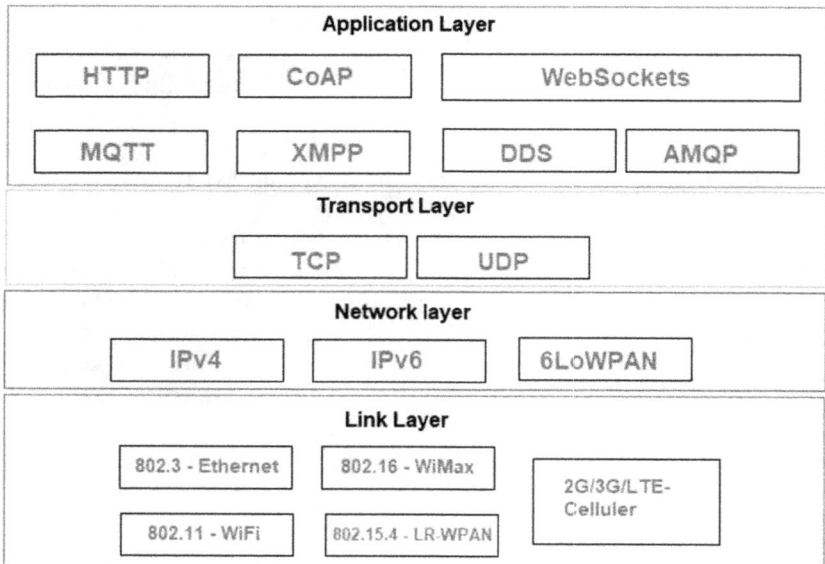

Application Layer		
HTTP	CoAP	WebSockets
MQTT	XMPP	DDS	AMQP

Transport Layer
TCP	UDP

Network layer
IPv4	IPv6	6LoWPAN

Link Layer
802.3 - Ethernet	802.16 - WiMax	2G/3G/LTE-Celluler
802.11 - WiFi	802.15.4 - LR-WPAN	

Figure 2.2 IoT protocol stacks.

consumption, and adaptability make it a popular choice for IoT applications requiring efficient and reliable communication.

Bluetooth Low Energy (BLE): BLE is a wireless communication protocol optimized for low-power applications with a short range. It is part of the Bluetooth 4.0 standard and is widely used in IoT devices such as fitness trackers, smart watches, medical sensors, and home automation systems. BLE is designed to transmit a small amount of data efficiently and allow the devices to run at minimum power over a longer period, often months or even years on one battery. BLE works in the ISM 2.4 GHz band and uses adaptive frequency jumping to reduce interference. Its typical range is 10–50 m indoors and up to 100 m in open spaces. BLE supports various topologies, including Point-to-Point, broadcast, and network, which are suitable for a variety of applications. The major strength of BLE is its fast connection setup, enabling devices to quickly exchange data and conserve energy. It also supports secure communication through features such as AES-128 encryption and pairing mechanisms. While BLE has limited data transfer speeds compared to classic Bluetooth, its energy efficiency and widespread acceptance make it an ideal choice for the IoT, though limited by a source requiring reliable, low-latency communication.

Long Range (LoRa): LoRa is a wireless communication protocol designed for long-term and low-energy IoT applications. It takes place in non-cultivated ISM bands (usually 868 MHz in Europe, 915 MHz in North America, and 433 MHz in Asia) and is ideal for scenarios where the device must transmit small amounts of data over long distances with minimal power consumption. LoRa can cover a range of up to 15 km in rural areas and 2–5 km in the urban environment. The protocol is based on the modulation of Chirp Spectrum (CSS), which provides excellent interference resistance and robust performance in noisy environment. LoRa is widely used in applications such as intelligent agriculture, environmental monitoring, industrial automation, and intelligent cities. The low data rate of the LoRa (ranging from 0.3 kbps to 50 kbps) is unsuitable for applications with high bandwidth, but is ideal for sensor-based use. LoRaWAN, a network layer protocol built on LoRa, adds support for scalability, security (AES-128 encryption), and device management in large deployments.

Near Field Communication (NFC): NFC is a wireless short-range communication technology that allows data to be replaced between devices within several centimeters. NFC, which acts on 13.56 MHz in the high-frequency (HF) band, supports low-energy interactions, ideal for applications such as contactless payments, access control, ticket sales, and data sharing. NFC works in three modes: (1) peer-to-peer, for direct data exchange between devices; (2) read/write, where one device reads data from another; and (3) card emulation, which allows the device to function as a contactless smart card. Its simple and tap-based interaction enhances usability and security, as physical proximity is required for communication. NFC's data transfer rate ranges from 106 kbps to 424 kbps, which is sufficient for small data packets. While limited in range compared to Bluetooth or Wi-Fi, NFC's advantages include lower energy consumption, faster setup (no pairing required), and inherent security due to its close-range operation.

IPv6 over Low-power Wireless Personal Area Networks (6LoWPAN): 6LoWPAN is an adaptation layer protocol that allows IPV6 communication over wireless networks limited to sources such as IEEE 802.15.4. It is specially designed for IoT applications and supports efficient data transfer for devices with limited power, memory, and energy. 6LoWPAN uses compression techniques and fragmentation of the header to reduce IPv6 packets, making them suitable for low-width networks. It supports Mesh, Star, and Peer-to-peer topology, increasing scalability and reliability. This protocol allows you to integrate the IoT with the wider Internet, allowing direct IP addressing and end-to-end communication. The common 6LoWPAN applications include intelligent houses, industrial automation, environmental monitoring, and intelligent cities. Thanks to its lightweight design and compatibility with the existing IP infrastructure, it makes it a basic technology for building large interoperable IoT networks in solving problems of low-energy and lossy environments. It requires efficient energy control for low-energy devices.

Routing Protocol for Low-Power and Lossy Networks (RPL): RPL is a distance vector specially designed for the IoT environment characterized by limited resources and unreliable network conditions. It is commonly used in applications such as intelligent networks, industrial automation, and environmental monitoring. RPL organizes a network into a structure of a controlled acyclic chart (DAG), optimizing paths based on different metrics such as energy consumption, connection reliability, and hop number. Devices can dynamically adapt routes to changing network conditions, ensuring reliable communication. The protocol supports bidirectional traffic, including point-to-point, point-to-multipoint, and multipoint-to-point communication, making it versatile for diverse IoT use cases. RPL includes mechanisms to conserve energy, such as parent selection strategies and trickle algorithms to minimize control traffic. While RPL is highly scalable and efficient in low-power and lossy networks, its complexity may introduce overhead in small-scale deployments. Nevertheless, it is a critical protocol for enabling robust and efficient IoT communication.

Message Queuing Telemetry Transport (MQTT): MQTT is a lightweight, publish/preparation communication protocol designed for IoT applications requiring efficient and reliable data exchange in constrained environments. MQTT, which operates TCP/IP, is optimized for low bandwidth, high-latency, and unreliable networks, ideal for intelligent houses, industrial automation, healthcare, and connected vehicles. In MQTT, clients publish reports on specific topics, while subscribers receive messages by subscribing to these topics through a central broker. This separate architecture simplifies communication and allows scalability in a large deployment of IoT. MQTT supports three levels of service quality (QoS), which ensures flexibility in the reliability of message delivery. It also includes functions such as permanent session support, latest clearance, and testament (LWT) for disconnection processing and optional security authentication mechanisms. The low overhead and simplicity of the protocol are highly efficient for equipment with limited resources. However, relying on a central broker may present a single failure point in some implementations.

Constrained Application Protocol (CoAP): CoAP is a lightweight, RESTful protocol designed for IoT devices with limited resources. It works via UDP and is optimized for low-energy networks, low-bandwidth, and high-priority applications, such as wireless sensor networks. CoAP is widely used in applications such as intelligent houses, industrial IoT, and environmental monitoring. RESTful architecture CoAP allows devices to perform standard web operations such as Get, Post, Put and Lubrication, making it compatible with HTTP-based systems. It uses a simple binary header format to reduce overhead and supports multicast communication for efficient data dissemination. There are several key features that include reliable messaging via retransmission mechanisms, resource discovery using well-known URIs, and security through DTLS (Datagram Transport Layer Security). CoAP also enables easy integration with web services and supports proxying between HTTP and CoAP. Its lightweight design makes CoAP ideal for constrained devices, though its reliance on UDP may limit its use in scenarios requiring guaranteed delivery.

Advanced Message Queuing Protocol (AMQP): AMQP is a robust protocol for sending messages on the Agnostic platform, designed for reliable, secure, and efficient communication in Enterprise and IoT. It supports asynchronous message queuing and facilitates message-oriented middleware for diverse use cases, including industrial IoT, financial services, and supply chain management. AMQP operates over TCP and ensures interoperability across systems by standardizing message formats and behaviors. It uses a broker-based architecture where producers send messages to a central broker, and consumers retrieve them, supporting point-to-point and publish/subscribe messaging patterns. Key features include message routing, queuing, and delivery acknowledgments, ensuring reliable and ordered message transfer. AMQP also supports transnationality, making it suitable for critical applications. Built-in security mechanisms, such as TLS and SASL, enhance communication safety. While AMQP offers rich functionality and reliability, its higher resource requirements compared to lightweight protocols such as MQTT make it more suitable for powerful devices and complex systems.

Lightweight M2M (LwM2M): LWM2M is a protocol designed for efficient IoT management and monitoring. It works over limited networks and devices, such as power with limited power, memory, and battery life. LWM2M, developed by the Open Mobile Alliance (OMA), uses the client–server architecture and promotes IP-based communication, such as UDP, TCP, and CoAP. The protocol defines essential functionalities such as device provisioning, configuration, firmware updates, and remote monitoring.Its object-oriented data model allows flexible and hierarchical representation of device resources, making it adaptable to various IoT use cases. Security is a key focus, with support for DTLS (Datagram Transport Layer Security) for encryption and authentication. LwM2M's lightweight design makes it ideal for applications in smart cities, industrial IoT, and utilities, where resource-constrained devices require scalable, efficient, and secure management.

Narrowband IoT (NB-IoT): NB-IoT is a low-energy wide-range (LPWAN) specially designed for IoT. Standardized by 3GPP, works on existing LTE or separate frequencies, which ensures wide coverage and minimum deployment costs. NB-IoT excels in connecting devices with low data requirements, such as smart meters, asset trackers, and environmental sensors. Its power-efficient design allows devices to operate for years on small batteries. The technology offers robust indoor penetration and wide-area coverage, making it ideal for urban and rural applications. It supports data rates up to 250 kbps and leverages techniques such as Power Saving Mode (PSM) and extended Discontinuous Reception (eDRX) to optimize battery life. NB-IoT also prioritizes security and scalability, accommodating millions of devices within a single cell. Its cost-efficiency and compatibility with existing cellular infrastructure make it a key enabler of smart cities, industrial IoT, and connected agriculture.

2.2 COMMON SECURITY WEAKNESSES IN IoT DEVICES

Common security weaknesses in IoT devices stem from their diverse use cases, limited computational resources, and lack of standardized security practices, making them prime targets for cyberattacks. These vulnerabilities not only compromise individual devices but also pose risks to entire IoT ecosystems and connected networks. These common security weaknesses need a concerted effort from manufacturers, users, and policymakers. IoT users should take proactive steps to secure their devices, such as changing default credentials, applying updates, and using network segmentation. Policymakers and industry leaders must work toward establishing universal IoT security standards to ensure consistent protection across devices. The IoT ecosystem can become more resilient to emerging threats, enabling safe and secure connectivity in a rapidly growing digital landscape. Some of the prevalent security weaknesses in IoT devices include the following.

Weak Authentication and Authorization: Weak authentication and authorization mechanisms are significant vulnerabilities in the IoT ecosystem, exposing devices and networks to unauthorized access and potential exploitation. Authentication refers to the process of verifying a user's or device's identity, while authorization determines the permissions granted to an authenticated entity. Many IoT devices employ minimal security protocols, often relying on default credentials, such as "admin/admin" or "user/password," which users frequently fail to change. These default settings are widely documented and easily exploited by attackers, enabling unauthorized control over devices. Furthermore, many IoT systems lack support for advanced authentication mechanisms, such as multi-factor authentication (MFA) or biometric verification, which could significantly enhance security. Authorization issues arise when devices or applications fail to implement proper role-based access controls (RBAC), granting excessive privileges to users or processes. This can lead to unauthorized data access, manipulation of device functions, or lateral movement within a network, enabling attackers to compromise other connected systems.

IoT devices often communicate with cloud platforms or mobile applications, where insecure APIs with inadequate authentication and authorization checks become a critical vulnerability. These weaknesses can result in data breaches, DoS attacks, and manipulation of critical operations, particularly in sensitive environments such as healthcare, industrial automation, and smart cities. Addressing these challenges requires manufacturers to implement robust authentication protocols, enforce password complexity requirements, and disable default credentials out of the box. IoT systems should support MFA and integrate with identity management solutions to ensure secure access. Similarly, authorization mechanisms must follow the principle of least privilege, granting users and processes only the access necessary for their roles. Encryption should be used to secure authentication tokens and communications, further safeguarding against interception and replay attacks. Continuous monitoring for unusual login attempts and failed access attempts can help detect and mitigate threats in real time. At a regulatory level, standardization efforts must enforce baseline authentication and authorization practices across IoT devices to ensure consistent protection. Finally, user awareness campaigns are vital, as many security lapses stem from a lack of understanding about the importance of changing default credentials and configuring devices securely. Weak authentication and authorization are central to many IoT-related attacks, including the formation of botnets like Mirai, which exploited default credentials to hijack thousands of devices for large-scale DDoS attacks. By prioritizing these security aspects, IoT systems can significantly reduce their vulnerability to threats, ensuring safer and more reliable operations across applications.

Inadequate Encryption: Insufficient encryption is a critical vulnerability in the IoT ecosystem, with sensitive data captured for manipulation and unauthorized access. Encryption is a process of converting data into a secure format to ensure confidentiality and integrity during storage or transmission. However, many IoT devices either completely lack encryption or implement weak, outdated algorithms that are easily compromised. This is often due to limited performance and memory of processing in IoT devices, which limits the use of robust cryptographic methods. Without proper encryption, data transmitted between devices, cloud platforms, and mobile applications can be captured through attacks such as eavesdropping or MITM. In addition, sensitive information such as user data, financial data, and health records stored on IoT devices or in their associated databases may be vulnerable to unauthorized access if encryption is missing or incorrectly applied. Insufficient encryption also exposes IoT devices to repetition of attacks, where the attacker captures and reuses valid data transmissions to obtain unauthorized access or manipulate equipment. To deal with this, manufacturers must accept modern encryption standards, such as the standard for advanced encryption (AES), and secure the transport layer (TLS) to ensure both data at rest and in transit. End-to-end encryption should be implemented to protect the data from the collection site, ensuring that even intermediaries cannot access information. In addition, robust key management procedures, including secure keys and rotation of the periodic key, are necessary to maintain the efficiency of encryption. IoT systems, by ensuring sufficient encryption, can significantly increase data security, protect user privacy, and build confidence in a rapidly expanding digital environment.

Outdated Software and Firmware: Outdated software and firmware are among the most significant security challenges in the IoT ecosystem, exposing devices to known vulnerabilities and exploitation. Firmware is the embedded software that controls IoT device operations, while additional software often governs applications and connectivity. When manufacturers fail to provide timely updates or patches, or users neglect to apply them, these systems remain susceptible to exploits targeting identified weaknesses. Outdated software can leave IoT devices vulnerable to malware, DoS attacks, and unauthorized access, as attackers can leverage publicly disclosed vulnerabilities or exploit codes to compromise the devices. The issue is compounded by the long lifecycle of many IoT devices, which often outlast their support periods, resulting in devices that are no longer maintained but remain connected to networks. Furthermore, many IoT devices lack mechanisms for automatic updates, relying on manual intervention by users who may be unaware of the need for updates or how to perform them. This neglect can lead to the widespread compromise of IoT devices, as seen in large-scale botnets like Mirai, which exploited outdated firmware to launch massive DDoS attacks. Addressing this issue requires manufacturers to prioritize security throughout the device lifecycle, including regular software updates, secure over-the-air (OTA) update mechanisms, and transparent communication of update availability. Users must also be educated on the importance of applying updates promptly and ensuring devices remain supported by manufacturers. Regulatory frameworks can further incentivize manufacturers to provide long-term support and maintain secure update practices. By tackling the problem of outdated software and firmware, the IoT industry can reduce vulnerabilities, protect devices and networks, and enhance overall trust in connected systems.

Lack of Secure Boot and Hardware Protections: The lack of secure boot and hardware protections in IoT devices is a significant security vulnerability, exposing them to unauthorized modifications, malicious firmware installations, and persistent threats. Secure boot is a mechanism that ensures only trusted and verified software is loaded during a device's startup process, using cryptographic signatures to validate the integrity of the firmware. Many IoT devices, however, lack this safeguard, allowing attackers to tamper with the firmware or load malicious software that bypasses security measures. Without secure boot, attackers can install rootkits or backdoors, gaining long-term control over devices and the ability to manipulate their operations or exfiltrate sensitive data. In addition to secure boot, hardware protections such as Trusted Platform Modules (TPMs) or secure enclaves are often absent in IoT devices. These hardware components provide secure storage for cryptographic keys and enable trusted execution environments that protect critical processes from tampering. The lack of such protections makes it easier for attackers to extract sensitive information, such as encryption keys or credentials, directly from the device through physical attacks or reverse engineering. IoT devices deployed in public or remote areas are especially vulnerable to these types of attacks, as they are more accessible to attackers. Addressing these vulnerabilities requires manufacturers to integrate secure boot mechanisms and hardware-based security features into their devices. This includes implementing tamper-resistant designs, secure key storage, and trusted execution environments to safeguard sensitive operations. Additionally, developers should adopt best practices for firmware signing and ensure firmware integrity checks are part of the device's regular operation. By incorporating these protections, IoT devices can resist unauthorized modifications, enhance overall security, and build trust in their resilience against emerging threats in increasingly connected environments.

Poor Network Security: Poor network security is a critical vulnerability in the IoT ecosystem, exposing devices, data, and interconnected systems to a wide range of cyberthreats. IoT devices often rely on networks to communicate and function, but many of these networks are inadequately secured, creating entry points for attackers. Common issues include the use of weak or outdated communication protocols, such as WEP or unencrypted HTTP, which allow attackers to intercept, modify, or steal data in transit through methods like MITM attacks. Open ports, unsecured device discovery protocols like Universal Plug and Play (UPnP), and poorly configured firewalls further exacerbate the risk by providing attackers with direct access to devices and networks. Inadequate network segmentation is another major problem. IoT devices are often connected to the same network as critical systems, enabling attackers who compromise an IoT device to move laterally and target sensitive assets. Moreover, the lack of strong access controls and authentication for networked devices leaves them vulnerable to unauthorized access, making them easy targets for exploitation in botnets or DoS attacks. IoT networks often lack intrusion detection and prevention systems, which are essential for identifying and responding to suspicious activities in real time. These deficiencies make it difficult to detect breaches or mitigate ongoing attacks. It includes encrypting all communications with modern protocols like TLS, implementing network segmentation to isolate IoT devices, and using firewalls to control traffic. Device discovery protocols should be configured securely or disabled when unnecessary. Regular monitoring and the use of intrusion detection systems (IDSs) can further enhance security by enabling prompt responses to threats. Strengthening network security is vital for safeguarding IoT ecosystems and preventing exploitation of connected devices.

Insufficient Physical Security: Insufficient physical security in IoT devices is a significant vulnerability that exposes them to unauthorized access, manipulation, and attacks. Unlike traditional computing devices, IoT devices are often deployed in distant, public, or easily accessible places, which makes them vulnerable to physical compromise. The attackers can get direct access to hardware and allow them to extract sensitive data, edit firmware, or install malicious software. This can lead to unauthorized control of the device, theft of cryptographic keys, or disruption of equipment operations. Physical security flaws include a lack of tamper-resistant enclosures, exposing internal components such as chips, memory modules, or debugging interfaces like JTAG and UART. These interfaces often remain active in production devices, allowing attackers to bypass software-based security measures. Furthermore, inadequate protection against side-channel attacks—such as power analysis or electromagnetic emission attacks—enables skilled attackers to infer sensitive information without directly accessing the device's data storage. Devices without secure storage for sensitive data, such as cryptographic keys or configuration files, are particularly vulnerable. Attackers can physically extract this information and use it to compromise not just the targeted device but also the entire IoT ecosystem it belongs to. Additionally, weak or absent protections against hardware tampering, such as anti-tamper switches or coatings, make it easier for attackers to alter the device's hardware or firmware undetected. Techniques such as hardware encryption, anti-tamper mechanisms, and detection of unauthorized access can further enhance security. By addressing physical security vulnerabilities, IoT systems can better safeguard their hardware, data, and functionality from physical threats in both consumer and industrial environments.

Lack of Standardized Security Frameworks: The lack of standardized security frameworks in the IoT ecosystem poses a significant challenge to ensuring the safety and reliability of connected devices and networks. IoT encompasses a diverse range of devices, manufacturers, and use cases, each with unique security needs. However, the absence of universally accepted guidelines or frameworks leads to inconsistent security implementations. Many manufacturers prioritize functionality and cost over security, resulting in devices with weak authentication, insufficient encryption, and vulnerabilities that attackers can exploit. Without standardized frameworks, interoperability between devices and systems is also hindered. Security protocols may vary widely, leaving gaps in communication channels or creating compatibility issues between devices from different vendors. These inconsistencies expose IoT ecosystems to threats such as unauthorized access, data breaches, and large-scale attacks like DDoS. The lack of a unified framework also complicates regulatory compliance and user confidence. Organizations struggle to meet varying regional or industry-specific security requirements, while end-users remain uncertain about the security of their devices. This fragmentation makes it difficult to establish best practices, conduct thorough risk assessments, or implement effective countermeasures against evolving threats. Frameworks like ISO/IEC standards or the National Institute of Standards and Technology (NIST) guidelines can serve as models for developing IoT-specific standards. Certification programs for devices adhering to these frameworks can further enhance trust and accountability. By adopting standardized security frameworks, the IoT industry can create a more secure, interoperable, and resilient ecosystem, enabling the widespread adoption of IoT technologies without compromising security.

Vulnerable APIs and Cloud Services: Vulnerable APIs and cloud services are critical weak points in the IoT ecosystem, exposing connected devices and their associated data to cyberthreats. Application Programming Interfaces (APIs) are essential for communication between IoT devices, mobile applications, and cloud platforms. However, poorly designed or inadequately secured APIs can provide attackers with a pathway to compromise the entire IoT ecosystem. Common vulnerabilities include insufficient authentication and authorization checks, lack of input validation, and weak encryption of data in transit. These flaws can enable attackers to execute unauthorized commands, gain access to sensitive data, or manipulate device functionality. Cloud services, which serve as the backbone for IoT data storage, analytics, and remote management, are attractive targets for attackers. Weak security configurations, such as misconfigured access controls or inadequate encryption, can expose cloud-hosted IoT data to breaches. In addition, cloud service security errors can lead to extensive attacks such as data theft or disruption of critical services that affect millions of devices simultaneously. The use of these vulnerabilities can result in serious consequences, including data violations, privacy violations, DOS attacks, and even physical damage in applications such as healthcare or industrial automation. Robust security measures are necessary to alleviate these risks. APIs should enforce strong authentication mechanisms such as OAuth or Token verification and verify all inputs to prevent attacks. Encryption protocols such as TLS must be used to ensure data transfer between devices and cloud services. Continuous monitoring and logging can help immediately detect and respond to unusual activities.

Over-Privileged Access and Permissions: Over-privileged access and permissions in the IoT ecosystem represent a significant security risk, as they grant users, applications, or devices more access than necessary to perform their intended functions. This violates the principle of least privilege, which recommends that entities be given only the permissions required for their specific tasks. When IoT devices, systems, or users operate with excessive permissions, the attack surface expands, increasing the likelihood of exploitation. This problem is exacerbated by poorly implemented access control mechanisms in many IoT systems. Default configurations often include administrative privileges or unrestricted access to connected systems, and these settings are rarely reviewed or adjusted by users. Additionally, shared accounts or hardcoded credentials on IoT devices can provide broad access to multiple systems, creating a single point of failure if compromised. Excessive permissions also increase the risk of insider threats, whether intentional or accidental. A legitimate user with over-privileged access could inadvertently modify critical settings or expose sensitive data. In large IoT deployments, such as smart cities or industrial IoT systems, these risks are magnified, potentially causing widespread disruption or safety hazards. Manufacturers must design IoT systems to implement least-privilege principles by default, ensuring that devices, users, and applications operate within their necessary boundaries. Robust logging and monitoring can further help detect and address anomalies, reducing the likelihood of misuse or exploitation.

Lack of Monitoring and Intrusion Detection System: The lack of monitoring and intrusion detection in the IoT ecosystem is a critical vulnerability that undermines the ability to detect, respond to, and mitigate security threats in real time. IoT devices, often deployed in large numbers across diverse environments, generate massive amounts of data and operate autonomously, making continuous monitoring essential to identify abnormal behavior or potential intrusions. However, many IoT systems lack built-in monitoring tools or integration with centralized security platforms, leaving them blind to unauthorized access, data breaches, or malicious activities. IDSs are crucial for identifying threats such as unauthorized device access, data exfiltration, or DoS attacks. However, the resource constraints of IoT devices, such as limited processing power, memory, and bandwidth, often prevent the implementation of traditional IDS solutions. The absence of monitoring exacerbates the impact of security breaches. For example, attackers can exploit vulnerabilities in IoT devices for extended periods without detection, as seen in botnet attacks like Mirai. These breaches can lead to widespread network disruptions, data theft, or control over critical infrastructure. It becomes difficult to trace the source of an attack or evaluate its scope, delaying response and recovery efforts. IoT systems must incorporate lightweight, resource-efficient monitoring solutions tailored for IoT environments. This includes behavior-based anomaly detection, device-specific IDS, and centralized logging systems that aggregate data from multiple devices for analysis. Real-time alerts, coupled with automated response mechanisms, can significantly enhance the ability to counter threats.

2.3 FIRMWARE AND SOFTWARE VULNERABILITIES

Firmware and software vulnerabilities on IoT devices are significant risks for the security and functionality of interconnected systems. These vulnerabilities arise due to flaws in the design, development, or implementation of device firmware and software, as well as inadequate maintenance practices.

They create exploitable entry points for attackers, jeopardizing user data, device operations, and the broader IoT ecosystem. The solution to these weaknesses requires a proactive approach that includes safe development procedures, continuous updates, and efforts to cooperate between manufacturers, users, and a wider community of cybersecurity professionals. In-depth consideration of routine firmware and software vulnerability in IoT devices includes the following.

Outdated Firmware and Software: Outdated firmware and software pose significant risks in IoT and IT systems, compromising security, performance, and reliability. They often contain unpatched vulnerabilities that hackers can exploit, leading to data breaches, malware attacks, or unauthorized access. Additionally, outdated software may lack compatibility with newer technologies, reducing system efficiency and limiting functionality. For IoT devices, this can lead to network disruptions and unreliable operations. Regular updates address bugs, enhance security, and improve features, ensuring optimal performance. Implementing automated update mechanisms and monitoring tools is critical to mitigate risks associated with outdated firmware and software, safeguarding devices and systems effectively.

Insecure Firmware Updates: Insecure firmware updates are a critical vulnerability in IoT and IT systems, potentially exposing devices to attacks. Without proper security measures, attackers can intercept or manipulate updates, injecting malicious code or backdoors. Risks arise from unencrypted update transmissions, lack of authentication, and weak integrity checks. This can lead to unauthorized access, compromise of the system, or device failure. Secure firmware updates should use encryption to protect data in transit, digital signatures to verify authenticity, and integrity to ensure that the updates are unchanged. To secure devices and networks, it is necessary to implement the mechanisms of secure updates, such as OTA Air updates (OPE) with robust cryptographic procedures.

Lack of Secure Boot Mechanisms: A lack of secure boot mechanisms exposes devices to significant security risks, such as unauthorized code execution or malware infiltration during the startup process. Secure boot ensures that only trusted and verified firmware or software is loaded by validating digital signatures against trusted certificates. Without it, attackers can tamper with the bootloader or firmware, compromising the device's integrity and functionality. This can lead to data breaches, system instability, or unauthorized access. To mitigate these risks, devices should implement secure boot with cryptographic validation, hardware-based root of trust, and protections against rollback to older, vulnerable software versions, ensuring a secure startup.

Buffer Overflows and Memory Management Issues: Buffer overflows are critical vulnerabilities in software, often leading to crashes, unauthorized access, or arbitrary code execution. A buffer overflow occurs when data exceeds a buffer's allocated size, overwriting adjacent memory and potentially exposing sensitive information or enabling malicious exploits.

Poor memory management, such as improper allocation, dangling pointers, or memory leaks, degrades performance and stability, increasing the risk of attacks. Preventive measures include border control, input verification, use of programming languages in memory, and compiler protection, such as stack channels and ASLR (randomization of address space layout). Correct coding and robust testing procedures are necessary to alleviate these risks.

Open Debugging Interfaces: Open debugging interfaces are a security risk, as they can provide attackers with unauthorized access to a device's internal systems. These interfaces, often left active in production environments, expose critical functions such as memory read/write, firmware loading, or system controls. Exploiting them allows attackers to bypass authentication, extract sensitive data, or install malicious code. Common examples include JTAG, UART, or other debug ports left unprotected. To mitigate risks, debugging interfaces should be disabled or securely locked in production, with access restricted through authentication or cryptographic controls. Regular security assessments can help identify and address exposed debugging interfaces, ensuring device protection.

Lack of Code Obfuscation: A lack of code obfuscation leaves software vulnerable to reverse engineering, exposing sensitive logic, proprietary algorithms, and security mechanisms to attackers. Without obfuscation, the source code or binary can be easily analyzed, revealing cryptographic keys, hardcoded credentials, or system vulnerabilities. This enables attackers to modify, exploit, or replicate the software. Obfuscation techniques, such as renaming variables, encrypting strings, and restructuring code, make reverse engineering significantly more difficult by concealing the software's logic. While not a standalone security solution, code obfuscation is a critical layer of defense, complementing other security practices to protect intellectual property and reduce the attack surface.

Insufficient Testing and Quality Assurance: It results in software and systems with vulnerabilities, bugs, and performance issues. Without rigorous testing, critical flaws may go unnoticed, leading to security breaches, system crashes, or poor user experiences. Neglecting QA increases the likelihood of unhandled edge cases, compatibility issues, and scalability problems. Comprehensive testing—covering functional, security, performance, and regression aspects—is essential to ensure reliability and resilience. Automated testing tools, manual reviews, and continuous integration practices improve coverage and efficiency. Investing in robust QA processes reduces risks, enhances product quality, and builds user trust by delivering secure, reliable, and high-performing solutions.

Poorly Designed APIs: Poorly designed APIs pose significant security and functionality risks in software systems. Weak authentication, inadequate input validation, and lack of rate limiting can expose APIs to attacks such as data breaches, injection, and denial of service. Poor documentation and inconsistent standards lead to developer confusion, integration errors, and reduced usability. Inefficient designs can result in high latency, increased resource consumption, and scalability issues. To mitigate these risks, APIs should follow secure design principles, enforce authentication and access controls, validate inputs rigorously, and implement rate limiting. Adhering to standards such as REST or GraphQL ensures consistency, while comprehensive documentation improves developer experience.

Insecure Default Configurations: Insecure default configurations are a common vulnerability in software and devices, leaving systems exposed to attacks. Defaults such as weak passwords, open ports, unnecessary services, or overly permissive settings create exploitable entry points for attackers. Users often fail to change these defaults, increasing the risk of unauthorized access, data breaches, or system compromise. Secure configurations should disable unused services, enforce strong authentication, and follow the principle of least privilege. Implementing security baselines, providing configuration guides, and prompting users to modify default settings during setup are critical steps to reduce risks associated with insecure default configurations and enhance overall system security.

Absence of Runtime Protections: The absence of runtime protections leaves systems vulnerable to attacks targeting applications during execution. Threats such as buffer overflows, code injection, and unauthorized memory access can exploit this gap, compromising security and stability. Without safeguards, attackers can manipulate active processes, execute malicious payloads, or exfiltrate sensitive data. Runtime protections, such as Data Execution Prevention (DEP), Address Space Layout Randomization (ASLR), and runtime integrity checks, are essential to prevent exploitation. These measures detect and block suspicious behavior, ensuring code execution adheres to expected patterns. Implementing runtime protections significantly enhances resilience against real-time threats and fortifies overall application security.

2.4 INADEQUATE AUTHENTICATION AND AUTHORIZATION

Insufficient verification and authorization represent the basic weakness in the IoT ecosystem and create serious vulnerabilities that threaten the security of the device, user privacy, and the integrity of the system. Verification is the process of authentication of the user, device, or application when attempting to access the system, while authorization determines what level of access or permissions is provided to a verified entity. In many IoT devices, these safety mechanisms are either poorly implemented or absent, so systems are exposed to unauthorized access, data violations, and harmful activities. One pervasive issue is the widespread use of default credentials, such as "admin" and "password," which are often hardcoded into devices and either overlooked or intentionally left unchanged by users. These default credentials are widely known and easily exploitable, enabling attackers to gain unauthorized access with minimal effort. Compounding this issue is the lack of strong password policies in many IoT systems, where devices may accept weak passwords that fail to meet basic security criteria, such as sufficient length, complexity, or periodic expiration, thereby increasing susceptibility to brute-force attacks.

Many IoT devices also lack support for robust authentication methods such as MFA, which combines something that the user knows (e.g., password) with something the user has (e.g., hardware token or smartphone) or something the user is (e.g., biometric data). Without MFA, even if one verification factor is at risk, there is no additional security layer to protect against unauthorized access. This deficiency is particularly concerning in high-stakes applications such as smart homes, industrial control systems, or healthcare devices, where unauthorized access can lead to safety risks, operational disruptions, or significant privacy violations.

The problem extends beyond authentication to authorization, where IoT systems frequently fail to enforce the principle of least privilege. This principle dictates that users, applications, or devices should have only a minimum level of access necessary to perform their specific tasks. In practice, however, IoT systems often grant broad or unrestricted permissions by default, resulting in over-privileged access. This creates an environment where a compromised device or user account can be leveraged to access critical system resources or sensitive data. For instance, an attacker gaining access to a smart thermostat could potentially manipulate other connected devices on the same network or extract personal information stored in the system. Such over-privileged access can also lead to insider threats, where legitimate users unintentionally or maliciously misuse their elevated privileges to compromise system security or data integrity.

Another major challenge lies in the absence of secure authentication and authorization frameworks designed specifically for IoT. Unlike traditional IT systems, IoT devices often operate under significant constraints, with limited power, memory, and energy capacity. These limitations make it difficult to implement advanced safety protocols or encryption methods that are standard in conventional computational environments. As a result, many IoT manufacturers prefer usability and cost-effectiveness over security, producing a device with minimal or no verification and authorization warranty. The lack of industry-wide standards further exacerbates this issue, leading to inconsistent security practices across different manufacturers and devices. For example, some IoT devices may implement proprietary authentication protocols that are poorly designed or inadequately tested, while others may forgo authorization mechanisms entirely, relying on network isolation as the sole line of defense.

The consequences of insufficient authentication and authorization in IoT systems are far-reaching and often devastating. The attackers can use these vulnerabilities to start extensive attacks, such as DDoS campaigns, using compromised devices within botnets. Mirai Botnet's incorrect attack, which focused on IoT with weak verification, is an example that disrupts the main websites and services by overwhelming them with the operation of a generated kidnapped devices. In addition to DDoS attacks, insufficient verification, and authorization, IoT systems expose risks such as data violations, unauthorized equipment management, and malware dissemination. These threats relate mainly to critical sectors, such as healthcare, where attackers could manipulate medical devices, or in intelligent cities, where the endangered infrastructure could lead to extensive disturbances and security risks.

Addressing these challenges requires a multifaceted approach. First and foremost, manufacturers must implement strong authentication mechanisms, including support for MFA and secure password policies. Default credentials should be disabled or require mandatory updates during the initial device setup, and devices should enforce password complexity requirements and encourage periodic password changes. RBAC should be adopted to limit permissions based on specific roles or tasks, ensuring that users and devices only have the access necessary to fulfill their functions. Sensitive actions, such as changing system settings or accessing personal data, should require additional verification steps to prevent unauthorized modifications.

From a design perspective, manufacturers must incorporate secure authentication and authorization protocols that are lightweight and efficient, making them suitable for resource-constrained IoT devices. Protocols such as OAuth 2.0, device attestation, and public key infrastructure (PKI) can be tailored to meet the unique needs of IoT environments. Additionally, secure boot mechanisms and hardware-based security modules, such as TPMs, can help ensure the integrity of authentication processes by protecting cryptographic keys and preventing unauthorized firmware modifications.

Standardization and regulatory efforts are also essential to improving IoT security. Industry stakeholders, governments, and standards organizations must collaborate to establish universal guidelines and certification programs for secure authentication and authorization in IoT systems. These standards should address the entire lifecycle of IoT devices, from secure design and manufacturing to regular updates and eventual decommissioning. User education is equally important, as many security breaches result from users' lack of awareness about the importance of changing default settings, enabling additional security features, or updating device firmware.

2.5 INSUFFICIENT DATA PROTECTION AND PRIVACY

Insufficient data protection and IoT privacy are significant risks for individuals, organizations, and society. IoT, which ranges from intelligent domestic devices to industrial sensors, collects and transmits a huge amount of personal, sensitive, and operational data. However, many of these devices are designed with minimal security and protection of privacy, which leaves them vulnerable to exploitation by malicious actors. These devices often lack strong encryption, secure data storage mechanisms, or corresponding access controls, making them targets for cyberattacks, data violation, and unauthorized access. In addition, the clear volume of data generated by IoT devices—combined with their ubiquity and integration into critical infrastructure—magnifies the potential impact of data compromises, as violations could lead to highly sensitive information such as health records, financial data, and personal behavior.

Insufficient privacy also causes IoT devices to be susceptible to the supervision, collection, and monitoring of individuals without their consent, often without the users being fully aware of the scope in which their data is collected, processed, and shared. Lack of transparency in data-processing procedures can undermine users' confidence and reduce the acceptance of IoT technologies. One of the primary challenges in providing data protection and privacy in IoT is the absence of standardized security protocols and personal data protection frameworks across the huge and fragmented IoT ecosystem. Many manufacturers prefer functionality, cost efficiency, and easy use before security and privacy, leading to poorly secure devices that are easily compromised. For instance, many IoT devices use default, easily guessable passwords and fail to prompt users to change them during initial setup. Others may store sensitive data, such as usernames, passwords, or encryption keys, in an unprotected form, leaving it vulnerable to extraction. Similarly, the communication channels between IoT devices and their associated platforms may be inadequately secured, allowing attackers to intercept or manipulate data transmissions, often without the user's knowledge. Moreover, weak or non-existent data encryption exposes information both at rest and in transit, leaving it open to theft or tampering. In some cases, IoT devices may lack the capability to support over-the-air (OTA) updates, making it difficult to patch vulnerabilities and address emerging security threats once the device is deployed in the field.

The problem of insufficient data protection is exacerbated by the increasingly interconnected nature of IoT devices. Many devices are part of larger ecosystems where data flows between multiple interconnected devices, servers, and third-party platforms. The complexity of these networks makes it difficult to track where data is stored, who has access to it, and how it is being used. For example, smart home systems may link sensors, cameras, thermostats, and voice assistants, all of which generate sensitive data. Without adequate protections, this data can be accessed by unauthorized users or third parties, raising concerns about surveillance, privacy violations, and exploitation. Similarly, IoT devices in industrial applications may be collecting data on manufacturing processes, employee activities, and machinery performance, which could be valuable to competitors or malicious actors seeking to disrupt operations. As the amount of data generated by IoT devices grows, the risks associated with data breaches and privacy violations increase, as there are more opportunities for sensitive data to be accessed or misused.

Another concern is the lack of user control over their data. Many IoT devices collect data continuously, often without clear consent or notification to the user. In some cases, users may not be aware of the extent to which their data is being shared with third parties or how long the data is retained. Without robust consent mechanisms, users have a limited ability to control how their personal data is collected, processed, and shared. This is particularly problematic in industries such as healthcare, where IoT can monitor sensitive information about the health and wellness of individuals. A lack of spending transparency and user control undermines the ethical principles of privacy and data security, exposing users to potential damage in case of violation. To deal with this, manufacturers must implement more robust personal data controls, such as clear personal data protection principles, granular consent mechanisms, and users' ability to easily access, remove, or modify their data.

They should also observe the Privacy Policy according to the proposal and ensure that the protection of personal data is integrated from the beginning into the development and deployment of IoT equipment. Legal and regulatory frameworks also play an important role in dealing with insufficient data protection and privacy on the IoT. While some regions, such as the European Union with its GDPR, have introduced comprehensive personal data protection laws, many countries lack strong and consistent regulations that would manage and use IoT data. This regulatory gap creates an environment in which manufacturers may not be responsible for violating personal data, and users have limited recourse in case of data violation. Stronger regulatory supervision is required to ensure that IoT manufacturers adhere to personal data protection standards, perform regular security audits, and provide consumers with clear and accessible information about their rights.

Global cooperation is essential to create international IoT security and privacy standards, which would help alleviate the fragmented regulatory environment and ensure consistent protection for users around the world. Finally, the lack of sufficient data protection and privacy on the IoT raises wider social concerns, especially in terms of potential for IoT devices to be used to supervise and collect bulk data. The extensive use of connected devices in households, workplaces, and public areas makes it easier to monitor the activities, behavior, and preferences of individuals. While the IoT can provide comfort and increase user experience, it also creates opportunities for invasive supervision, leading to concerns about individual freedom and autonomy. Without strong privacy, IoT equipment could become instruments for governments, corporations, or malicious actors to monitor individuals without their knowledge or consent, creating significant dilemmas and civil rights. Lack of security functions, procedures for handling data, and user control over personal data can lead to data violation, supervision, and exploitation. Manufacturers must prefer security and privacy in the design, deployment, and maintenance of IoT equipment, while a regulatory framework and users' education are necessary to ensure that IoT technologies are used responsibly and ethically. The solution to these concerns is essential to support trust in IoT and ensure its safe integration into everyday life.

2.6 THE ROLE OF MANUFACTURERS IN IOT SECURITY

Manufacturers play a decisive role in ensuring the security of IoT, as they are the first line of defense against potential threats that could endanger the integrity, privacy, and functionality of interconnected systems. As creators of these devices, manufacturers are responsible for incorporating robust safety measures throughout the product life cycle, from design and development to deployment and management at the end of life. One of the basic aspects of IoT security that the manufacturer must deal with is to ensure that the device is designed from the very beginning with security. This includes the integration of secure introduction mechanisms, hardware-based security, and secure firmware that protects the device from unauthorized access, handling, or harmful code injections. In addition, manufacturers must implement strong encryption standards for rest and transit data, ensuring that sensitive information between devices and networks is protected from capture.

A crucial aspect of securing IoT devices is ensuring they receive timely firmware and software updates, which is an area where manufacturers have a significant responsibility. Devices deployed in the field often become vulnerable over time as new security vulnerabilities are discovered. Manufacturers must establish secure and reliable mechanisms for updating firmware and software remotely, ensuring that devices can be patched without compromising their functionality or security. In addition, manufacturers should implement mechanisms such as digital signatures and encryption to ensure that updates are authentic and are not manipulated by harmful actors. By providing timely security updates, manufacturers can mitigate the risks of vulnerabilities and reduce opportunities for attackers to use the weaknesses in their facilities.

In addition to secure design and timely updates, manufacturers must also prefer the use of strong mechanisms for authentication and access control to avoid unauthorized users accessing or controlling the IoT device. This includes the use of MFA, if possible, ensuring that the default passwords are secure or, ideally, are not preset at all. The reliance on weak or common passwords is a significant security vulnerability in IoT devices, and manufacturers have the responsibility to ensure that users are prompted to change default credentials during the initial setup process. Manufacturers should also avoid hardcoding credentials in the firmware or software, as these can be easily extracted and exploited by attackers.

Another critical area in which manufacturers have a role is ensuring that IoT devices are built with scalability and interoperability in mind, while still maintaining robust security. As IoT ecosystems grow in complexity, the number of devices and data exchanges increases exponentially, which can create new vulnerabilities if proper security measures are not incorporated into the overall architecture. Manufacturers need to design their devices to work securely within these large-scale networks, ensuring that they are compatible with industry standards and can be managed effectively by end-users or operators. This includes implementing standardized communication protocols, secure APIs, and effective data governance practices that allow devices to communicate securely with each other and with centralized platforms, without exposing sensitive data or functionality.

Manufacturers also have a role in ensuring the physical security of their devices, particularly in environments where devices may be deployed in remote or insecure locations. Physical tampering with IoT devices can lead to devastating security breaches, as attackers may be able to extract sensitive data or install malicious firmware. Manufacturers should consider using tamper-resistant hardware and embedding security features such as secure elements or TPMs that store cryptographic keys and authentication credentials securely, preventing unauthorized access even in the event of physical compromise. Additionally, manufacturers must ensure that device lifecycle management includes secure decommissioning and disposal practices, such as wiping stored data and securely erasing cryptographic keys, to prevent sensitive information from being accessed after the device is no longer in use.

Collaboration with other stakeholders in the IoT ecosystem, including developers, service providers, and regulatory bodies, is also crucial for manufacturers to foster a secure environment. As IoT security is a shared responsibility, manufacturers must work together with other industry players to establish best practices, standards, and regulations that promote security across the entire IoT ecosystem. For instance, manufacturers can engage in industry initiatives that focus on developing security frameworks and protocols, such as the IoT Cybersecurity Improvement Act, which aims to set standards for the security of IoT devices in various sectors. In addition, manufacturers can cooperate with cybersecurity and researchers to perform regular security audits, evaluation of vulnerabilities and penetration testing, ensuring that their equipment is constantly evaluated to potential risks.

Finally, manufacturers must also prioritize educating consumers and enterprises about IoT security best practices. Even the most secure devices can be compromised if users fail to implement security measures, such as changing default passwords or enabling encryption. Manufacturers should provide clear, easy-to-understand instructions for device setup, security configuration, and ongoing maintenance. This empowers users to take ownership of the security of their devices and ensures that they are using the technology securely and responsibly. By designing devices with built-in security features, providing timely updates, ensuring strong authentication, collaborating with industry partners, and educating consumers, manufacturers can significantly reduce the risks posed by insecure IoT devices. Their proactive involvement in addressing security concerns ensures the safe deployment of IoT technology and builds trust with consumers, allowing the IoT to continue to thrive as an enabler of innovation and connectivity across various sectors.

2.7 CONCLUSION

IoT vulnerabilities and issues stem from a variety of factors, including insecure device design, inadequate data protection, weak authentication mechanisms, insufficient software updates, and a lack of regulatory oversight. These weaknesses expose IoT devices and networks to a wide range of risks, such as unauthorized access, data breaches, cyberattacks, privacy violations, and even physical tampering. The interconnected nature of IoT ecosystems further amplifies these risks, as compromised devices can serve as entry points for attacks across entire networks. To address these vulnerabilities, manufacturers, developers, and regulators must collaborate to implement robust security protocols, enhance user privacy protections, establish comprehensive security standards, and ensure that devices are continuously monitored and updated. Only by prioritizing security throughout the entire lifecycle of IoT devices can we mitigate the associated risks and unlock the full potential of IoT technology while ensuring the safety and trust of its users.

Chapter 3

Understanding IoT botnets

3.1 ANATOMY OF A BOTNET

A botnet is a network of compromised devices—often referred to as "robots" or "zombies"—remotely controlled by a cybercriminal or attacker. These devices, which can include computers, smartphones, the IoT, and servers, are infected with malware, which allows the attacker to control them without the user/owner knowing it. Botnet anatomy includes several key components, starting with a vector of infection, where malware is supplied to target devices. Figure 3.1 shows the anatomy of the botnet and emphasizes the hierarchical and modular nature of the botnet. This can happen through phishing emails, malicious websites, or vulnerabilities in network software. Once the device is infected, it becomes part of the botnet and waits for instructions from the command-and-control (C&C) server—a central system operated by an attacker. The process begins with an attacker who serves as an orchestrator of the botnet. The attacker publishes commands on the C&C server (Step 1), which acts as a central hub to coordinate botnet activities. The C&C server communicates and manages compromised devices (Step 2) to instruct them on how to operate and perform specific harmful tasks. The infected device communicates with the C&C server and receives commands, often via encrypted or masked channels to avoid detection.

The C&C server is the core of the botnet, and it can be distributed or centralized. In a centralized botnet, a single server is responsible for managing and issuing commands to all the compromised devices, while in a decentralized botnet (often using peer-to-peer communication), the botnet's control is distributed across many nodes, making it harder to dismantle. The C&C server instructs the infected devices on tasks, which can range from launching Distributed Denial of Service (DDoS) attacks, sending spam emails, stealing sensitive data, or executing additional malware. Botnets are highly adaptable, with many bots capable of self-propagating by spreading the malware to new devices through methods such as brute force attacks or exploiting known vulnerabilities in software.

A key element of a botnet's anatomy is command propagation and redundancy, which ensures that even if one C&C server is shut down, others can

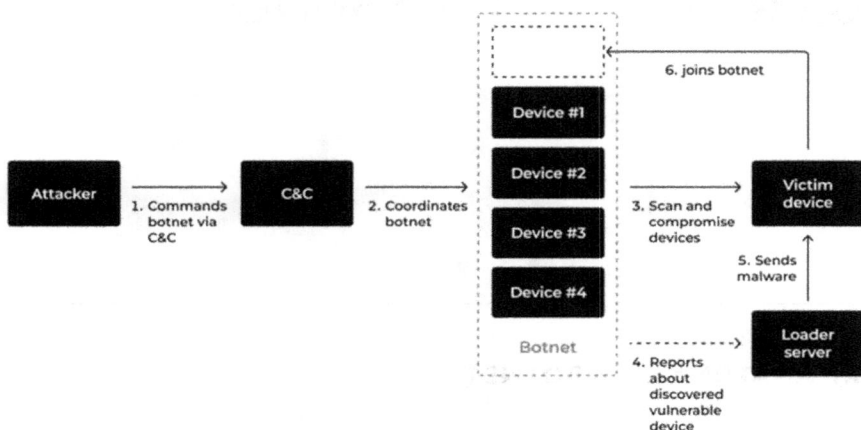

Figure 3.1 Anatomy of a botnet.

take over. Botnet creators employ techniques such as fast-flux networks, where the IP addresses of C&C servers change rapidly, or they use the Tor network or other anonymizing tools to hide the location of the control infrastructure. Once the botnet is active, it can perform a range of malicious activities. DDoS attacks are a common form of exploitation, where a botnet overwhelms a targeted server, network, or website with a flood of traffic, causing service disruption or even a total outage. Some botnets are used to carry out data exfiltration campaigns, stealing private information such as login credentials, personal data, or financial information. Other botnets may be employed for cryptocurrency mining, using the computing resources of infected devices to mine digital currencies, thereby generating illicit profit for the attacker. In more sophisticated botnets, rootkits and bootkits can be employed to deepen the compromise, providing stealth and persistence by embedding malicious code into the operating system, making it harder to detect or remove.

In this framework, the botnet comprises multiple devices, labeled as Device #1 through Device #4, which are already compromised and under the attacker's control. These devices play a crucial role in expanding the botnet by scanning for additional vulnerable devices in their network vicinity or across the Internet (Step 3). Once a vulnerable victim device is identified, the loader server comes into play. The loader server facilitates the delivery of malware to the vulnerable device (Step 5), ensuring it becomes compromised. Following the malware installation, the victim device joins the botnet (Step 6), becoming another "zombie" device that can be remotely controlled by the attacker through the C&C server. In addition, the loader server is responsible for reporting back to the Botnet infrastructure of any newly discovered vulnerable devices (Step 4). This step allows the attacker to maintain the current list of equipment that can be compromised and ensure that the botnet continues to grow. The feedback loop from the loader server to the C&C server is necessary to coordinate and optimize the propagation of malware over the network. Since multiple devices are threatened and added to the botnet, its size and the ability to perform harmful activities such as DDoS attacks, theft of data, or spamming significantly increase.

The C&C server acts as a command relay system, ensuring the attacker can manage the botnet remotely while remaining undetected. The attacker typically employs advanced techniques, such as encryption or obfuscation, to hide their communications with the C&C server, making it difficult for cybersecurity experts to track or disrupt the botnet's activities. The loader server, on the other hand, specializes in identifying and exploiting new vulnerabilities, continuously feeding fresh devices into the botnet, and ensuring its persistence. Botnets are often designed to be resilient and stealthy. Many employ advanced techniques to avoid detection by antivirus software, intrusion detection systems, or network traffic analysis tools. They can hide their activity by using encrypted communication channels, polymorphic code (which changes the bot's signature), or cloaking mechanisms to remain unnoticed while still performing malicious tasks. Moreover, the attackers controlling the botnet often use anonymity and obfuscation methods to protect their identity and location, including using compromised proxy servers or virtual private networks (VPNs) to hide their true origin.

Botnets can be rented out on the black market to other cybercriminals, enabling them to launch attacks without having to build their own network of compromised devices. The scale and power of botnets have grown over time, with some large botnets comprising millions of devices. The financial incentives behind botnet operations drive continuous innovation in their design, making them a persistent and evolving threat in the cybersecurity landscape. Overall, the anatomy of a botnet highlights its complexity, adaptability, and the diverse ways in which attackers exploit the power of large-scale, distributed networks of compromised devices for malicious gain. By representing the key entities and their roles in the lifecycle of a botnet, the figure provides a clear visualization of how these networks are structured and operated. It highlights the importance of vulnerable victim devices in sustaining botnets and underscores the cyclical nature of their growth and control mechanisms.

3.2 TYPES OF BOTNETS: FROM PC-BASED TO IoT BOTNETS

Botnets are networks of compromised devices controlled remotely by cyber-criminals to perform malicious activities. These networks have evolved significantly over the years, transitioning from traditional PC-based botnets to more sophisticated IoT-based botnets, exploiting the vulnerabilities of modern connected devices. Each type of botnet has unique characteristics, attack vectors, and potential impacts. There are distinct botnet types with their evolution and roles in the modern cyberthreat landscape.

PC-Based Botnet: PC-based botnets were the earliest and most common type of botnets in the early days of cybercrime. These botnets target personal computers running traditional operating systems such as Windows, macOS, or Linux. They exploit vulnerabilities in software, browsers, or email systems to infect devices with malware. Once a PC is compromised, it becomes part of the botnet and performs tasks such as sending spam, launching DDoS attacks, or distributing additional malware. Early PC-based botnets often relied on centralized C&C servers to manage and coordinate activities. In these botnets, infection typically occurs through phishing emails, malicious attachments, or drive-by downloads. These botnets were widely used for spamming, credential theft, and launching DDoS attacks. Botnets such as Storm, Conficker, and Zeus are suitable examples of PC-based botnets that wreaked havoc during their time. PC-based botnets were prevalent, but advancements in cybersecurity and operating system protections have made it more challenging for attackers to maintain large networks of infected PCs.

Server-based Botnets: Server-based botnets are networks of compromised servers controlled by attackers to carry out malicious activities. Unlike traditional botnets that rely on personal computers, server-based botnets exploit the higher bandwidth, computational power, and continuous uptime of servers, making them ideal for large-scale and persistent attacks. These botnets often target servers running outdated software, misconfigured applications, or weak security protocols, such as unpatched vulnerabilities in web servers or content management systems such as WordPress. Once compromised, these servers are integrated into the botnet and used for tasks such as launching DDoS attacks, hosting, distributing malware, sending spam emails, or stealing sensitive data. A key advantage of server-based botnets for attackers is their capacity to amplify attacks due to the robust infrastructure of servers. Attackers often employ techniques such as fast-flux DNS, which rapidly changes the IP addresses of the servers or leverages encrypted communication channels to make detection and takedown efforts more challenging. Some server-based botnets also act as control hubs for managing IoT or mobile botnets, creating a layered and resilient network. Some examples of server-based botnets include the Mirai botnet, which initially targeted IoT devices but also used vulnerable servers to amplify its impact, and Dark Nexus, which exploits compromised servers for advanced attacks. To address these botnets, organizations must prioritize server security through timely software updates, strong access controls, regular vulnerability assessments, and network monitoring to detect unusual activity before it escalates. Servers can handle higher data volumes, making them ideal for DDoS attacks and hosting illegal content. Servers often run outdated software or applications, providing long-term access for attackers.

These botnets frequently exploit vulnerabilities in web applications, databases, or content management systems such as WordPress.

Mobile Botnets: Mobile botnets are networks of compromised mobile devices that attackers control to perform harmful activities without knowing the owner of the device. These botnets use the growing prevalence of smartphones, tablets, and other mobile devices that often lack robust security measures and are often associated with the Internet. Cybercriminals use techniques such as phishing, harmful downloads, or the use of unknown vulnerabilities to infect malware, turn them into robots or "zombies." After being infected, these devices can perform various tasks, including DDoS attacks, sending spam or phishing messages, theft of sensitive data, and fraud with clicks. Mobile botnets are a primary concern due to the large amount of personal data stored on mobile devices, such as login data, financial information, and location information. Attackers often leverage these botnets for financial gain or to create backdoors into corporate networks. Advanced mobile botnets can hide their presence using stealth techniques like encryption, evading detection by antivirus software. The increased use of mobile IoT devices further exacerbates the issue, as these devices often operate on outdated firmware and lack adequate security protocols. Combatting mobile botnets requires multifaceted strategies, including user education, regular software updates, app vetting by app stores, and the implementation of network-based monitoring and anomaly detection systems to identify and neutralize malicious activity. The global penetration of smartphones provides attackers with a vast pool of potential victims. Malicious apps distributed through app stores or third-party platforms are a common infection vector. Mobile botnets often focus on stealing sensitive information, such as banking credentials, or spying on users. Infected devices can be used to send spam SMS messages to propagate the malware further. HummingBad, Triada are examples of mobile botnets.

IoT Botnets: IoT botnets are networks of compromised IoT devices controlled remotely by attackers to execute large-scale malicious activities. These devices, including smart cameras, thermostats, routers, and industrial sensors, often have weak security measures, making them easy targets for exploitation. Cybercriminals infect IoT devices with malware, such as Mirai or Mozi, through methods such as exploiting default credentials, unpatched vulnerabilities, or insecure communication protocols. Once infected, these devices are integrated into a botnet and controlled via C&C servers to perform tasks such as DDoS attacks, data theft, credential harvesting, or spreading malware. IoT botnets are particularly alarming due to the clear volume and ubiquity of the IoT devices that continue to grow exponentially. Unlike traditional computing devices, many devices do not have robust hardware sources for advanced safety measures, which makes it difficult to detect and alleviate threats. In addition, these devices often work continuously and autonomously and offer attackers persistent support in the network. The infamous Mirai botnet is an example of the destructive potential of an IoT botnet, having launched some of the largest DDoS attacks ever recorded. The decentralized nature of IoT ecosystems and the lack of standardized safety frameworks worsen this problem. Attackers exploit these vulnerabilities to build resilient and scalable botnets capable of evading traditional defense mechanisms. IoT botnets also pose a significant threat to critical infrastructure, as compromised industrial IoT devices can disrupt essential services such as energy, transportation, and healthcare. Mitigating IoT botnets requires a multilayered approach involving manufacturers, network administrators, and end-users. Device manufacturers must prioritize security by enforcing secure coding practices, offering regular firmware updates, and implementing features such as secure boot and encrypted communication. Network administrators can deploy intrusion detection systems, segment IoT devices, and monitor anomalous traffic patterns to identify potential botnet activity. Educating end-users to change default passwords and keep devices updated is also crucial in reducing the attack surface. Proactive collaboration between stakeholders and adherence to emerging security standards are essential to curb the growing threat of IoT botnets. One of the most infamous IoT botnets, Mirai, exploited default credentials on IoT devices to build a botnet that launched some of the largest DDoS attacks in history. It is a peer-to-peer IoT botnet that targets routers and other IoT devices to perform DDoS attacks and data exfiltration.

Peer-to-Peer (P2P) Botnets: Botnets P2P are decentralized networks of infected devices (robots) that communicate directly with each other rather than rely on a centralized C&C server. This decentralized architecture causes P2P botnets to be more resistant to the spread of effort because there is no single failure. Each robot in Botnet P2P acts both as a client and a server, which allows attackers to distribute commands and updates in the network without even depending on the central infrastructure. This design allows the botnets to remain functional, even if the network parts are disturbed or endangered. P2P botnets pose significant challenges for cybersecurity due to their adaptability and robustness. Traditional mitigation strategies, such as targeting and disabling C&C servers, are ineffective against P2P botnets because the removal of one bot does not disrupt the entire network. These botnets can self-heal by redistributing communication routes among remaining bots, making them highly resilient. Furthermore, advanced encryption techniques and obfuscation mechanisms are often used in P2P botnets to evade detection and analysis. Attackers use P2P botnets for various malicious activities, including DDoS attacks, data theft, cryptocurrency mining, and the distribution of spam or malware. P2P botnets such as Storm, Waledac, and Gameover Zeus have demonstrated the ability to infect millions of devices and sustain long-term operations. The lack of a centralized control point also allows attackers to evade law enforcement efforts, complicating attribution and mitigation. Defending against P2P botnets requires a combination of advanced threat detection, network monitoring, and collaborative efforts between organizations and law enforcement. Techniques such as sinkholing, where traffic from infected devices is redirected to controlled servers, can help disrupt botnet communications. Additionally, implementing strong endpoint security, regular software updates, and user education can reduce the attack surface. As P2P botnets continue to evolve, ongoing research and innovation in cybersecurity are essential to counter their sophisticated techniques and mitigate their growing threat. The decentralized nature of P2P botnets poses a significant challenge for cybersecurity experts, as traditional methods of disrupting botnets, such as taking down C&C servers, are ineffective.

Hybrid Botnets: Hybrid botnets are advanced networks of compromised devices that combine features of both centralized and decentralized architectures to maximize resilience, scalability, and effectiveness. By leveraging the strengths of centralized C&C servers and decentralized P2P communication, hybrid botnets offer attackers increased flexibility and robustness against detection and takedown efforts. In these botnets, a central server may issue high-level commands or updates, while individual bots communicate with each other using P2P mechanisms to execute tasks and propagate instructions. This dual approach ensures the botnet can remain operational even if part of its infrastructure is disabled. The hybrid design addresses key weaknesses in purely centralized or P2P botnets. Centralized botnets are vulnerable to takedowns targeting the C&C server, while P2P botnets, though resilient, can be complex to manage. Hybrid botnets overcome these challenges by decentralizing operational tasks such as malware updates or data exfiltration while retaining centralized elements for more efficient control. This combination makes hybrid botnets harder to disrupt, as attackers can shift between centralized and decentralized modes based on defensive measures they encounter. Hybrid botnets are used for a variety of malicious activities, including DDoS attacks, cryptocurrency mining, ransomware distribution, and data theft. Notable examples, such as the Kraken and TDL-4 botnets, have showcased how hybrid architectures can enable large-scale, stealthy, and persistent operations. These botnets often employ sophisticated techniques such as encryption, fast-flux DNS, and stealth communication protocols to evade detection and analysis. Mitigating hybrid botnets requires a multifaceted approach involving real-time monitoring, advanced threat intelligence, and collaboration between cybersecurity organizations. Techniques such as traffic analysis, honeypots, and sinkholing can help disrupt botnet communications. Additionally, promoting secure coding practices, enforcing regular updates, and educating users about phishing and malware risks are essential preventive measures. As hybrid botnets continue to evolve, proactive and collaborative defenses are critical to countering their increasingly sophisticated and adaptive threat capabilities. Hybrid botnets highlight the evolving sophistication of cybercriminals and their ability to adapt to changing security measures.

Cloud-based Botnets: Cloud-based botnets represent a modern and highly potent evolution of traditional botnet architectures, leveraging cloud computing infrastructure to amplify their scalability, efficiency, and stealth. Unlike conventional botnets that rely on compromised physical devices, cloud-based botnets utilize rented or hijacked cloud servers to orchestrate malicious activities. These botnets benefit from the vast computational power, high bandwidth, and global reach of cloud platforms, making them particularly effective for large-scale attacks such as DDoS, cryptocurrency mining, spam campaigns, and data exfiltration. Cloud-based botnets represent a growing threat as organizations increasingly rely on cloud infrastructure, highlighting the need for strong cloud security practices. One of the key advantages of cloud-based botnets is their ability to disguise malicious traffic within legitimate cloud services, making them harder to detect and mitigate. Attackers exploit vulnerabilities in cloud-hosted applications or abuse stolen cloud credentials to gain unauthorized access to server resources. Once established, cloud-based botnets can quickly scale up by provisioning additional virtual machines, leveraging the pay-as-you-go model of cloud computing to their advantage. The elasticity and redundancy of cloud infrastructure further enhance the resilience of cloud-based botnets. Even if individual nodes are identified and taken down, attackers can swiftly deploy new instances in different regions, maintaining operational continuity. Additionally, cloud-based botnets often use advanced encryption and obfuscation techniques to evade detection by security tools. Organizations should secure cloud credentials, adopt multi-factor authentication (MFA), and deploy continuous monitoring solutions to identify unauthorized activities. As cloud adoption continues to rise, cloud-based botnets pose an escalating threat, blending the capabilities of advanced botnet design with the immense resources of cloud platforms. Proactive and collaborative measures are essential to mitigate this evolving cyberthreat landscape. Cloud-based botnets exploit misconfigured cloud servers or use stolen credentials to deploy malware across virtualized environments. Cloud botnets can compromise virtual machines in the cloud which can be used for DDoS attacks, cryptojacking, or data theft.

Table 3.1 shows the different types of botnets that evolved from basic PC-based networks to sophisticated and diverse systems that exploit the vulnerabilities of modern technologies. The rise of IoT botnets, P2P botnets, and cloud-based botnets demonstrates how attackers adapt to technological advancements, leveraging the ubiquity and connectivity of devices. Each type of botnet presents unique challenges to cybersecurity, emphasizing the need for robust security measures, including strong authentication, regular software updates, and network monitoring. As botnets continue to evolve, combating them will require a combination of advanced technologies, regulatory oversight, and collaborative efforts across industries.

Table 3.1 Types of botnets

Botnet type	Architecture of botnet	Major attacks	Attack vectors	Tools
PC-Based Botnet	Client–Server	DDoS attacks, spam campaigns, data theft	Phishing emails, malicious attachments	Zeus, SpyEye, Cutwail
Server-based Botnets	Centralized (command from servers)	Credential harvesting, financial fraud	Exploited web servers, malicious scripts	BlackEnergy, Kelihos
Mobile Botnets	Client–Server or decentralized	SMS fraud, surveillance, ad fraud	Malicious apps, SMS trojans	DroidDream, ZitMo, FakeInst
IoT Botnets	Decentralized or Peer-to-Peer	DDoS attacks, network disruption	Default credentials, unpatched firmware	Mirai, Mozi, BASHLITE
Peer-to-Peer (P2P) Botnets	Peer-to-Peer	DDoS, spam, crypto mining	File-sharing, vulnerable applications	Storm, ZeroAccess, Gameover Zeus
Hybrid Botnets	Hybrid	Complex attacks (multivector), espionage	Mixed (email, web, IoT, mobile)	Tofsee, Necurs
Cloud-based Botnets	Virtualized cloud infrastructure	Account takeovers, cryptojacking, DDoS	Cloud misconfiguration, stolen credentials	Cloudbot, Lucifer

3.3 COMMON BOTNET ATTACKS: DDoS, SPAM, AND DATA THEFT

There are several IoT botnet attacks that are vary in their methods and objectives, including DoS, DDoS, spam campaigns, cryptojacking, credential stuffing, and data theft which are among the most common and impactful. These attacks exploit IoT networks of compromised devices (botnets) to execute large-scale malicious operations. The widespread availability of vulnerable devices and the sophistication of modern botnets make these attacks increasingly pervasive. The mitigation of this malware requires robust security practices, including network monitoring, endpoint protection, and user education, along with proactive measures to secure IoT devices and prevent their exploitation in botnet operations.

DDoS: These attacks are a form of cyberattack intended to disrupt the normal functioning of a targeted server, network, or website by overwhelming it with traffic from multiple sources. Unlike traditional DOS attacks that come from a single source, DDoS attacks use a distributed network of compromised devices known as a botnet to create excessive traffic. These botnets often consist of infected devices of IoT, computers, and servers that attackers control remotely. The mere volume of traffic generated during the DDoS attack runs out the target sources, such as bandwidth, processing, or memory, which is inaccessible to legitimate users. DDoS attacks may take different forms, including volume attacks that saturate high-operation bandwidth; protocol attacks use vulnerability in network protocols; and attacks on a layer of applications focus on specific web applications. The consequences of DDoS attacks are significant, from financial losses and operational downtime to damage to the reputation of companies and organizations. These attacks are particularly difficult to alleviate because of their distributed nature, making it difficult to distinguish harmful traffic from legitimate requirements. To combat DDoS attacks, organizations implement strategies such as filtering, speed limitation, load leveling, and CDN use. Advanced threat detection tools, combined with collaboration between cybersecurity teams and ISPs, are essential to effectively identify and neutralize such attacks.

Spam Campaigns: Spam campaigns are large-scale operations in which attackers use compromised devices, often organized into botnets, to send massive volumes of unsolicited messages. These messages are primarily distributed via email, but they can also target other platforms such as social media, instant messaging apps, and SMS. The content of spam campaigns varies widely, ranging from advertisements for counterfeit goods or dubious services to phishing links and malware-laden attachments. Attackers aim to exploit recipients by tricking them into revealing sensitive information, clicking on malicious links, or downloading harmful files, which can lead to data breaches, financial fraud, or malware infections. Botnets play a pivotal role in spam campaigns by automating the process and allowing attackers to distribute spam globally while evading detection. By using thousands or even millions of infected devices as relay points, attackers bypass traditional email filters that block bulk messages originating from a single source. Botnets such as Cutwail and Rustock have been responsible for some of the most prolific spam campaigns in history, sending billions of spam emails per day. The consequences of spam campaigns extend beyond individual victims. Organizations may experience resource strain due to the sheer volume of incoming spam, while end-users may suffer financial losses or identity theft. Spam also degrades the performance of infected devices, as bots consume significant computational and network resources. To combat spam campaigns, organizations and individuals must adopt proactive measures such as using advanced spam filters, regularly updating software, and implementing email authentication protocols such as SPF, DKIM, and DMARC.

User education is equally critical to help recipients identify and avoid phishing attempts. Coordinated efforts between cybersecurity firms, ISPs, and law enforcement agencies are essential to dismantle botnets and disrupt spam campaigns at their source.

Data Theft: Data theft involves the unauthorized access, acquisition, or exfiltration of sensitive information by malicious actors. This stolen data can include personal details, financial information, trade secrets, intellectual property, and login credentials. Data theft is typically executed through methods such as phishing attacks, malware infections, or exploiting vulnerabilities in networks, software, or devices. Botnets often play a critical role in large-scale data theft, as attackers can deploy spyware, keyloggers, or other malware on compromised devices to silently monitor user activity and steal valuable information. The consequences of data theft are serious for individuals and organizations. This may result in identity, financial fraud, and privacy violations. In companies, data theft may lead to damage to reputation, loss of customer credibility, regulatory fines, and significant financial losses. Sensitive corporate information, such as customer data, financial records, or proprietary technologies, is often aimed at obtaining competitive benefits or selling on a dark website for profit. Data theft has become more sophisticated with the rise of IoT and cloud computing. The attackers use unsecured IoT devices and incorrectly configured cloud environments to get access to a huge amount of data. In addition, advanced techniques such as double blackmail ransomware, data penetration, and threats to escape them complicate this problem. Mitigating data theft requires a multilayered approach to security, including strong encryption protocols, robust authentication measures, regular software updates, and employee training to identify phishing schemes. Organizations must also prioritize implementing intrusion detection systems, data loss prevention solutions, and access control policies. By fostering a culture of security awareness and staying vigilant against emerging threats, both individuals and businesses can reduce the risk of falling victim to data theft.

Cryptojacking: It is a form of cyberattack where malicious actors hijack a victim's computational resources to mine cryptocurrencies without their knowledge or consent. This unauthorized activity can occur on any Internet-connected device, including computers, smartphones, IoT devices, and servers. Attackers either inject cryptojacking malware directly into a system or embed malicious scripts in websites, which execute mining operations when unsuspecting users visit the page. Unlike ransomware or other overt attacks, cryptojacking is stealthy, operating in the background while exploiting the victim's hardware for financial gain. The most mined cryptocurrency in cryptojacking attacks is Monero, favored for its privacy features and lower computational requirements compared to Bitcoin. Cryptojacking causes devices to slow down, overheat, or experience reduced battery life due to the intensive resource usage involved in mining. For organizations, cryptojacking can result in increased electricity costs, reduced operational efficiency, and potential hardware damage. The rise of cryptojacking is fueled by the profitability of cryptocurrency mining combined with the difficulty of detecting these attacks. Attackers often distribute cryptojacking malware via phishing emails, malicious downloads, or compromised websites. Once inside a system, the malware is designed to avoid detection by throttling its resource consumption or operating intermittently. Preventing cryptojacking requires robust cybersecurity measures, including up-to-date antivirus software, firewalls, and browser extensions that block mining scripts. Organizations should monitor network traffic for unusual activity, enforce strict access controls, and implement endpoint protection solutions. Educating users to recognize phishing attempts and suspicious links is also critical to minimizing the risk of infection. As cryptocurrency adoption continues to grow, cryptojacking remains a pervasive threat, highlighting the need for proactive defenses and vigilance against this insidious form of cybercrime.

Credential stuffing: It is a type of cyberattack in which hackers use automated tools to test large sets of stolen usernames and passwords on multiple websites and applications to gain unauthorized access to accounts. This attack exploits the widespread practice of password reuse, where individuals use the same credentials across different platforms. Hackers typically obtain these credentials from data breaches or leaks and then deploy bots to systematically attempt login combinations across various online services. If the same credentials are used on multiple sites, attackers can successfully breach accounts with minimal effort. The consequences of credential stuffing are severe, leading to unauthorized access to sensitive information, financial loss, identity theft, and potential reputational damage for affected organizations. Successful attacks can compromise user accounts, resulting in fraudulent transactions, data theft, or misuse of services. For businesses, this can lead to customer dissatisfaction, regulatory fines, and increased operational costs associated with remediation efforts. Credential stuffing attacks are particularly challenging to detect because they often mimic legitimate login behavior. Attackers may use proxies or distributed bots to disguise the origin of the login attempts, making it harder for security systems to identify patterns. To combat credential stuffing, organizations must implement multilayered security measures, including rate limiting, IP blocking, and CAPTCHA challenges to thwart automated login attempts. Enforcing MFA significantly enhances account security by requiring an additional verification step beyond passwords. Password-less authentication methods and encouraging users to create strong, unique passwords also reduce the risk of successful attacks. On an individual level, users should employ password managers to generate and store unique passwords for each platform, regularly update credentials, and monitor accounts for suspicious activity. As credential stuffing attacks continue to rise, a combination of user vigilance and robust security practices is critical for mitigating this pervasive threat.

3.4 COMMAND-AND-CONTROL INFRASTRUCTURE

Command-and-Control (C&C) infrastructure is the backbone of many modern cyberattacks, providing a mechanism for attackers to communicate with and control compromised devices, systems, or networks (Figure 3.2). This infrastructure is pivotal in the execution and maintenance of malicious campaigns such as botnet operations, ransomware attacks, spyware, and advanced persistent threats (APTs). By enabling remote control over infected systems, C&C infrastructure facilitates a wide range of malicious activities, from data theft and espionage to DDoS attacks and cryptocurrency mining. This explanation delves into the key components, operational mechanisms, types, and mitigation strategies for C&C infrastructure, offering a detailed analysis of its role in the cyberthreat landscape.

The primary purpose of a C&C infrastructure is to establish a reliable communication channel between the attacker and the compromised systems. This infrastructure acts as a central nervous system for malware operations, allowing attackers to

- Issue commands to infected devices (bots or zombies).
- Retrieve sensitive data or results from compromised systems.
- Update malware or deploy additional payloads.
- Monitor the status of an ongoing attack.
- Coordinate large-scale actions such as DDoS attacks or spam campaigns.

There are several key components of C&C Infrastructure involved in the process that typically comprise distinct components that work together to maintain the attacker's control over the compromised network. The C&C server is the central node that issues commands and receives information from infected devices. It can be a physical server, a virtual machine, or even a cloud-based instance. The bots are the infected devices that form part of a botnet. They communicate with the C&C server to receive instructions or send back stolen data. The communication channels rely on communi-

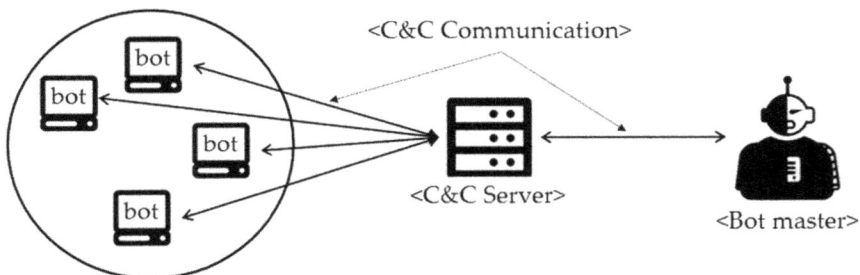

Figure 3.2 C&C infrastructure.

cation protocols such as HTTP, HTTPS, IRC, DNS, or custom encrypted protocols. These channels ensure a steady flow of information between the attacker and the infected systems. To evade detection, attackers may use relay points such as proxy servers or peer devices to obfuscate the true location of the C&C server. The functioning of a C&C infrastructure involves several stages:

- *Infection and Setup*: The infection and setup phase of a cyberattack is the initial stage where attackers compromise a system and establish their malicious presence. This process begins with the exploitation of vulnerabilities, such as weak passwords, unpatched software, phishing attacks, or malicious links. Once access is gained, malware is delivered to the target device or network, often disguised as legitimate files or applications. After delivery, the malware executes its payload, setting up persistence mechanisms to maintain access even after system reboots. These mechanisms may include registry modifications, scheduled tasks, or backdoors. During this phase, the malware often communicates with its C&C server to receive instructions, download additional components, or send data about the infected system. The infection and setup phase is critical for attackers to solidify control, evade detection, and prepare for the next steps, such as lateral movement or the execution of their primary objectives, like data theft or sabotage. Attackers first compromise devices through phishing, malware downloads, or exploiting vulnerabilities. The malware then establishes a connection to the C&C server, often through an initial "beaconing" process to notify the server of the infection.
- *Command Execution*: Command execution is a critical stage in cyberattacks where attackers gain control over compromised systems and execute malicious commands to achieve their objectives. After establishing a foothold during the infection phase, the attacker uses tools, scripts, or malware to issue instructions to the infected system, often through a C&C infrastructure. These commands can include downloading additional malware, stealing sensitive data, capturing screenshots, logging keystrokes, or disrupting operations. In advanced attacks, command execution may involve leveraging built-in administrative tools such as PowerShell or exploiting remote access protocols to avoid detection. Attackers also use encrypted channels or custom protocols to transmit commands, further evading security monitoring. This phase is highly adaptive, with attackers dynamically tailoring their actions based on system responses and defenses encountered. Successful command execution not only solidifies the attacker's control but also enables the escalation of the attack, such as spreading to other systems or launching targeted payloads. Once connected,

the C&C server can send commands to the infected devices. These commands could involve stealing data, downloading additional malware, or executing malicious scripts.

- *Data Exfiltration*: It is the unauthorized transfer of sensitive information from a compromised system to an attacker-controlled location. After successfully infiltrating a system, attackers identify and extract valuable data, such as personal information, financial records, intellectual property, or trade secrets. This process often involves compressing, encrypting, and disguising the data to evade detection by security systems. Attackers use various exfiltration methods, including direct transmission via malware, hidden channels like DNS tunneling, or leveraging legitimate network protocols such as HTTP, HTTPS, or FTP. In some cases, attackers exfiltrate data in small, incremental amounts to avoid raising alarms, while others conduct mass data dumps. Advanced attackers may use encrypted communication channels to ensure confidentiality during transfer. Data exfiltration poses significant risks, including financial losses, reputational damage, regulatory penalties, and compromised privacy for individuals or organizations. Preventing exfiltration requires robust monitoring, encryption, and anomaly detection to identify and block suspicious activities in real time. Infected devices send stolen information or operational updates back to the C&C server. This data is often encrypted to avoid detection.

- *Persistence and Evasion*: Persistence and evasion are essential tactics attackers use to maintain control over compromised systems while avoiding detection. Persistence ensures the attacker's access survives system reboots, software updates, or user actions. Techniques for persistence include creating scheduled tasks, modifying system registries, installing backdoors, or leveraging legitimate tools such as Remote Desktop Protocol (RDP). Attackers may also use fileless malware that resides in memory to minimize their footprint. Evasion tactics focus on bypassing security mechanisms such as firewalls, IDS, or antivirus software. These include encrypting or obfuscating malicious code, mimicking legitimate processes, using anti-analysis techniques, and employing polymorphic or metamorphic malware that changes its structure to avoid detection. Attackers may also exploit gaps in monitoring, use encrypted communication channels, or route traffic through anonymization networks like Tor. When combined, persistence and evasion allow attackers to remain undetected for extended periods, increasing the success of data theft, surveillance, or further exploitation. To maintain longevity, attackers design C&C infrastructures to avoid detection by security tools. This could involve using encrypted communication, domain fluxing (frequently changing C&C server domains), or P2P networks.

The C&C infrastructure can be classified into several types based on its design and operational strategy, such as the following.

- *Centralized C&C*: A traditional setup where all infected devices communicate with a single or small group of centralized servers. While simple to manage, this design is vulnerable to single points of failure— if the C&C server is detected and taken down, the botnet is disrupted. A centralized C&C infrastructure is a framework used by attackers to manage and coordinate malware-infected systems or botnets. In this model, all infected devices (bots) communicate with a single, central server or a small set of servers to receive instructions and report back data. The centralized server acts as the control hub, where attackers issue commands for tasks such as data exfiltration, launching DDoS attacks, or downloading additional payloads. This type of infrastructure is relatively easy for attackers to set up and manage, making it a popular choice for small- to medium-scale botnets. However, its reliance on a central point of communication is also its greatest weakness. Security professionals can effectively neutralize the entire botnet by locating and taking down the central server, a process known as a sinkhole. Attackers often mitigate this risk by hosting their servers in jurisdictions with weak cybersecurity laws, using dynamic IP addresses, or employing domain generation algorithms (DGA) to create rotating addresses. Despite its simplicity and efficiency, the centralized C&C infrastructure is less resilient than decentralized models, as it is highly susceptible to disruption and detection by modern security tools and coordinated defensive actions.
- *Decentralized C&C*: A decentralized C&C infrastructure is a more resilient and sophisticated model used by attackers to manage malware-infected systems or botnets. Unlike the centralized approach, decentralized C&C eliminates reliance on a single control server by distributing command and communication responsibilities across multiple nodes within the network. Often implemented using P2P protocols, each infected device (bot) in the network can act as both a client and a server, communicating directly with other bots and sharing control commands. This model significantly enhances the survivability of the botnet, as there is no single point of failure. Even if some nodes are identified and taken down, the remaining network continues to function and propagate. Attackers further secure decentralized networks by encrypting communications and embedding mechanisms to locate new peers dynamically, making it challenging for defenders to intercept or dismantle the botnet entirely. Despite its robustness, decentralized C&C infrastructures are more complex to design and maintain, requiring sophisticated protocols and mechanisms to synchronize commands and prevent detection. Malware such as Conficker and Gameover Zeus are notable examples of leveraging decentralized

models. These infrastructures are harder to mitigate and track, posing a significant challenge for cybersecurity professionals in combating advanced botnet operations. The utilization of P2P communication allows bots to communicate with each other instead of a central server. This makes the botnet more resilient to takedown efforts, as there is no single point of failure.

- *Fast-Flux C&C Networks*: Fast-Flux C&C networks are a sophisticated technique used by attackers to increase the resilience and anonymity of their malicious infrastructure. These networks leverage a rapidly changing set of IP addresses associated with a single domain name to hide the location of their C&C servers. By frequently altering the DNS records—sometimes every few minutes—Fast-Flux networks make it difficult for defenders to track, block, or shut down the malicious servers. There are two primary types of Fast-Flux networks: single-flux and double-flux. Single-flux involves continuously rotating IP addresses for the same domain, while double-flux extends this technique by adding another layer of obfuscation, rotating both the DNS servers and the end-host IPs. Attackers use this method to hide phishing sites, malware delivery servers, or botnet C&C servers behind a constantly shifting network of compromised systems acting as proxies. Fast-Flux networks offer attackers significant advantages, including resistance to takedown efforts and the ability to operate in a more distributed manner. However, their reliance on large numbers of compromised machines and rapid DNS updates makes them detectable by advanced threat intelligence systems. Combating Fast-Flux networks requires collaboration between DNS registrars, ISPs, and cybersecurity organizations to identify and disrupt the underlying infrastructure. This method frequently changes the IP addresses associated with the C&C servers, making it harder for defenders to block or trace the infrastructure.
- *DGAs-Based C&C*: It is a sophisticated technique used by attackers to dynamically generate domain names for their C&C servers. Instead of hardcoding a fixed server address into the malware, DGAs enable the malware to generate a list of potential domain names based on predefined algorithms and parameters, such as date, time, or specific seeds. The attacker registers only a few of these domains, allowing the malware to locate and connect to the active C&C server. This approach provides significant resilience to takedown efforts, as security teams must identify and block every possible domain generated by the algorithm, a daunting and resource-intensive task. DGAs make it difficult to disrupt the communication channel between the malware and its C&C infrastructure because even if one domain is blocked, the malware can attempt others in its list. However, DGAs also have their limitations. The algorithm itself may leave a fingerprint that cybersecurity experts can analyze to predict future domain names and preemptively block or sinkhole them. Advanced DGAs use encryption

and randomization to make detection and analysis more challenging. This technique has been employed in notorious malware families such as Conficker, Dyre, and Kraken, posing ongoing challenges to security defenses worldwide. Attackers register only a few of these domains for the C&C servers, making it challenging for defenders to predict and block the active domains.

- *Cloud-Based C&C*: Cloud-based C&C infrastructures include cloud services, such as Google Drive, Dropbox, or Microsoft Azure, to manage malware-infected devices or botnets. This method allows attackers to blend malicious activities with legitimate cloud traffic, making detection significantly harder for security systems. Instead of traditional C&C servers, attackers use cloud storage, messaging platforms, or web-based APIs to issue commands, receive data, or distribute updates to compromised systems. The appeal of cloud-based C&C lies in its ability to exploit the trusted reputation of cloud providers. Security systems are less likely to block traffic from well-known cloud platforms, providing attackers with a secure and reliable communication channel. Additionally, cloud services often offer scalability and high availability, enabling attackers to manage large botnets effectively. To execute this model, malware retrieves commands or uploads stolen data to specific cloud accounts controlled by the attacker. These accounts can be accessed globally, allowing seamless management of infected devices across different regions. Furthermore, attackers can use encryption to obfuscate the data, making analysis and interception even more challenging. Defending against cloud-based C&C requires advanced monitoring tools capable of distinguishing malicious traffic from legitimate cloud usage, as well as coordinated efforts between cybersecurity teams and cloud providers to detect and shut down abusive accounts.

The detection and mitigation of C&C infrastructure is a challenging task due to several distinct reasons such as the following.

- *Stealthy Communication*: Stealthy communication is a critical technique used by attackers to maintain covert interactions between malware and its C&C infrastructure, evading detection by security systems. This method involves masking malicious traffic to appear as legitimate, thereby avoiding raising alarms. Common techniques include encrypting communications, using standard network protocols such as HTTP, HTTPS, or DNS, and embedding malicious instructions within seemingly innocuous data packets or legitimate application traffic. Attackers often leverage encryption and obfuscation techniques to hide the content of their communications, making it difficult for IDS to analyze the traffic. Advanced methods, such as domain fronting, route malicious traffic through reputable domains to further disguise its origin. Additionally, some malware employs timing-based communication, where messages are sent at irregular intervals to avoid detection by traffic pattern analysis. Another approach is the use of covert channels, such as embedding commands in metadata, social media posts, or even in steganographically altered images. These techniques ensure that malicious activities remain hidden within the noise of legitimate network traffic. Stealthy communication significantly enhances the longevity of malware operations, enabling attackers to maintain control over infected systems and execute their objectives undetected. Counteracting this requires advanced anomaly detection, behavioral analysis, and threat intelligence to identify subtle patterns of malicious activity. Encrypted traffic and legitimate communication protocols such as HTTPS make it harder to identify malicious activity.

- *Dynamic Behavior*: Dynamic behavior in malware refers to its ability to adapt and modify its operations based on the environment it encounters, making detection and mitigation significantly more challenging. This behavior allows malware to respond to security measures, evade analysis, and optimize its attack strategies. For instance, dynamic malware can detect if it is running in a sandbox or virtualized environment, commonly used by security analysts, and then alter its behavior to appear benign or go dormant, delaying its malicious actions until it escapes scrutiny. It also includes polymorphism and metamorphism, where malware changes its code or appearance with each infection or execution, making signature-based detection methods ineffective. Additionally, some malware dynamically downloads new modules, updates itself, or alters its communication protocols to adapt to evolving defenses or to increase its effectiveness. The other aspect of dynamic behavior is the ability to exploit specific system vulnerabilities or configurations in real time, tailoring attacks based on the target's characteristics. For example, ransomware might dynamically select which files to encrypt based on their importance. This adaptability ensures that dynamic malware remains a persistent threat, requiring defenders to rely on advanced behavioral analysis, machine learning, and heuristic-based detection systems to identify malicious actions rather than static indicators of compromise.

- *Distributed Nature*: The distributed nature of modern cyberthreats, particularly botnets, refers to their reliance on a decentralized network of compromised devices working collaboratively to execute attacks. This architecture makes such threats resilient, scalable, and harder to detect or dismantle. In a distributed system, infected devices, or bots, are spread across diverse geographic locations and networks, reducing reliance on a central point of control. Each bot acts as an independent node, capable of performing specific tasks, such as launching attacks, propagating malware, or reporting stolen data. First, it increases the scale of attacks, enabling the execution of high-volume DDoS attacks or widespread spam campaigns. Second, it makes takedown efforts challenging, as defenders must identify and neutralize each bot or disrupt the underlying C&C infrastructure. Third, distributed systems are resilient; even if some nodes are taken down, the remaining bots can continue functioning. The distributed nature also enhances anonymity for attackers, as traffic and commands are routed through multiple nodes, obscuring their origin. Countering such threats requires a multilayered defense strategy, including global threat intelligence sharing, advanced anomaly detection, and real-time response mechanisms to identify and mitigate attacks across dispersed networks effectively.

- *Hidden Channels*: Hidden channels, also known as covert channels, are communication pathways used by attackers to secretly exchange information between malware and its C&C infrastructure without being detected. These channels exploit legitimate systems, protocols, or services to mask malicious activities, allowing attackers to evade traditional security measures. Hidden channels can be implemented in a variety of ways, including embedding commands in seemingly benign data or leveraging underutilized parts of communication protocols. For example, attackers may use DNS tunneling to encode and transmit commands or stolen data within DNS queries and responses, exploiting the fact that DNS traffic is often trusted and rarely inspected. Similarly, HTTP or HTTPS traffic is frequently used as a covert channel, as it blends with regular web activity and is protected by encryption. Attackers may also use steganography to hide malicious data within images, audio files, or videos shared through legitimate services. Hidden channels are highly effective in bypassing firewalls, IDS, and other security measures because they operate within legitimate traffic flows. Their use poses significant challenges for defenders, requiring advanced tools and techniques, such as deep packet inspection, anomaly detection, and machine learning-based behavioral analysis, to identify and disrupt covert communication without disrupting legitimate operations. Attackers often use unconventional channels such as DNS tunneling, social media platforms, or even IoT devices to maintain communication.

The mitigation of C&C infrastructures is crucial in defending against modern malware campaigns and botnet activities. C&C systems serve as the backbone of cyberattacks, enabling attackers to control infected systems, execute commands, and exfiltrate data. To counter these threats, organizations and cybersecurity experts employ a comprehensive range of strategies that involve detection, disruption, and prevention mechanisms. The mitigation of C&C infrastructure needs to integrate reactive and proactive methods such as the following.

- *Threat Intelligence Sharing*: The intelligence of threats and timely detection are the basic components of modern cybersecurity strategies, allowing organizations to identify, assess, and alleviate potential risks that could escalate into significant incidents. The intelligence of threats includes the collection, analysis, and use of information about potential and active cyberthreats so as to improve the security level of the organization. This proactive approach helps to identify compromise indicators (IOC), such as malicious IP addresses, domains, hash files, and behavior patterns that can signal the presence of malware, phishing attempts, or other forms of cyberattacks. The use of such intelligence can implement measures to prevent attackers from using vulnerabilities or gaining access to their systems. Early detection focuses on identifying anomalies and suspicious activities as soon as they occur, thereby minimizing the attacks at the time of harm. It includes deployment of advanced tools and technologies such as security information and event management (SIEM) systems and endpoint detection and response (EDR). These tools collect and analyze protocols, monitor network traffic, and examine the activities of endpoints for signs of harmful behavior. For example, unusual login attempts, unauthorized access to sensitive data, or abnormal traffic patterns can serve as red flags. With timely detection, security teams can quickly explore and respond to incidents, reducing their scope and impact.

The synergy between threat intelligence and early detection is essential for robust cybersecurity. Threat intelligence provides context and insights that inform detection mechanisms, making them more precise and effective. For example, threat intelligence feeds can be integrated into SIEM systems to automatically correlate known IOCs with ongoing activities, alerting security teams to potential threats. Similarly, advanced behavioral analysis, supported by machine learning, can detect subtle anomalies that traditional signature-based systems might miss. This is particularly critical in identifying zero-day attacks and APTs, where attackers use sophisticated methods to evade conventional defenses. Organizations often participate in threat intelligence sharing communities, such as Information Sharing and Analysis Centers (ISACs) or global cybersecurity initiatives, to exchange insights about emerging threats. Collaborative efforts enhance collective defenses, as threat intelligence shared by one entity can help others proactively protect against similar attacks. Additionally, automation in threat intelligence, such as using APIs to integrate threat feeds with security tools, ensures real-time updates and responses, significantly reducing the window of vulnerability.

In addition, the growing acceptance of ML and AI has revolutionized the intelligence of threats and early detection. AI-controlled systems can process a huge amount of data from different sources, and identify formulas and trends indicating potential threats. These systems may prefer warnings, filter out false positives, and provide special knowledge, allowing security teams to focus on critical problems. For example, AI can analyze phishing campaigns, identify common characteristics, and predict future attack vectors. Despite its effectiveness, the implementation of intelligence on threats and early detection comes with challenges. Organizations must ensure that they have the right expertise, tools, and processes for interpreting and acting on news data. In addition, the total volume of threat data can be stunning, so it is necessary to prioritize and contextualize information. Cybercriminals also adapt to defensive measures using tactics such as encryption, confusion, and polymorphism to avoid detection. The organization, therefore, must constantly update and improve its intelligence and threat detection to stay in front of opponents. By proactive identification and threat alleviation, organizations can significantly reduce their risk exposure, protect critical assets, and maintain operational continuity. The integration of advanced technologies, cooperation, and strategic focus on special knowledge ensures that this effort remains effective in the developing threat.

- *Network Traffic Analysis*: It is a critical part of modern cybersecurity procedures that allows organizations to monitor, detect, and respond to potential threats in their digital infrastructure. It includes exploring data packets passing through networks to identify formulas, anomalies, and harmful activities that could endanger security or performance. This process provides network behavior visibility and helps security teams to understand how devices and systems interact while revealing unauthorized or suspicious activities. By analyzing network traffic, organizations can detect, identify malware, prevent data exfiltration, and optimize network performance, making it a major aspect of maintaining a safe and efficient IT environment. The core of the network traffic analysis lies in its ability to identify deviations from normal behavior. By determining the basic line of regular network activities, safety tools can indicate anomalies, such as unexpected tips, unusual data streams, or communication with known harmful IP addresses or domains. These anomalies often indicate potential threats such as DDoS attacks, data violations, or botnet activity. Techniques such as DPI inspections (DPI) allow analysts to examine the content of data packets, reveal built-in malware, unauthorized file transfers, or C&C communication. In addition, the analysis of the transport flow provides knowledge into which devices create or receive unusual amounts of data, emphasizing the potential sources of compromise. ML and AI can improve the capabilities of network traffic analysis by identifying formulas and trends in huge amounts of data. ML models can be trained to recognize the signatures of well-known attacks and detect previously invisible threats based on their behavior. For example, driven AI tools can identify hidden activities such as exfiltration of slow data or secret side movements in the network. These technologies also reduce fake positives and ensure that security teams can focus on real threats without being distracted by irrelevant warnings.

Another important aspect of network traffic analysis is encrypted traffic monitoring. With the rise of SSL/TLS encryption, much of today's network traffic is encrypted, which poses challenges for traditional inspection tools. However, advanced solutions now allow organizations to decrypt and analyze encrypted traffic while maintaining privacy and compliance. This capability is essential for detecting malicious activities concealed within encrypted channels, such as malware payloads or phishing attempts. Moreover, metadata analysis, which examines attributes such as packet size, timing, and destination without decrypting the contents, can also uncover suspicious patterns in encrypted traffic. Many regulations, such as GDPR, HIPAA, and PCI DSS, require organizations to monitor their networks for unauthorized access and data breaches. Traffic analysis helps demonstrate compliance by providing detailed logs and reports of network activity. The sheer volume of data generated by modern networks can overwhelm traditional tools, making it difficult to process and analyze traffic in real time. To address this, organizations often employ scalable solutions, such as cloud-based traffic analysis platforms, that can handle high volumes of data and provide real-time insights. Another challenge is the increasing use of evasion techniques by attackers, such as encrypting malware communications or using legitimate cloud services for malicious activities. This necessitates continuous updates to detection mechanisms and the integration of threat intelligence feeds to stay ahead of evolving threats. By providing visibility into network activities, it enables organizations to detect and respond to threats, maintain compliance, and optimize performance. The integration of advanced technologies like AI, coupled with a focus on encrypted traffic and scalability, ensures that network traffic analysis remains effective in addressing the complexities of today's digital landscape. As cyberthreats continue to evolve, investing in robust traffic analysis capabilities is essential for safeguarding organizational assets and maintaining operational resilience.

- *Endpoint Protection*: It is a critical part of modern cybersecurity aimed at protecting devices such as desktop computers, laptops, smartphones, tablets, and computer threat servers. These endpoints serve as entry points to organizational networks, making them the main goal for attackers trying to use vulnerability, get unauthorized access, or deploy malware. The solution of endpoint protection includes a combination of technology, processes, and procedures for the detection, prevention, and alleviation of security risks associated with the endpoints, ensuring the integrity and confidentiality of organizational data. With the growing prevalence of remote work, bringing your own facilities (BYOD) and IoT, the protection of the endpoint has become more critical than ever. Protection of endpoints in its core includes the use of software or agents on endpoints to monitor, detect, and respond to threats. Modern endpoint protection platforms (EPPs) offer a wide range of features, including antivirus and anti-malware capabilities, IPS, real-time behavior, and monitoring. These platforms use detection based on signatures to identify known threats and heuristics or machine learning to detect vulnerabilities and APTs. The protection of endpoints exceeds the traditional antiviral solution by integrating with centralized management consoles, allowing security teams to monitor and control all endpoints in the organization from one interface. One of the key components of endpoint protection is EDR, which focuses on continuous monitoring and analysis of endpoint activities to detect and respond to advanced threats. EDR solutions provide insight into suspicious behavior, allowing security teams to explore potential incidents and carry out immediate steps, such as isolating compromised equipment or malicious processes.

This proactive approach helps to mitigate the damage caused by cyberattacks and prevent attackers from gaining a foothold within the network. Another important aspect of endpoint protection is data encryption and secure authentication. By encrypting sensitive data stored on endpoints and enforcing strong authentication protocols, organizations can prevent unauthorized access, even if devices are lost or stolen. MFA further increases security by requiring users to provide other verification factors, such as biometrics or one-time passwords, before accessing sensitive resources. The protection of endpoints is also dealt with by challenges that represent remote work and cloud environments. As employees approach business resources from various locations and facilities, the organization must ensure consistent security measures at all endpoints. Solutions such as VPNs, secure web gateways, and platforms for protection of endpoints delivered by the cloud help ensure remote connection and recovery from policies. Furthermore, endpoint protection integrates with broader security frameworks, such as zero-trust architectures, to ensure continuous verification of user and device identities. Despite its effectiveness, endpoint protection is not without challenges. Cybercriminals constantly evolve their tactics, employing sophisticated techniques to bypass security measures. For instance, fileless malware, which resides in memory instead of being stored on disk, can evade traditional detection methods. Additionally, managing and securing many endpoints across geographically dispersed locations can strain IT resources. To address these challenges, organizations must adopt advanced endpoint protection solutions that incorporate AI-driven threat intelligence, automated responses, and regular updates to keep pace with emerging threats. Securing endpoint devices against a wide range of threats helps organizations safeguard their networks, data, and operations. Modern endpoint protection solutions, with features such as EDR, encryption, and AI-based detection, provide comprehensive defenses while enabling centralized management and scalability.

As cyberthreats continue to evolve, investing in advanced endpoint protection measures is crucial for ensuring resilience in an increasingly digital and interconnected world.

- *Application and API security*: This is a vital aspect of modern cybersecurity, focusing on protecting applications and their underlying APIs from vulnerabilities, unauthorized access, and malicious exploitation. As applications become increasingly central to business operations and APIs serve as the connective tissue between systems, ensuring their security is paramount to safeguard sensitive data, maintain operational continuity, and prevent cyberattacks. Application and API security encompasses a range of measures, tools, and best practices designed to mitigate risks, address vulnerabilities, and ensure secure communication between applications, services, and users. Applications, particularly web and mobile ones, are prime targets for attackers due to the valuable data they process and the widespread access they provide. Normal threats for applications include injection attacks, cross-site scripting (XSS), unsecured databases, and incorrect configurations. These vulnerabilities can lead to data violation, system compromise, or even complete loss of the application. In order to resolve these risks, developers must accept secure encoding procedures, perform regular code checks, and evaluate vulnerability using tools such as Static Application Security Testing (SAST) and Dynamic Application Security Testing (DAST). In addition, web application firewalls provide an added layer of monitoring and filtering of harmful traffic. APIs, which enable communication between different software systems, are equally susceptible to threats. APIs expose endpoints that attackers can exploit if not properly secured, leading to data leakage, unauthorized access, or DoS attacks. As businesses increasingly rely on APIs for integration, particularly in cloud-native and microservices architectures, the attack surface for API-related threats has grown. Common API vulnerabilities include improper authentication, excessive data exposure, broken access control, and lack of input validation. To secure APIs, organizations must implement strict access controls, such as OAuth 2.0 and API keys, to ensure that only authorized users and applications can access them. Rate limiting and throttling mechanisms help prevent abuse, such as API scraping or DoS attacks.

  A key component of application and API security is adopting a "shift-left" approach, where security is integrated into the development lifecycle from the beginning. This includes conducting threat modeling, implementing secure design principles, and leveraging DevSecOps practices that embed security testing within CI/CD pipelines. Automation tools, such as API gateways and runtime application self-protection (RASP), help monitor and mitigate threats in real time by identifying suspicious activity and enforcing security policies. The rise of serverless architectures and third-party integrations has further underscored the importance of application and API security.

These technologies often rely on external dependencies, which can introduce additional risks if not vetted or maintained. Regular patching and updates are crucial to address known vulnerabilities in both custom-built and third-party components. Additionally, ensuring compliance with industry standards and regulations, such as OWASP API Security Top 10, GDPR, or PCI DSS, helps organizations align their security practices with best-in-class recommendations. A comprehensive approach that integrates secure development practices, advanced tools, and continuous monitoring is essential to address the dynamic nature of threats in an increasingly interconnected world. As cyberattacks evolve, proactive application and API security measures are critical for mitigating risks and enabling secure innovation.

- *DNS Security*: DNS security is a critical aspect of cybersecurity, focused on protecting the DNS from threats, vulnerabilities, and misuse. While essential for Internet functionality, DNS is inherently vulnerable to various attacks and exploits due to its open and decentralized design. DNS security involves implementing measures to safeguard DNS infrastructure, prevent malicious activities, and ensure the integrity and availability of DNS services, thereby protecting users and organizations from data breaches, service disruptions, and cyberattacks. One of the primary DNS security threats is spoofing or cache poisoning, where attackers put fake DNS records into the server cache and redirect users to malicious websites. This can lead to phishing, malware distribution, or data theft. To alleviate this, the organizations use the Domain Name System (DNSSEC) to add cryptographic signatures to DNS records, ensure their authenticity, and prevent tampering. DNSSEC works by verifying the integrity of DNS responses and ensuring that users are focused on legitimate sources. However, DNSSEC adoption requires consistent implementation across DNS servers, which remains a challenge for widespread deployment.

  Another significant DNS-related threat is DDoS attacks targeting DNS infrastructure. By overwhelming DNS servers with massive volumes of requests, attackers can disrupt the resolution of domain names, rendering websites and online services inaccessible. To counter this, organizations utilize redundant DNS infrastructure, load balancing, and Anycast routing to distribute traffic across multiple servers, ensuring resilience against DDoS attacks. Additionally, DNS firewall solutions monitor DNS traffic, identifying and mitigating malicious activities such as volumetric attacks, data exfiltration, or C&C communication from botnets. DNS tunneling is another technique that exploits DNS to covertly transmit data or commands, often used by attackers to bypass traditional network defenses. Through DNS queries, data can be encoded and transmitted between compromised endpoints and malicious servers. Detecting and preventing DNS tunneling requires advanced threat intelligence, behavioral analysis, and monitoring tools that identify anomalous patterns in DNS traffic.

The rise of malicious domain registrations, such as typo-squatting, domain squatting, or newly registered domains used for phishing, further complicates DNS security. Cybercriminals often use these tactics to make users visit false websites or disclose sensitive information. Organizations can mitigate these threats by implementing the domain monitoring tools that detect suspicious registrations or block access to known harmful domains using intelligence channels. Secure DNS configurations also play a key role in DNS security. The correct DNS configuration prevents unauthorized zones from accessing unauthorized zones, which could expose the entire DNS structure to attackers. To enforce strict access controls and the use of secure communication protocols such as DNS over HTTPS (DoH) or DNS via TLS (DOT), encrypt DNS questions, preventing eavesdropping and man-in-the-middle (MITM) attacks. Despite these measures, DNS security is a permanent challenge due to the evolving tactics of attackers and the complexity of DNS infrastructure. Organizations must accept multilayer access, integrate DNSSEC, monitor tools, firewall gates, and encryption to protect their ecosystem DNS. Regular audits, updates, and compliance with proven procedures are necessary to maintain DNS resistance and protection of users from cyberthreats. Since the attackers continue to use DNS vulnerabilities, proactive measures and advanced technologies are decisive for risk alleviation and ensuring the integrity and availability of DNS services. Organizations that prefer DNS security can increase their overall posture of cybersecurity, protect sensitive data, and maintain the trust and reliability of their online presence.

Behavioral Analysis: It is a critical cybersecurity technique that involves monitoring and analyzing the behavior of users, systems, and networks to detect anomalies, identify potential threats, and mitigate risks. Unlike traditional methods that rely on signature-based detection of known threats, behavioral analysis focuses on identifying unusual patterns or deviations from baseline behaviors, making it highly effective against zero-day attacks, APTs, and other sophisticated cyberthreats. This approach leverages ML, AI, and data analytics to provide real-time insights into the activities within an environment, enabling organizations to respond proactively to potential threats before they escalate. The core concept of behavioral analysis is establishing a baseline of normal activity. For instance, in a network, this might include typical login times, data transfer volumes, or access to specific applications. By continuously monitoring and comparing real-time behaviors against this baseline, behavioral analysis tools can identify anomalies, such as an employee accessing sensitive data outside of regular working hours or a device suddenly communicating with an unknown server. These deviations often signal potential malicious activities, such as insider threats, compromised accounts, or malware infections.

Behavioral analysis is widely used in endpoint security, network monitoring, and application security. In endpoint security, it helps detect unauthorized actions on devices, such as unusual file modifications, installation of suspicious software, or unexpected changes in device configurations.

In networks, behavioral analysis identifies traffic patterns that deviate from the norm, such as sudden spikes in data transfers, unauthorized connections, or attempts to access restricted resources. Similarly, in applications, it monitors user activities to detect fraudulent transactions, account takeovers, or misuse of privileges. One of the most significant advantages of behavioral analysis is its ability to detect unknown threats. Traditional signature-based solutions are limited to identifying threats that match pre-defined signatures, leaving organizations vulnerable to new or polymorphic malware. In contrast, behavioral analysis focuses on the actions and intentions of entities, allowing it to identify previously unseen threats based on suspicious behaviors. This capability is especially valuable in addressing modern attack techniques, such as fileless malware, where malicious activities occur entirely in memory and leave little to no trace on disk.

To increase its efficiency, behavior analysis often integrates with other security technologies, such as SIEM systems, EDR tools, and user behavior analytics (UEBA). These integrations allow organizations to correlate data from multiple sources and provide a more comprehensive view of potential threats, and allow for faster response times. For example, if the UEBA platform detects unusual login behavior and the EDR tool identifies a suspicious process at the same endpoint, combined knowledge can help security teams quickly determine the main cause and alleviate the threat. Despite its advantages, the analysis of the behavior of the challenge has. One common problem is the potential for false positives where benign activities are marked as suspicious due to atypical behavior. This can amaze the security teams and lead to fatigue. To solve this, advanced solutions to analyze behavior use AI and machine learning to improve detection algorithms, reducing false positives while maintaining high detection accuracy. Another challenge is the complexity of the deployment and management of tool analysis, which often requires considerable resources and expertise. Monitoring and analyzing the behavior of users, systems, and networks allows proactive threat detection and increases overall security. As cyberthreats continue to evolve, accepting behavior analysis in combination with other advanced technologies will remain necessary for staying against attackers and protecting critical assets.

Regulatory Compliance and Standards: For organizations operating in today's digital environment, providing sensitive data protection, maintaining trust with customers and avoiding legal and financial sanctions, and avoiding legal and financial sanctions are essential. Consistency involves compliance with legal, regulatory, and contractual obligations concerning the organization and geography of the organization, while the standards provide frameworks and instructions to ensure security, privacy, and operational efficiency. For organizations that process sensitive information, such as financial institutions, healthcare providers, or technology companies, compliance with regulatory compliance and standards is not only a legal requirement, but also a critical aspect of risk management and social responsibility. These regulations outline specific data protection requirements, secure data storage, and user privacy, and ensure that organizations take the necessary steps to protect customer and operational data. For example, GDPR mandates strict data processing rules requiring that organizations take measures such as encryption, pseudonymization, and inspection of access to personal data protection. Failure to comply can result in stiff fines and damage to the reputation, which makes regulatory adherence the top priority.

Beyond regulations, standards such as ISO/IEC 27001, NIST Cybersecurity Framework, and SOC 2 provide organizations with comprehensive guidelines for establishing and maintaining robust security practices. These standards focus on critical aspects such as risk assessment, incident response, encryption protocols, and employee training, enabling organizations to create a systematic and consistent approach to security. Achieving certifications for such standards not only demonstrates an organization's commitment to security but also provides a competitive advantage by instilling confidence in customers and stakeholders. One of the key challenges in regulatory compliance is the dynamic nature of the regulatory environment. As technologies and cyberthreats evolve, regulations and standards are constantly updated to address emerging risks. Organizations must stay vigilant, continuously monitor changes in compliance requirements, and adapt their policies and practices accordingly. This requires investment in dedicated compliance teams, legal expertise, and technology solutions that automate compliance monitoring and reporting. Tools such as Governance, Risk, and Compliance (GRC) platforms help streamline compliance processes by centralizing documentation, tracking compliance status, and ensuring audit readiness. Another challenge is the complexity of complying with multiple regulations and standards, especially for organizations operating in multiple jurisdictions or industries. Overlapping requirements, regional variations, and cross-border data transfer rules often complicate compliance efforts. To address this, organizations adopt a unified approach by mapping common requirements across different frameworks, enabling them to implement controls that satisfy multiple compliance obligations simultaneously. Collaboration with third-party auditors and consultants also helps in navigating the intricacies of compliance and achieving alignment with industry best practices. Compliance is not a one-time effort but an ongoing process that requires continuous monitoring, regular audits, and periodic updates to security measures. Training employees to understand compliance requirements and fostering a culture of security awareness are also critical components of maintaining regulatory compliance. By proactively addressing regulatory obligations and aligning with standards, organizations can reduce the risk of breaches, enhance customer trust, and demonstrate accountability to regulators and stakeholders.

C&C infrastructure is a cornerstone of modern cybercrime, enabling attackers to manage and scale their operations with precision. Its adaptability and evolution, particularly with the advent of IoT and cloud technologies, make it a persistent and formidable challenge for cybersecurity professionals. Combating C&C infrastructure requires a proactive, multilayered approach that includes advanced detection techniques, global threat intelligence sharing, and robust defense mechanisms. By understanding its intricacies, organizations can better prepare to detect and mitigate the threats posed by this critical element of cyberattacks.

3.5 INFECTION VECTORS AND PROPAGATION TECHNIQUES

Infection vectors and propagation techniques are central to the dissemination of malware and cyberattacks. They define how attackers breach systems, install malicious software, and spread their payload across devices or networks. Understanding these mechanisms is crucial for defending against ever-evolving cyberthreats, as attackers continue to exploit technological vulnerabilities and human behavior to achieve their goals. The examples of malware propagation are WannaCry ransomware, NotPetya, and Mirai botnet. The WannaCry ransomware propagated through the EternalBlue exploit, and WannaCry rapidly infected networks worldwide by exploiting SMB vulnerabilities in unpatched Windows systems. NotPetya is a destructive malware that spreads via a compromised software update from a legitimate Ukrainian company, affecting global operations. The Mirai botnet leveraged weak IoT device credentials to propagate and create a massive botnet capable of launching large-scale DDoS attacks. It explores the key infection vectors and propagation methods, offering insights into their working mechanisms, impact, and prevention.

3.5.1 Infection vectors: Entry points for malicious software

Vectors of infection are methods or paths through which malware (malware) infiltrates devices, networks, or systems. These entry points are used by attackers to obtain unauthorized access, disrupt operations, or extract sensitive data. Understanding the vectors of infection is essential for the development of effective defense against malware because they are the first step in the compromise chain. Malware developers are constantly developing their tactics to use vulnerabilities in the behavior of software, hardware, and users, which is essential for organizations and individuals to remain alert and proactive in ensuring their digital assets. An in-depth exploration of common infection vectors, their mechanisms, and the strategies used to mitigate their risks is needed.

Phishing and Social Engineering: Phishing is one of the most prevalent and effective infection vectors, leveraging human psychology rather than technical vulnerabilities. Attackers send fraudulent emails, messages, or links that appear to originate from legitimate sources, such as banks, colleagues, or popular brands. These messages often contain malicious attachments or direct users to fake websites designed to steal credentials or deliver malware. Social engineering techniques exploit trust, urgency, or curiosity to manipulate users into clicking malicious links, downloading infected files, or divulging sensitive information. For instance, a phishing email may claim a user's account has been compromised, urging them to log in through a provided link, which is controlled by the attacker. Once credentials are stolen, attackers can access systems or spread malware further.

Exploiting Software Vulnerabilities: Outdated or poorly maintained software is a significant infection vector for malware. Cybercriminals scan for vulnerabilities in operating systems, applications, or firmware and exploit them using techniques such as buffer overflows, SQL injection, or remote code execution. Zero-day vulnerabilities—flaws unknown to the software vendor—are particularly dangerous, as they can be exploited before patches are available. Attackers often use exploit kits, automated tools that scan for vulnerabilities and deploy payloads to compromise targets. For example, a vulnerable web browser may inadvertently download and execute malicious code when visiting a compromised website, allowing attackers to gain control over the device or network.

Drive-By Downloads: The unit downloads when the user visits a compromised or malicious site, and malware is automatically downloaded and executed without their knowledge. These attacks usually use a vulnerability in web browsers, plugins, or extensions, often focusing on obsolete versions of the software. Drive-by downloads are stealthy and require no user interaction, making them particularly effective for spreading malware. Attackers may embed malicious scripts in legitimate websites through vulnerabilities or create fake websites designed to lure victims. Users are commonly directed to such sites via phishing emails, social media links, or malvertising—malicious advertisements placed on legitimate ad networks.

Removable Media: Removable media, such as USB drives, external hard drives, or SD cards, are frequently used as infection vectors, especially in targeted attacks. Malware can be preloaded onto a device and executed automatically when connected to a system. For instance, the infamous Stuxnet worm was spread via infected USB drives to compromise industrial control systems. Organizations that lack strict policies governing the use of removable media are particularly vulnerable. Attackers may strategically drop infected devices in public places, relying on the curiosity of individuals who pick them up and connect them to their computers.

Malicious Attachments and File Downloads: Attachments in emails or messages are a common vector for spreading malware. These files often masquerade as legitimate documents, such as invoices, resumes, or official notices, and are designed to trick users into opening them. Once opened, malicious macros, scripts, or executables embedded within the file activate, delivering the malware payload. Similarly, downloading files from untrusted or suspicious sources can lead to malware infections. Freeware, cracked software, or pirated media often contain hidden malicious code, exposing users to threats such as ransomware, spyware, or trojans.

Network-based Attacks: Attackers frequently exploit weaknesses in network configurations, protocols, or security measures to deliver malware. Open ports, misconfigured firewalls, and unprotected Wi-Fi networks can serve as entry points for malicious traffic. Network-based infection vectors include MITM attacks, where attackers intercept and manipulate data between two parties, and DDoS attacks, which often act as distractions while malware is deployed. Worms and botnets also propagate through networks by exploiting vulnerabilities in connected devices.

Mobile Devices and IoT: The increasing adoption of mobile devices and IoT devices has expanded the attack surface for malware. Mobile malware often spreads through malicious apps, phishing links, or compromised app stores. IoT devices, which often lack robust security features, are vulnerable to exploitation via weak credentials, outdated firmware, or insecure communication protocols. Once compromised, mobile and IoT devices can be used as entry points to broader networks, enabling attackers to access sensitive data or launch further attacks.

Supply Chain Attacks: Supply chain attacks target vulnerabilities in third-party vendors, suppliers, or service providers to compromise their customers. For example, attackers may embed malware in software updates, hardware components, or developer tools, which are then distributed to end-users. The SolarWinds attack is a prominent example, where attackers compromised a software update to distribute malware to thousands of organizations, including government agencies and Fortune 500 companies.

Cloud and Remote Access Exploits: The shift to cloud services and remote work has introduced new infection vectors for malware. Misconfigured cloud storage, weak remote access credentials, or insecure VPNs provide opportunities for attackers to infiltrate systems. Phishing attacks targeting remote access credentials, such as those for RDP or SSH, are also on the rise.

3.5.2 Propagation techniques: How malware spreads

Propagation techniques refer to the methods and strategies employed by malware to spread from an initial infected device to other systems or networks. Understanding these techniques is crucial for designing effective defenses, as they allow malware to amplify its impact and maximize its reach. Cybercriminals use a wide variety of propagation methods, exploiting software vulnerabilities, network weaknesses, human errors, and technological interconnectivity. There are several common malware propagation techniques used to mitigate the risks such as:

> *File-based Propagation*: One of the oldest and simplest techniques, file-based propagation relies on infecting files shared between systems. Malware can embed itself in executable files, documents, or archives

and spread through physical media (e.g., USB drives) or digital channels (e.g., email attachments or file-sharing platforms). Attackers often use social engineering tactics to trick users into opening infected files. For instance, a malicious email attachment disguised as an invoice or resume may execute malware upon opening. Worms, such as the infamous "Lottery" worm, rely heavily on file-based propagation by exploiting human trust and curiosity. Mitigation strategies include implementing antivirus solutions, scanning files before opening them, and educating users on recognizing suspicious files.

Network-Based Propagation: Malware frequently exploits network connectivity to propagate itself. Network-based propagation techniques involve spreading through LAN, WAN, or the Internet. This can be achieved using the following methods, such as exploiting open ports, brute force attacks, and self-replication. Malware scans for open ports or unsecured services to infiltrate networks. For example, the WannaCry ransomware exploited a vulnerability in the SMB protocol to spread rapidly across networks. Malware may attempt to guess weak passwords to gain access to networked devices or shared resources. Worms are particularly adept at network-based propagation, as they can replicate themselves and spread to connected devices without user interaction.

To mitigate network-based propagation, organizations can deploy firewalls, IDS/IPS, and network segmentation to limit the spread of malware.

Email and Messaging Systems: Email remains one of the most effective vectors for malware propagation. Attackers use phishing techniques to distribute malicious attachments or links that, when opened, execute malware or redirect victims to compromised websites. Messaging platforms, including instant messaging apps and social media, are also exploited for malware distribution. For example, malware can spread via links shared in chats or by hijacking accounts to send messages to a victim's contacts. Advanced email security solutions, such as spam filters and phishing detection tools, are essential for mitigating risks. Users should also be educated on identifying phishing attempts and avoiding clicking on unknown links or downloading suspicious attachments.

Removable Media and Hardware Devices: Physical media such as USB drives, external hard drives, and SD cards are popular tools for malware propagation. Malware can be preloaded onto these devices and automatically executed when connected to a computer or other systems. The infamous Stuxnet worm is an example, as it propagated through infected USB drives to target specific industrial control systems. Attackers may also drop malicious USB drives in public places, relying on human curiosity to spread the malware. Organizations can mitigate these risks by restricting the use of removable media, implementing endpoint detection solutions, and disabling autorun features on devices.

Drive-By Downloads: These attacks are a stealthy method of malware propagation. They occur when users visit compromised or malicious websites, and malware is automatically downloaded and executed without their consent or knowledge. These attacks often exploit vulnerabilities in web browsers, plugins, or extensions. Malvertising, a form of drive-by attack, uses legitimate online ad networks to deliver malware. A user may encounter malicious ads on otherwise trustworthy websites, exposing them to malware infections. To counter drive-by downloads, organizations should enforce regular software updates, block access to suspicious websites, and use web content filtering tools.

Peer-to-Peer (P2P) Networks: P2P networks are another common method for malware propagation. Attackers use these decentralized networks to distribute malware among connected devices. Malware embedded in shared files, such as pirated software or media, can quickly infect multiple systems within a P2P network. For example, the Gameover ZeuS botnet used P2P technology to spread malware and establish resilient C&C communication.

Mitigating P2P-based propagation involves monitoring network traffic, avoiding the use of untrusted P2P platforms, and enforcing endpoint protection measures.

Exploiting Software Vulnerabilities: The attackers continuously seek vulnerabilities in operating systems, applications, or firmware that can be used to spread malware. Relays with zero day that are not unknown to software suppliers are particularly valuable for attackers. Using kits, such as Angler or Blackhole Kits, automates the process of identifying vulnerability and deployment of useful malware load. Once the exploitation is successful, malware can spread to other systems by using a similar vulnerability. Effective patch management, regular vulnerability evaluation, and use of virtual repair tools are necessary to alleviate software vulnerabilities.

Supply Chain Attacks: Supply chain attacks are sophisticated methods of malware propagation that target third-party vendors, suppliers, or service providers. Malware can be embedded in software updates, hardware components, or development tools and distributed to end-users. The SolarWinds attack is a prime example, where attackers compromised a software update to spread malware to thousands of organizations. To mitigate supply chain risks, organizations should vet their vendors, enforce strict security standards, and monitor third-party integrations for potential vulnerabilities.

Cloud Services and Remote Work Tools: The shift to cloud computing and remote work has introduced new opportunities for malware propagation. Attackers may exploit misconfigured cloud storage, weak remote access credentials, or insecure collaboration tools to spread malware. For example, ransomware attacks on cloud-based services often propagate through shared files or compromised user accounts. RDP brute force attacks are also a common method for accessing systems and deploying malware. Mitigating these risks requires enforcing strong access controls, encrypting data, and implementing zero-trust security models.

3.5.3 Impacts of infection vectors and propagation

Infection vectors and propagation techniques are critical components of malware operations that allow malicious software to infiltrate systems and spread across networks. These methods, employed by attackers, have significant impacts on various aspects of technology, businesses, individuals, and society. The consequences can range from data breaches and financial losses to disruption of critical services and erosion of trust. Economic losses are one of the most evident impacts of malware infection vectors, and propagation is the economic damage inflicted on organizations and individuals. Cyberattacks that exploit infection vectors often lead to significant financial costs, including data recovery, business disruption, ransomware, and litigation. The data recovery and system restoration may require allocating substantial resources to recover lost or corrupted data and restore affected systems. Malware propagation through networks can cause prolonged system outages, halting operations and reducing productivity. Ransomware attacks, a common form of malware propagation, often result in victims paying large sums to regain access to their encrypted data. Data breaches result from infection vectors that may expose organizations to lawsuits and regulatory fines due to non-compliance with data protection laws. For example, the 2017 WannaCry ransomware attack caused billions of dollars in losses globally by exploiting a vulnerability in Windows systems, propagating rapidly across networks, and disrupting critical services, including healthcare and transportation.

Data breaches and loss of confidentiality often spread to access and exfiltrate sensitive data. Infection vectors such as phishing emails or drive-by downloads are commonly used to infiltrate systems and steal valuable information. Personal identity theft can use stolen personal information to commit fraud or identity theft. Businesses may suffer from stolen intellectual property, trade secrets, or customer data. Sensitive government or defense data compromised by malware propagation can threaten national security. Data breaches undermine trust and can lead to reputational damage for organizations, which may lose customers and partners due to the perception of weak security practices. The disruption of critical infrastructure targets to the critical infrastructure, such as energy grids, transportation systems, healthcare facilities, and communication networks, can have devastating consequences. Malware propagation through IoT devices, for instance, has proven particularly dangerous, as these devices often lack robust security measures. Transportation systems affected by malware propagation can cause accidents or delays, endangering lives and causing significant inconvenience. Disruptions in utilities such as water and electricity can ripple through economies, affecting businesses and households alike.

Data breaches can spread misinformation and manipulate through malware propagation using networks of compromised devices to launch attacks. These botnets can spread misinformation or manipulate public opinion by disseminating fake news or propaganda. Infection vectors targeting social media platforms or messaging services enable malware to propagate and spread harmful content widely and quickly. The effectiveness of infection vectors and propagation techniques has fueled the growth of cybercrime, enabling threat actors to scale their operations and launch sophisticated attacks. Cybercriminals now offer ransomware propagation tools on the dark web, allowing even non-technical actors to carry out attacks. Malware propagation tools have facilitated the rise of organized cybercrime groups that operate across borders. The accessibility of these tools makes it easier for cybercriminals to target individuals, small businesses, and large enterprises, leading to a global increase in cybercrime incidents.

These infections lead to compromised privacy as malware collects and transmits sensitive personal data without consent. Malware that propagates to mobile devices or PCs can monitor user activity, capturing keystrokes, browsing habits, and private conversations. Malware targeting IoT devices, such as smart cameras or speakers, can turn these devices into tools for unauthorized surveillance. The erosion of privacy due to malware infections undermines user trust in technology and raises ethical concerns about data usage. The distributed and sophisticated nature of malware propagation creates significant challenges for law enforcement and cybersecurity professionals. Identifying the perpetrators of malware attacks is often difficult, especially when attackers use advanced techniques such as encryption or decentralized C&C infrastructure. The rapid propagation of malware forces organizations and governments to allocate substantial resources to incident response, diverting attention from other priorities.

In order for organizations to deal with the impact of infectious vectors and promotion techniques, they must accept proactive and multilayer access to cybersecurity, including regular updates, employee training, network security, endpoint protection, and threat intelligence. User education about phishing, social engineering, and secure online practices can reduce human mistakes, a key factor in infection. Robust antivirus and endpoint detection solutions can identify and neutralize threats at entry points. Ensuring software and firmware are up to date reduces vulnerabilities that malware exploits for propagation. Collaborative efforts between organizations and governments enhance collective defenses against evolving threats.

Infection vectors and propagation techniques are fundamental aspects of cyberattacks, enabling attackers to infiltrate systems and spread malware across networks. From phishing and software vulnerabilities to IoT exploitation and lateral movement, these methods evolve alongside technological advancements, presenting ongoing challenges to cybersecurity. Mitigation requires a multilayered approach, combining proactive defenses, user education, and advanced detection capabilities.

3.6 PERSISTENCE AND EVASION TACTICS

Persistence and evasion tactics are critical strategies employed by cybercriminals and threat actors to maintain control over compromised systems while avoiding detection. These tactics are central to ensuring the longevity and effectiveness of malicious campaigns, whether for data theft, ransomware deployment, botnet operations, or espionage. Understanding these techniques is essential for organizations to design robust defense mechanisms and countermeasures.

Persistence Tactics: Persistence refers to the ability of malware or a threat actor to remain in a system after a successful compromise, even though system reboots, updates, or user actions intended to remove the threat. Achieving persistence ensures the attacker can maintain their foothold and continue malicious activities over time. The boot and startup modifications are threat actors that often modify boot processes or system configurations to automatically launch malicious code upon system startup. Techniques such as altering the Windows registry, adding malicious files to startup folders, or creating scheduled tasks ensure that malware executes every time the system boots. Attackers frequently install backdoors in compromised systems to regain access if initial entry points are closed. These backdoors may involve remote administration tools (RATs) or specially crafted applications that allow attackers to bypass authentication mechanisms and reconnect to the system. Rootkits are sophisticated tools that embed themselves deep within the operating system, often at the kernel level, to ensure persistent control. Rootkits are difficult to detect as they hide malicious processes, files, or network activity from monitoring tools and the user.

Malware may register itself as a legitimate service in operating systems such as Windows or Linux. These services run in the background and restart automatically, ensuring that the malware continues to function even if terminated manually. Attackers utilize built-in scheduling mechanisms, such as Windows Task Scheduler or cron jobs in Unix/Linux systems, to execute malicious scripts or programs at specific intervals or during system events. This ensures the consistent execution of malware. Fileless malware operates directly in system memory rather than being installed on disk, which allows it to evade traditional antivirus solutions. Fileless persistence often leverages native tools such as PowerShell or Windows Management Instrumentation (WMI) to maintain its foothold. Injecting malicious code into legitimate processes or replacing system Dynamic Link Libraries (DLLs) with tampered versions ensures that malware persists while piggybacking on trusted applications. This approach makes detection more challenging. Malicious browser extensions or plugins can be used to inject ads, steal credentials, or track user activity. Since browser extensions persist across sessions, they provide an effective means of maintaining a presence on a user's device. Organizations increasingly adopt cloud services; attackers exploit cloud environments for persistence. They may create rogue accounts, APIs, or containerized instances to remain within the infrastructure undetected.

Evasion Tactics: Evasion tactics are designed to help attackers and malware avoid detection by security systems, monitoring tools, and human oversight. These techniques ensure that malicious activities can be carried out without being interrupted or identified by defenders. Malicious actors use encryption and obfuscation to hide their activities and payloads from antivirus tools and IDS. For example, malware may encrypt its communications to avoid being flagged by network monitoring tools or obfuscate its code to make analysis difficult for researchers. The polymorphic malware changes its code structure during propagation or execution to evade signature-based detection systems. Metamorphic malware takes this further by rewriting its entire codebase, creating a unique version of itself each time it executes. Malware often includes mechanisms to detect whether it is being run in a sandbox or debugged by analysts. If a sandbox environment is detected, the malware may delay execution, terminate itself, or exhibit benign behavior to avoid detection. Threat actors increasingly rely on legitimate system tools (e.g., PowerShell, WMI, or Bash) to execute malicious activities. This approach minimizes the need for external files or applications, making the activity appear as part of normal system behavior. Injecting malicious code into legitimate processes allows attackers to hide within trusted applications. Code packing and compression are also used to hide the malicious code within a file that looks safe. These packed files decompress the payload only at runtime, evading static analysis by traditional security tools.

Advanced attackers use tactics such as domain fronting, encrypted tunnels, and steganography to evade network-level defenses. Domain fronting disguises malicious traffic as legitimate by routing it through well-known domains, while steganography hides malicious data within seemingly innocuous files such as images or videos. Malware may employ time-based triggers to delay execution until specific conditions are met, such as a certain time of day, an IP address, or user activity. This tactic ensures that the malware executes under circumstances where detection is less likely. Modern evasion tactics also target AI-driven security systems by exploiting their training data or introducing adversarial inputs. By subtly modifying malicious files or traffic, attackers can trick machine learning algorithms into classifying threats as benign. Malware often includes environmental checks to identify whether it is running in a virtualized environment or on a real machine. If a virtual environment is detected, the malware may cease operations to avoid detection. Threat actors use anonymized networks such as Tor or P2P communication channels to manage compromised devices.

These techniques make it challenging for defenders to trace or block communications between attackers and their malware. Malware may display fake error messages or use names that mimic legitimate applications to mislead users. For example, a malicious process may name itself like a system file (e.g., svchost.exe) to avoid scrutiny.

Addressing persistence and evasion tactics challenges in cybersecurity requires a multilayered, proactive approach to identify, prevent, and mitigate threats that aim to remain undetected while maintaining control over compromised systems. Persistence tactics, such as modifying system boot processes, using rootkits, or creating scheduled tasks, ensure malware or attackers maintain access to targeted systems over extended periods. Evasion tactics, on the other hand, leverage techniques such as encryption, code obfuscation, polymorphism, process injection, and living-off-the-land strategies to hide malicious activity from detection systems. To combat these threats effectively, organizations must employ robust endpoint protection, network monitoring, threat intelligence, and advanced detection mechanisms. A critical first step is implementing EDR solutions that monitor system behavior in real time, flagging suspicious activities such as unauthorized modifications to registry files, unusual scheduled tasks, or hidden malicious processes. Behavioral analysis complements this by focusing on deviations from baseline patterns, particularly for fileless malware and stealthy attacks that evade signature-based detection.

Additionally, threat intelligence plays a vital role in staying ahead of adversaries. Organizations must utilize up-to-date intelligence about emerging persistence and evasion techniques to adapt their defenses. By integrating this intelligence into automated tools and workflows, security teams can proactively identify and block new attack vectors. Regular software and firmware updates are essential in closing vulnerabilities that attackers exploit for persistence. These updates prevent attackers from using outdated software, including insecure libraries, as entry points. Furthermore, strong network segmentation ensures that even if one part of a network is compromised, the attack cannot spread to critical systems. Segmenting sensitive data and applications into isolated zones with access controls limits lateral movement, a common evasion method.

Another key measure is the use of advanced anomaly detection systems that use AI and ML to identify unusual behavior or formulas that may indicate harmful activity. Machine learning can analyze extensive datasets of normal activities to detect fine, avoidable threats. Organizations must also implement strict control and policies of the least privileges to minimize offensive surfaces. This includes limitation of administrative permissions and ensuring that users and applications have only the minimum authorization necessary for their functions, which reduces the opportunities for malware to obtain endurance. The secure starting mechanisms that verify the integrity of the system firmware during startup are effective against rootkits and bootkits designed to create persistent core support.

Comprehensive incident response plans are vital for the rapid detection and containment of attacks. These plans should include predefined steps to isolate infected systems, remove malicious files, and restore operations while preventing further exploitation. Organizations should also conduct regular penetration testing and red team exercises to uncover vulnerabilities and test their ability to detect and mitigate persistence and evasion tactics. Finally, employee training on recognizing phishing and social engineering attempts is crucial since attackers often rely on human error to deploy their malicious payloads. By integrating these measures, organizations can build a resilient defense system capable of combating the sophisticated persistence and evasion techniques employed by modern threat actors.

3.7 CONCLUSION

This chapter focused on the comprehensive understanding of IoT botnets, their anatomy, types, and common attacks, underscoring the growing complexity and severity of threats in an increasingly interconnected digital landscape. IoT botnets, formed by exploiting the vulnerabilities of IoT devices, highlight the risks posed by the rapid adoption of smart technologies without robust security measures. The anatomy of these botnets reveals their core components—infected devices, C&C infrastructure, and the mechanisms for executing malicious activities—all designed to exploit the inherently weak security of IoT ecosystems. Examining the different types of IoT botnets, such as centralized, decentralized (P2P), hybrid, and cloud-based botnets, reveals how attackers adapt their strategies to increase scalability, stealth, and resilience against takedown efforts. Each type presents unique challenges, with decentralized and hybrid models being particularly difficult to neutralize due to their distributed nature. Common IoT botnet attacks, including DDoS, spam campaigns, data theft, cryptojacking, and credential stuffing, demonstrate the versatility and impact of these malicious networks. These attacks disrupt businesses, compromise sensitive data, and strain network infrastructure, often with devastating consequences. This analysis emphasizes the importance of proactive mitigation strategies, such as implementing secure device configurations, strong authentication protocols, and regular software updates, to combat the proliferation of IoT botnets. Additionally, fostering awareness among users and manufacturers about the critical need for security-by-design principles is essential to fortify the IoT ecosystem. By combining technological advancements, regulatory measures, and user education, stakeholders can effectively counter the threat of IoT botnets, ensuring the safety and resilience of smart networks. Ultimately, addressing these challenges is not merely about responding to existing threats but about creating a secure foundation for the continued evolution of IoT technologies.

Chapter 4

Real-world IoT botnet case studies

4.1 THE MIRAI BOTNET

Botnet Mirai is a threat of cybersecurity that has developed significantly over the years and one of the most famous cyberthreats in recent history. Mirai, that was first discovered in 2016, is a sophisticated Botnet IoT, which was responsible for some of the greatest DDoS attacks in history. Its impact on the landscape of cybersecurity was significant, raising concerns about the security of IoT devices and the vulnerabilities they introduce. This chapter provides an in-depth analysis of Mirai botnet, including its origin, functioning, attack methodology, impact, relief techniques, and future consequences. The Mirai botnet was first discovered by malware researchers in August 2016. They were created by three university students—Paras Jha, Josiah White, and Dalton Norman—originally with an intention of gaining an advantage in hosting Minecraft servers. However, the control quickly got out and became a global threat of cybersecurity. The term "Mirai" means "the future" in Japanese and the source code of the botnet was publicly released in September 2016 by Jha, which is accessible to cybercriminals around the world. The release of its source code led to the creation of many Mirai variants, increasing its proliferation. The Mirai botnet primarily targets IoT devices, such as IP cameras, DVR, and routers, using their weak security configurations. It continuously scans the Internet for IoT devices that are vulnerable due to the default login data or a weak password. It is attempted to log in using a pre-configured list of commonly used default usernames and passwords (e.g., admin/admin, root/12345). After obtaining access, the device is infected and accepted into the botnet. After infection, a compromised device determines communication with the C&C server, which is controlled by attackers. The C&C server issues commands with an infected device and directs them to perform various harmful activities.

The main functionality of Mirai involves executing massive DDoS attacks. Through massive network traffic and service overloads, the attacks create necessary disruptions or full network system downtime. Different DDoS attack forms are possible through the botnet such as UDP floods together with TCP SYN floods joined by HTTP GET/POST floods and self-preservation and

DOI: 10.1201/9781003631460-4

detection evasion capabilities. Between them the Dyn DNS attack together with OVH attack and KrebsOnSecurity stand as the primary assaults executed through the Mirai botnet. A notorious Mirai attack struck Dyn in October 2016 causing the massive disruption of US Internet services together with European service availability. Twitter together with Reddit and Netflix and GitHub along with Airbnb were some platforms affected by the attack. In September 2016 Brian Krebs' website KrebsOnSecurity faced a DDoS attack at 620 Gbps, which proved to be a record-breaking assault at that time. The thermal attack served to show how destructive Mirai could be. The attack against French web hosting company OVH was responsible for one of the biggest DDoS attacks in history with a 1.1 Tbps volume that still stands as a historical record. The attack leveraged a massive number of compromised IoT devices, highlighting the scale of Mirai's capabilities. The impact of Mirai botnet significantly raised distinct landscape such as increased awareness of IoT vulnerabilities, strong security policies, and reduction of financial and operational losses (Figure 4.1).

The C2 server of Mirai operates independently from discovery and loading functions of its code. A new version of the botting engine received adjustments which led to the development of an efficient and rapid asynchronous telnet brute force engine that performs 500 attempts per second. Mirai advances its scalability and operational speed through the combination of Go (Golang) programming assets with traditional C language in its essential server module. The Mirai C2 server allows users to access a MySQL database that stores user accounts and attack history through its customer-oriented API. Operators who use Mirai can divide their botnet into various sections for customers to make flexible pricing options possible based on client-selected botnet segment sizes.

To counteract Mirai and its evolving strains, researchers, security professionals, and organizations have developed multiple mitigation strategies and defense mechanisms, which can be broadly categorized into device-level security, network-based defenses, anomaly detection systems, and proactive regulatory measures. At the device level, securing IoT devices is the first line of defense against Mirai infections. Most Mirai attacks originate due to weak authentication mechanisms, default credentials, and outdated firmware. Device manufacturers must enforce strong password policies, requiring users to set unique and complex passwords during device setup. Additionally, MFA can provide an extra layer of security against unauthorized access. Automatic firmware updates and patch management are critical to fixing known vulnerabilities that Mirai exploits. Many IoT devices operate on outdated software, making them vulnerable to known exploits. Implementing secure boot mechanisms ensures that only trusted firmware is executed, preventing unauthorized modifications to the device. Disabling unnecessary services and ports is another effective technique, as Mirai often exploits open Telnet (port 23) and SSH (port 22) connections to spread malware.

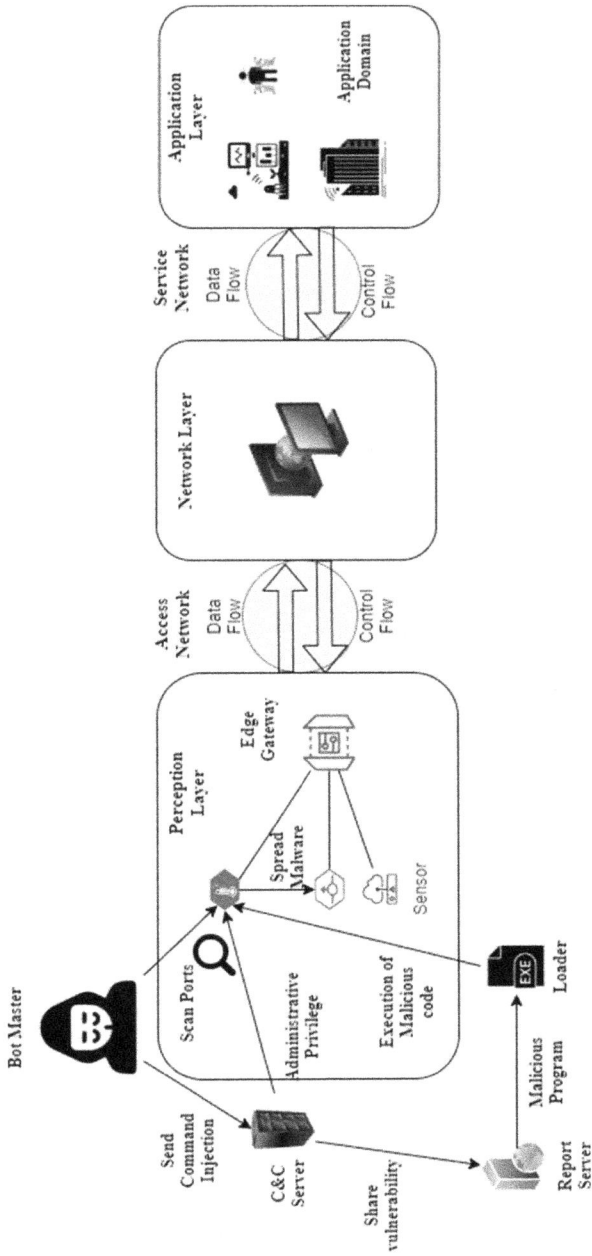

Figure 4.1 Mirai botnet blueprint.

At the network level, firewalls, IDS, and IPS play a vital role in mitigating Mirai botnet threats. Network segmentation helps isolate IoT devices from critical infrastructure, reducing the risk of lateral movement in case of an infection. Implementing access control lists (ACLs) ensures that only trusted devices communicate within the network. Deep packet inspection (DPI) and traffic filtering mechanisms help identify malicious traffic associated with Mirai infections. Rate limiting and traffic shaping techniques can mitigate the impact of DDoS attacks by restricting excessive traffic from specific sources. Additionally, blacklisting known malicious IP addresses and blocking communication with Mirai's C&C servers can significantly reduce the effectiveness of the botnet.

The application of AI and ML in anomaly-based detection systems has proven effective in detecting and mitigating Mirai botnet activities. Traditional signature-based systems are trying to keep up with the rapidly developing variants of the botnets, while AI-driven models can identify behavioral anomalies in network traffic. Learning techniques under supervision and unattended, such as random forest, LSTM, and CNN, can detect deviations from normal operation formulas and potential botnet activities. Behavioral analysis techniques, such as analysis of time intervals between packets arrival, flow entropy, and unusual network spikes, help detect infected botnet before performing large attacks. Botnet-based detection allows many organizations to work together with models without sharing sensitive network data, increasing privacy and improving the intelligence of threats. Honeypot-based strategies also play a key role in Mirai's monitoring and alleviating. IoT honeypots such as IoTPOT and HoneyD simulate vulnerable IoT devices, attracting Mirai-infected bots and capturing their attack patterns. Security researchers can analyze these captured botnets to develop improved defense mechanisms. Threat intelligence sharing platforms, such as MITRE ATT&CK and VirusTotal, enable organizations to share IoT botnet indicators of compromise (IoCs) in real time, helping security teams proactively mitigate emerging threats.

In order to overcome the use of unsecured IoT devices, blockchain technology has become a potential solution. Decentralized authentication systems by blockchain eliminate individual failure points, reducing the risk of taking the botnet. Intelligent contracts can be used to enforce security principles across IoT networks, which ensures that only credible devices participate in network communication. Additionally, blockchain-based anomaly detection systems can create an immutable log of network behaviors, making it difficult for botnets to remain undetected. From a regulatory and policy perspective, government agencies and cybersecurity organizations have implemented various frameworks to mitigate Mirai botnet threats. The European Union's Cybersecurity Act, NIST Cybersecurity Framework, and IoTSF guidelines provide best practices for securing IoT ecosystems. Many countries have introduced IoT security certification programs, ensuring that manufacturers integrate secure-by-design principles in their products.

The US IoT Cybersecurity Improvement Act mandates minimum security standards for IoT devices used in federal networks, reducing the risk of large-scale botnet attacks. Another crucial aspect of Mirai botnet mitigation is DDoS attack prevention and mitigation strategies. Cloud-based DDoS protection services, such as Cloudflare, Akamai, and AWS Shield, provide real-time traffic analysis and filtering mechanisms to mitigate large-scale Mirai-induced DDoS attacks. Anycast-based traffic distribution disperses attack traffic across multiple servers, reducing the impact on individual networks. Additionally, sinkholing techniques redirect botnet traffic to controlled environments where it can be analyzed and neutralized without affecting real services.

Digital forensics techniques, such as reverse engineering malware samples, analyzing C&C communication patterns, and identifying attack signatures, help cybersecurity experts track botnet operators. Law enforcement agencies have successfully dismantled several Mirai botnet variants by tracing financial transactions linked to botnet operators and collaborating with international cybersecurity organizations. As Mirai botnet variants continue to evolve, future mitigation strategies must focus on proactive defense mechanisms. Emerging technologies such as Zero Trust Architecture (ZTA) enforce strict authentication and least privilege access, reducing the risk of IoT device exploitation. SDN can dynamically detect and mitigate botnet activities by segmenting infected devices in real time. Post-quantum cryptography (PQC) can enhance IoT security by enabling devices resistant to future quantum computing-based cyberthreats. By integrating these strategies, organizations and individuals can significantly reduce the risk of Mirai infections, ensuring a secure and resilient IoT ecosystem. Future research should focus on real-time botnet detection, automated remediation techniques, and cross-industry collaborations to stay ahead of evolving botnet threats. With continuous advancements in AI, blockchain, and cybersecurity frameworks, the fight against Mirai and similar IoT botnets will become increasingly effective, leading to a more secure digital landscape.

4.2 THE HAJIME BOTNET

Security researchers found Hajime shortly before the Mirai attacks on Dyn and three days after the public release of Mirai source code occurred in October 2016. Security researchers gave this discovery its official name as "Hajime." The original malware creator learned about their research and used some findings to maintain and improve his own botnet while choosing the Hajime title. Following the research report, the botnet periodically displays this terminal message. The highly sophisticated Hajime botnet automatically spreads itself through IoT devices which have inadequate security protocols. Unlike traditional botnets such as Mirai, which are used for launching DDoS attacks, Hajime functions as a P2P decentralized network, making it stealthy and more resistant to takedown efforts. It is unique because, rather than being overtly malicious, it operates as a gray-hat botnet, securing infected devices by blocking common attack vectors and closing vulnerable ports. However, its exact intentions remain unknown, raising concerns about potential misuse.

- *Infection Mechanism and Propagation*: Hajime spreads through brute-force attacks on Telnet and SSH ports, targeting IoT devices such as routers, IP cameras, and DVRs that have default or weak credentials. The botnet scans the Internet for vulnerable devices, and once a target is identified, it attempts to log in using a set of predefined username-password pairs. If successful, Hajime gains access and executes a malicious payload. Unlike Mirai, which directly reports to a C&C server, Hajime does not rely on a centralized control mechanism, making it much harder to dismantle. The botnet's propagation process follows some steps such as target discovery, brute force attack, malware injection, execution, and p2p formation. Hajime continuously scans the Internet for open Telnet (port 23) and SSH (port 22) services. Then it attempts to log in using commonly used or factory-default credentials using brute force attack. Once access is obtained, the botnet injects its payload into the device. Hajime operates entirely in-memory, meaning it does not create persistent files on the infected device, making detection difficult. The infected device joins the botnet's decentralized network, enabling secure communication without relying on a single C&C server.
- *Decentralized P2P Communication*: One of Hajime's most advanced features is its P2P network architecture. Unlike traditional botnets that rely on centralized C&C servers, Hajime utilizes a BitTorrent-based Distributed Hash Table (DHT) protocol for communication. This allows infected devices to exchange data without needing a central controller, making it extremely resilient against law enforcement takedowns. In p2p communication, each infected device (peer) stores a small portion of the botnet's control data. These devices periodically update each other using DHT queries, ensuring that control commands are distributed across multiple nodes. Instead of using hardcoded IP addresses for communication, Hajime dynamically generates network paths, further improving its stealth.
- *Payload and Functionality*: Hajime's payload is designed primarily to harden IoT devices against other malware rather than perform destructive actions. Once a device is infected, the malware does the following: the telnet and SSH ports are closed to prevent future infections by other botnets such as Hajime. Blocks access known Mirai C&C servers, effectively acting as a counter-botnet defense mechanism and runs stealthily in the background, avoiding unnecessary CPU or memory consumption. Despite these seemingly protective actions, the true intentions of Hajime remain unclear. While it does not currently

engage in DDoS attacks, data exfiltration, or ransomware activities, the botnet's decentralized nature means it could be reprogrammed at any time to carry out malicious actions.

- *Evasion Techniques*: Hajime employs several sophisticated anti-detection mechanisms, making it one of the most resilient IoT botnets such as encrypted communication, polymorphic behavior, rootkit capabilities, and fileless malware execution. Hajime runs entirely in-memory, meaning it disappears when the device is restarted. The encrypted communication has been conducted in all p2p communications that preventing security breaches from intercepting the command transmissions. Hajime frequently updates itself, modifying its code to evade signature-based detection by antivirus and IDS systems. It actively hides its processes and disables system logs, making it difficult for administrators to detect infected devices. These evasion techniques make Hajime one of the most persistent and stealthy IoT botnets, capable of staying hidden for extended periods.
- *Security Implications and Potential Threats*: Although Hajime does not currently exhibit malicious behavior, its sheer size and control over thousands of infected devices pose a serious security risk. However, several potential threats are included in the Hajime botnet such as weaponization, unknown operator, and uncontrolled growth. The botnet could be updated remotely to launch DDoS attacks, cryptocurrency mining, or data theft. Since Hajime continues to spread autonomously, it could potentially infect millions of devices worldwide. And the author of Hajime remains anonymous, making it impossible to determine their true intentions.

The Hajime botnet represents a new generation of decentralized, stealthy malware that differs from traditional botnets by securing infected IoT devices rather than exploiting them for attacks. Its P2P architecture, in-memory execution, and advanced evasion techniques make it extremely difficult to detect and mitigate. While its current behavior appears benign, security experts remain cautious, as the botnet could be reprogrammed for malicious purposes at any time. The best defense against Hajime is proactive security measures, including strong authentication, network monitoring, and regular firmware updates. As IoT adoption continues to rise, addressing vulnerabilities in smart devices remains a top priority to prevent large-scale botnet infections.

4.3 THE REAPER BOTNET

The Reaper botnet, also known as IoT Reaper or simply Reaper, is a sophisticated and evolving botnet that primarily targets IoT devices by exploiting known vulnerabilities instead of relying on weak or default passwords, which was the hallmark of earlier botnets such as Mirai. Discovered in late 2017, Reaper demonstrated a more advanced approach to botnet creation and control by incorporating modular components and an ability to propagate autonomously through various exploits, making it significantly more dangerous than its predecessors. Unlike Mirai, which utilized brute-force attacks on Telnet ports, Reaper actively scanned for vulnerabilities in networked devices such as routers, IP cameras, and network-attached storage (NAS) devices. The malware behind the Reaper botnet is a Lua-based script running on infected devices, allowing flexible control, remote execution, and easy modification. The C&C infrastructure of Reaper is centralized, where attackers can send commands to bots dynamically, enabling them to conduct DDoS attacks, exfiltrate data, and even launch further malware infections.

The malware spreads through CVEs found in well-known IoT device manufacturers, such as D-Link, Netgear, TP-Link, Linksys, AVTECH, GoAhead, and MikroTik. This makes Reaper particularly insidious because it does not rely on guessing credentials but instead infiltrates devices through unpatched security flaws. The Reaper botnet employs a modular architecture, allowing attackers to dynamically update payloads and add new exploits without requiring a full redeployment. This flexibility enables it to evolve quickly and target newly discovered vulnerabilities efficiently. The propagation mechanism of Reaper consists of an advanced network scanning engine that actively looks for vulnerable devices using concurrent scanning threads. When an exploitable device is found, Reaper injects its payload using remote command execution (RCE) techniques, allowing it to take control of the device remotely. The infected device then joins the botnet and starts scanning for new targets, creating a self-replicating infection cycle. The payloads used by Reaper vary depending on the attacker's objective, but common functionalities include DDoS attack modules, crypto mining scripts, credential harvesters, and back-door access mechanisms. The primary attack vector used by the Reaper botnet is its ability to manipulate HTTP, TCP, and UDP-based DDoS attack methods, which enables it to flood targeted servers with malicious traffic, making them unavailable to legitimate users. One of the most concerning aspects of Reaper is its ability to create persistent infections on IoT devices, meaning that even a system reboot does not remove the malware. Unlike Mirai, which operates primarily in memory and disappears when the device restarts, Reaper can modify system files to ensure persistence. This is achieved by embedding malicious scripts in the startup process or leveraging cron jobs and systemd services to relaunch its components after a reboot.

The C&C infrastructure of Reaper is controlled via hardcoded domain names and IP addresses, but it also supports domain generation algorithms (DGA), allowing it to frequently change C&C server addresses, making it difficult to disrupt the botnet. This feature significantly enhances Reaper's resilience against takedown attempts by cybersecurity firms and law enforcement agencies. The Lua scripting engine embedded in Reaper provides a flexible attack framework, enabling adversaries to execute custom scripts, issue arbitrary commands, and even update the botnet with new functionalities remotely. This means that Reaper is not limited to a single attack method but can be adapted for espionage, ransomware deployment, credential theft, and more. The botnet's ability to interact with third-party malware payloads makes it a potent tool for advanced persistent threats (APTs) and cybercriminal organizations. One of the key reasons why Reaper remains a significant threat is the slow adoption of security patches in IoT ecosystems. Many IoT manufacturers fail to provide timely firmware updates, and even when patches are available, end-users often neglect to apply them, leaving their devices vulnerable. This, combined with the absence of built-in security mechanisms in many IoT devices, provides an ideal breeding ground for Reaper's expansion. Researchers analyzing Reaper found that its infection process involves a multistage execution chain, where an initial reconnaissance phase is followed by payload injection, privilege escalation, command execution, and botnet integration.

Unlike traditional botnets that rely on simple script-based propagation, Reaper employs multithreaded execution, allowing it to scan, exploit, and compromise devices at a much faster rate. The threat landscape of IoT-based botnets has significantly evolved due to Reaper, as it has introduced polymorphic attack strategies, adaptive learning techniques, and exploit automation. Some cybersecurity experts believe that Reaper represents a blueprint for future IoT botnets, where attackers shift from brute-force approaches to exploitation-based infections, making mitigation more challenging. Traditional security measures such as firewalls, IDS, and basic endpoint protection are often insufficient against Reaper because the malware operates stealthily, blends with normal network traffic, and employs obfuscation techniques to evade detection. Mitigation strategies for Reaper involve a combination of network segmentation, timely firmware updates, disabling unnecessary services (such as Telnet and SSH), and deploying advanced behavioral-based anomaly detection systems. Security firms and governments have been working on sinkholing C&C servers, implementing kill-switch mechanisms, and improving threat intelligence sharing to counter the spread of Reaper.

However, due to its high adaptability, modularity, and decentralized infection methods, complete eradication remains difficult. The implications of the Reaper botnet extend beyond DDoS attacks; it can be repurposed for corporate espionage, supply chain attacks, ransomware delivery, and critical infrastructure sabotage. Given the rapid proliferation of IoT devices worldwide, the risks posed by Reaper continue to grow, making it a top concern in cybersecurity. If left unchecked, Reaper could serve as a foundation for next-generation cyberwarfare tactics, where adversaries leverage IoT-based botnets for large-scale disruptions. The best defense against Reaper lies in a proactive security approach, involving both manufacturers and end-users in enforcing stricter security standards, promoting patch management, and deploying next-generation IPS. As IoT ecosystems expand, the need for AI-driven cybersecurity solutions to counter threats such as Reaper becomes even more critical. Researchers and cybersecurity firms must continue reverse-engineering botnet payloads, monitoring exploit patterns, and collaborating on global botnet takedown efforts to mitigate the impact of Reaper and its successors.

Detecting and mitigating the Reaper botnet requires a multilayered cybersecurity approach due to its advanced propagation techniques, modular architecture, and ability to exploit vulnerabilities in IoT devices. Unlike traditional botnets that rely on brute-force attacks, Reaper infiltrates devices by utilizing the CVEs in routers, IP cameras, and networked storage systems, making its detection more challenging. NIDS and HIDS are crucial for identifying anomalous traffic patterns that indicate Reaper's scanning, exploitation, or communication with its C&C servers. Behavioral anomaly detection, which used ML models, can help in recognizing unusual spikes in outbound traffic, unauthorized system modifications, and unexpected network connections that could signify botnet activity. Signature-based detection methods, including YARA rules and IoC monitoring, can also be employed to identify known malware components of Reaper in IoT firmware. Since Reaper botnet operates with Lua-based scripting engines, security solutions must incorporate script analysis mechanisms to detect unauthorized script executions within IoT environments.

Mitigation strategies primarily involve patch management, as Reaper propagates through known vulnerabilities. Organizations and individuals must regularly update their firmware and software to prevent infections. Additionally, network segmentation can limit the spread of Reaper by isolating IoT devices from critical infrastructure. Disabling unnecessary services, such as Telnet, SSH, and UPnP, can significantly reduce the attack surface. Firewalls and ACLs should be configured to block malicious IP addresses and restrict inbound/outbound communication to known and trusted endpoints. Deploying honeypots can aid in early threat detection by tricking Reaper into revealing its infection techniques and payloads. ISPs and cybersecurity firms can work together to sinkhole Reaper's C&C servers, disrupting its operation. AI-driven threat intelligence platforms can facilitate proactive monitoring by analyzing real-time attack patterns and preventing infections before they escalate. Organizations should enforce ZTA to ensure that every device attempting to connect to the network undergoes strict verification. Traffic filtering using DPI can help in identifying malicious communications between infected devices and C&C servers. Automated IoT security solutions can be deployed to quarantine infected devices and prevent further propagation.

4.4 ANALYSIS OF RECENT IoT BOTNET ATTACKS

The largest known botnet was the 911 S5 botnet that was dismantled in 2024. At its peak, it had about 19 million active bots operating in 190 countries. 911 S5 was spread through infected VPN applications, such as MaskVPN, DewVPN, ShieldVPN, and a few more. A botnet might include personal computers, business servers, mobile devices, and IoT devices such as smart thermostats, cameras, and routers. The composition of the botnet depends on the malware. For example, the new Eleven11bot botnet only uses HiSilicon-based devices running TVT-NVMS9000 software, because the malware is designed to exploit a single vulnerability running on these devices. This limits the composition and size of the botnet, though the botmaster may be adding new capabilities to grow the network. In comparison to 2023, the overall number of DDoS attacks in 2024 rose by 53%. With a peak speed of 1.14 Tbps, the most potent DDoS assault of 2024 was 65% faster than the previous year's record of 0.69 Tbps.

Compared to the greatest botnet in 2023, which comprised "just" over 136,000 devices, the largest botnet we detected in 2024 had 227,000 devices. The increasing number of antiquated gadgets in emerging nations is the cause of this botnet's explosive expansion. In January 2025, reports highlighted the activities of the "Murdoc botnet," which posed a significant threat to IoT security worldwide. This botnet exploited known vulnerabilities in IoT devices to conduct high-impact DDoS attacks, including record-breaking volumes of malicious traffic. The Murdoc botnet's evolution underscored the critical need for robust security practices in managing IoT devices, as its sophisticated tactics allowed it to remain undetected while amassing a substantial network of compromised devices. Table 4.1 shows the recent IoT botnet attacks with their impact and characteristics.

Table 4.1 IoT botnet attacks

Attack	Year	Target	Impact	Characteristics
Mirai	2016	DNS provider Dyn, IoT devices	Massive DDoS attack disrupting major websites	Used default credentials, spread via telnet, open-source variant
Mozi	2019–2022	IoT routers, DVRs, and IP cameras	Persistent botnet with DDoS and payload injection	Peer-to-peer architecture, uses DHT protocol
VPNFilter	2018	Routers and network-attached storage	Data theft, device destruction, DDoS capabilities	Multistage malware, used SSL interception
Dark Nexus	2020	IoT devices (e.g., video recorders, routers)	DDoS attacks and remote control	Mimics legitimate processes, sophisticated evasion techniques
Hajime	2016–2024	IoT devices (Telnet ports)	Competes with Mirai, strengthens device security	Decentralized, uses encrypted communications, no DDoS payload

In April 2024, the New Jersey Cybersecurity and Communications Integration Cell (NJCCIC) identified a LockBit-branded ransomware campaign delivered by the Phorpiex botnet. This was one of the most notable Phorpiex attacks in 2024. It was back online by December of that year, although it reemerged as a variant called "Trik" or "Twizt." It operates using a decentralized C&C infrastructure that enables it to control a vast network of infected devices across the globe. The botnet is well-known for distributing malware such as GandCrab ransomware, pony information stealer, and various strains of cryptojacking malware, exploiting compromised devices to generate illicit profits for its operators. Phorpiex propagates through multiple infection vectors, including phishing emails, malicious attachments, drive-by downloads, and exploitation of software vulnerabilities. Once a device is infected, the botnet establishes persistent access by modifying system settings, injecting malicious code into legitimate processes, and disabling security defenses to evade detection. One of its most infamous campaigns involved sextortion scams, where infected devices were used to send fraudulent emails claiming to have compromising footage of the victim, demanding payment in cryptocurrency to prevent public exposure. The botnet also engages in cryptocurrency mining by hijacking the processing power of infected machines, secretly mining digital currencies such as Monero. Furthermore, it has been observed conducting massive botnet-driven DDoS attacks, using its network of compromised systems to overwhelm targeted services. Phorpiex's modular architecture allows it to adapt to evolving cybersecurity defenses, making it a persistent threat in the cyber landscape. Its operators continuously enhance its capabilities, integrating new exploit techniques and leveraging anonymized communication channels such as TOR to mask their activities. The botnet's ability to monetize infections through multiple revenue streams, including ransomware-as-a-service (RaaS) and spam-based monetization, makes it a highly lucrative tool for cybercriminals. Despite efforts to curb its spread, Phorpiex remains an active and evolving threat, exploiting unpatched vulnerabilities, weak credentials, and human negligence to propagate further. The protection of Phorpiex botnets depends on proactive defense methods which include network segmentation together with endpoint detection and response (EDR) systems, scheduled updates, and user training programs according to cybersecurity professionals. Organizations need to maintain constant alertness against upcoming threats because botnet strategies continue to advance thus requiring a comprehensive security model to successfully combat cyber dangers.

The newly discovered Mirai malware strain called Murdoc botnet currently exploits security weaknesses in AVTECH IP cameras as well as Huawei HG532 routers during its attacks. The botnet attacks these security vulnerabilities which consist of CVE-2024-7029 in AVTECH cameras alongside CVE-2017-17215 in Huawei routers to gain unauthorized entry and deploy malicious payloads. Once compromised, these devices are co-opted into a network of infected systems, enabling the botnet to launch large-scale DDoS attacks and facilitate further malware distribution. The Murdoc botnet employs a multistage attack mechanism, utilizing command-line injections to fetch, execute, and subsequently remove shell scripts on targeted devices, thereby maintaining stealth and persistence within the infected systems. Since its emergence in mid-2024, the botnet has compromised over 1300 devices globally, with significant concentrations in Malaysia, Thailand, Mexico, and Indonesia. The C&C infrastructure Murdoc botnet consists of more than 100 distinct servers, to manage communications with compromised hosts and distribute the Mirai malware payloads. The rapid proliferation and adaptability of Murdoc underscore the critical need for robust cybersecurity measures, including regular firmware updates, vigilant network monitoring, and the implementation of strong, unique passwords for IoT devices.

4.5 RESEARCH FINDINGS FROM CASE STUDIES

The research findings from IoT botnet case studies provide deep insights into the evolving nature of botnet attacks, their impact on critical infrastructure, and the strategies used to detect and mitigate such threats. Several case studies have analyzed large-scale IoT botnets such as Mirai, Reaper, Hajime, and Torii, revealing the mechanisms through which these botnets compromise IoT devices. One of the most notable cases is the Mirai botnet, which exploited weak authentication protocols by leveraging default credentials in millions of IoT devices. The Mirai-based attack on Dyn in 2016 disrupted major online services such as Twitter, Netflix, and PayPal by launching a massive DDoS attack. Case studies analyzing Mirai found that attackers leveraged a combination of brute-force credential stuffing and command injection vulnerabilities to spread across insecure IoT devices. Research findings indicated that most IoT botnets exhibit modularity, allowing them to evolve and incorporate new exploitation techniques. The Reaper botnet case study revealed how it used known exploits instead of brute force to gain access to IoT devices, making it more sophisticated than Mirai. Studies on Hajime, a peer-to-peer botnet, demonstrated that some botnets operate without a centralized C&C server, making them more resilient to takedown efforts. The Torii botnet case study highlighted the ability of some IoT botnets to evade detection by employing advanced obfuscation and persistence techniques. Another significant case study analyzed the VPNFilter malware, which targeted industrial IoT devices and routers, indicating that IoT botnets are increasingly used for cyberespionage and infrastructure attacks.

These studies also emphasized the economic impact of IoT botnets, including financial losses due to downtime, data breaches, and ransomware distribution. Furthermore, case studies on IoT botnet detection techniques found that ML-based approaches, such as deep autoencoders and convolutional neural networks, improved detection accuracy by identifying abnormal traffic patterns. The N-BaIoT dataset, which captured real-time IoT botnet traffic, was extensively used in research to benchmark intrusion detection systems. A key takeaway from these studies is that IoT botnet infections often go undetected due to the limited security capabilities of IoT devices, making real time anomaly detection critical for effective mitigation. Additionally, research on IoT botnet mitigation strategies suggested a multi-layered security approach, including network segmentation, firmware updates, strong authentication mechanisms, and automated threat intelligence sharing. Some case studies explored blockchain-based solutions for secure device authentication and decentralized botnet resistance.

The findings from these studies indicate that IoT botnets are evolving toward increased stealth, complexity, and adaptability. Attackers are now leveraging zero-day vulnerabilities and sophisticated payload delivery techniques to maintain long-term persistence in compromised devices. Moreover, case studies on legal and policy aspects of IoT botnets suggest that regulatory measures, such as mandatory security standards for IoT manufacturers, could significantly reduce the threat surface. The growing adoption of AI-powered cybersecurity solutions has also been highlighted as a crucial factor in future botnet defense mechanisms. Overall, research findings from IoT botnet case studies stress the urgent need for proactive security measures, continuous monitoring, and interdisciplinary collaboration between cybersecurity experts, policymakers, and IoT manufacturers to counter the growing threat of botnet-driven cyberattacks.

Chapter 5

Detection techniques for IoT botnets

5.1 SIGNATURE-BASED DETECTION

Signature or Misuse-based detection is designed to examine network behavior, traffic activity, online transactions, or network patterns for pre-defined and well-known attack patterns. The traffic data is collected from distinguished sources, pre-processed, and then converted into a pattern for detecting the attacking pattern. Sniffer data is processed by data processing engines or tools that may generate patterns for intrusion detection systems (IDSs). The IDS also has some pre-defined attacking patterns with new or updated rules of attacks. If the known behavior or generated pattern matches, then the IDS triggered an alarm or report to the system administrator as suspicious activity or take some corrective action as shown in Figure 5.1. There may be multiple botnets showing identical behavior but with different signatures. These approaches are very effective in case of known behavior of the attacks. Misuse detection is successful for known attacks which means low false positives while, it generates high false negatives due to very less detection rate for unknown attacks.

Most of the extensive research has been carried out on signature-based IDS for traditional network devices. There are two popular open-source IDS tools such as Snort and Bro which can gather information and detect using signature-based method in the traditional network. In the year 1999, Roesh, introduced a signature-based IDS which can maintain the signature database and detect the attack by comparing the signature with incoming packet payloads. Traditional detection is not sufficient for the detection of intrusion in an IoT environment. So, here we consider some work done by the researchers in the last decade. Behal et al. proposed an IDS mechanism N-EDPS in the year 2010 to capture the network-based intrusion which analyzes outbound traffic. It monitors the institute network traffic and stored log files in the database. If a match is found with the existing signature, then there is an alert for the administrator. This system is implemented using Snort and Bothunter tools. The major drawback of the system is it was not able to detect encrypted C and C channels and for unknown signatures. In 2011, Liu et al. detected the security threat using artificial immune systems in an IoT environment. The authors simulated an environment for

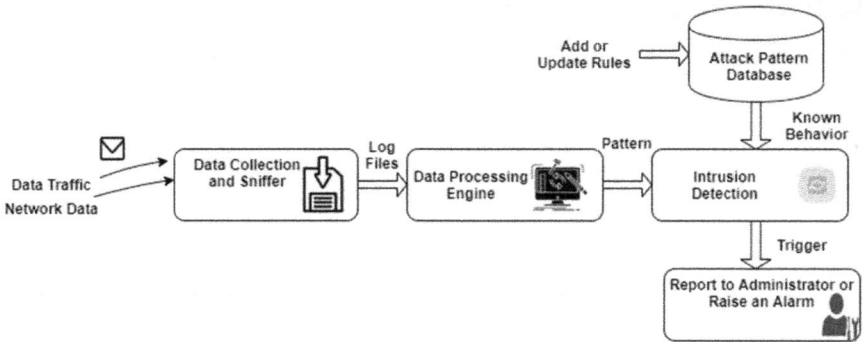

Figure 5.1 Signature-based IDS.

self-adaption and self-learning in the immune system and developed a model which was able to classify datagrams as malicious or non-malicious activity. The major disadvantage of this approach is it can generate some computational overheads for the execution of the process. In 2013, Kasinathan et al. proposed a solution to detect the DoS attacks in a 6LoWPAN-based network architecture. Suricata is an open-source IDS tool which can support IPv6 addresses, multithreading mechanisms, and intrusion prevention systems adapted by the authors into a 6LoWPAN network for known signatures. Once the protection manager receives an alert message, the attack detection can be confirmed and is able to diminish the false positive rates. This technique is made available for simulation only, so, there is a requirement of real-time implementation of such kind of IoT scenarios.

In 2014, Oh et al. proposed two techniques auxiliary shifting and early detection as distributed lightweight IDSs for IoT botnets. In the proposed method, the performance improvements can be achieved by reducing the number of unnecessary matching operations which may performed among packet payload and signature of attack. Auxiliary shift can be achieved by using a pattern in the prefix values that may enable early detection of the signature in the packet payloads. However, this technique may lead to performance degradation due to limited resource constraints. Abbas et al. proposed a less complex method which suggested that instead of storing the complete signature, only a subset may be stored. The system works in two phases, the first phase is offline extraction of signature from system call traces and removal of duplicate signature, and in the second phase extracted signatures are used to detect IoT botnet attacks. The proposed method improves the efficiency of the system and gives 100% detection rate with false positive detection. This method works well for detecting intrusions in an IoT environment but is not able to detect unknown malware.

Ioulianou et al. proposed a signature-based detection method that works in the Cooja Simulator for implementing a hybrid IDS module. The authors implemented a DoS attack scenario as Hello flood attack and version number modify in IoT devices which exploits the RPL protocol used for routing in low-powered IoT networks. In the implemented system, the router functions as a detector when traffic flows between the router and IoT devices. The router will determine and decide whether the traffic is coming from a malicious or normal node. One of the main drawbacks of the system is that it has only been simulated and not implemented in a real-time scenario. Jia et al. proposed a three-factor authenticated key exchange protocol and proved its security using a security model. To prove the security of the model, the authors considered three entities in the scheme: a user, a gateway node, and sensing devices. An authenticated user registers on a sensing device using a session key through a gateway node. A three-key exchange is secured even when two factors out of the three are compromised by the attacker. In the presented paper, the authors also demonstrated the challenges in designing a secured and lightweight key-exchange protocol using previous unknown vulnerabilities. However, the presented system does not provide resilience against the offline password guessing attacks and privileged insider attacks. Signature-based detection approaches provide efficient solutions for the detection of intrusion in the IoT environment. But it may generate high false negative rates due to poor detection of unknown malware. Table 5.1 shows the different IDS utilized for the signature-based mechanism.

Table 5.1 Signature-based IDS for IoT botnet detection

IDS technique	Detection method	Botnet detected	Pros	Cons
Snort	Rule-based packet inspection	Mirai, Mozi, Gafgyt, etc.	Open-source, real-time detection, extensive rule sets	Ineffective against zero-day and unknown botnets
Suricata	Deep packet inspection (DPI)	Known IoT botnet signatures	Multithreaded, high performance, protocol analysis	Requires frequent signature updates
OSSEC	Host-based signature matching	File changes from botnet infiltration	Customizable scripting, logs detailed traffic behaviors	Limited to host-based threats, not full network visibility
Bro/Zeek	Signature and behavior hybrid	Known IoT attacks, malware traffic	Lightweight, good for endpoint security	Higher learning curve, less plug-and-play
Cisco Secure IDS	Network-based signature detection	Industrial IoT botnets, large-scale	Enterprise-grade, integrates with Cisco security suite	Expensive, may require expert configuration and tuning

5.2 ANOMALY AND BEHAVIOR-BASED DETECTION

An anomaly detection system is based on identifying patterns in the system's behavior and continuously updating them recursively. Outliers or deviation from the pre-defined pattern come under the category of abnormal behavior or anomaly pattern. For example, a user generally logins to their system between working hours from somewhere in India, so, the model of the system might record the time and location of the user for normal behavior. But, if the same user logins from a very far location or in an odd time (such as mid night rather than working hours), then the anomalous behavior of the system will be flagged. These techniques are different from the misuse techniques as they are not having any pre-defined attacking pattern. These techniques are very much concerned about determining Self-intelligence-based network behavior and program-based behavior. The behavior analysis can be done by using two modules: static and dynamic analysis. The static analysis module can extract the network and program behavior by packet unpacker and code reverse engineering. This module can extract static features such as function calls or API calls. The dynamic analysis can capture network traffic and analyze the memory or host log files by executing some codes in the virtual environment such as sandbox. The unruffled pre-processed data is passed to the detection engine which can process the data and apply some algorithm to determine the pattern in host behavior or network behavior. Based on the data pattern, the system can take decision either it is a normal traffic or malicious traffic. If it contains some malicious behavior, then the system may alert to the administrator or kill the process or can take necessary action. The background working of the anomaly detection IDS is shown in Figure 5.2. A detailed discussion on the self-intelligence-based network behavior and programmed-based behavior is provided in the following section.

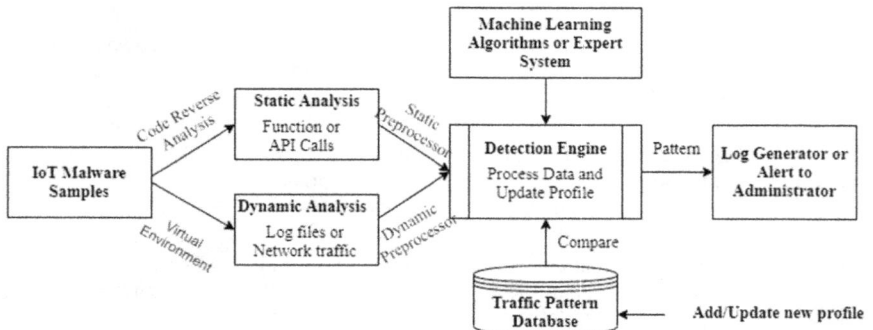

Figure 5.2 Anomaly detection IDS.

5.2.1 Self-intelligence-based behavior

As the name suggests, the system learns itself by analyzing and observing the network traffic or network call traces for a time span. These kinds of techniques can be applied to analyze the network behavior based on incoming and outgoing traffic in the IoT environment. The traffic can segregate based on some predefined features such as port address, IP address, or segment number, etc. Anomaly detection based on self-intelligence can be classified as follows:

- *Machine-Learning-Based Techniques*: IoT-based smart devices supplemented through various innovative technologies such as data mining or machine learning algorithms. Machine learning-based approaches can be applied to the system where manual analytics of the system is not possible due to large volume of data. Machine learning-based IDS employs the self-improvement ability and higher degree of effectiveness. However, a detailed description of machine learning algorithms is beyond the scope of this article. There are several surveys available for the discussion of machine learning algorithms in IDS. In this section, we discuss some machine learning or data mining-based IDSs proposed or implemented by researchers.

  Ranjan et al. proposed a strategy for analyzing the historical network data and obtained labels to identify the known attacks. For this purpose, the authors used a heuristic approach to determine features for a dataset in real time and assign the labels to them. After assigning the labels, the system is able to categorize the data unit to detect the botnet label. The major drawback of the proposed method is it is unable detect botnets when the system is based on a multilayer perceptron. Livadas et al. distinguished the traffic as IRC-based traffic or non-IRC-based traffic and between botnets or real-IRC traffic using machine learning-based classification. For the implementation of the chat-based botnet, the authors setup an IRC server, code server, 13 bots executing Kaiten botnet, a victim device, and an attacker. For the chat-based classification, the authors compare J48, Bayesian network classifier, or Naïve Bayes classifier to determine the features which can achieve good performance parameters. To differentiate botnet traffic from IRC traffic, researchers used several indicators in the flow label that indicates whether it belongs to suspicious or legal traffic. The Naïve Bayes classifier performed best in distinguishing between IRC and non-IRC-based traffic, achieving both a low FNR and a low FPR. However, the authors were not able to classify the botnet and real-IRC flows.

  IDSs play an important role in identifying the attacker when the cryptography is broken. Lopez-Martin et al. proposed a method which is based on an Intrusion Detection Conditional Variational Autoencoder (ID-CVAE), includes a definite architecture, and consolidates the intrusion labels within the decoder layers. To improve the performance and flexibility of the system, the authors rely on two inputs such as the intrusion class label and intrusion features, instead of using intrusion features only. This approach is used to create a single model with a single training step which is able to employ all training without the concern of associated labels. ID-CVAE is an unsupervised machine learning technique trained in a supervised manner due to the labels of the class during the training. The proposed approach is able to reconstruct the features (Data-recovery) with high accuracy of approximately 99%. The model was demonstrated on NSL-KDD datasets using well-known algorithms such as linear SVM, logistic regression, random forest, and multilayer perceptron. The unbalanced distribution of the dataset may create some problems to recover the task. Fu et al. proposed a uniform intrusion detection automata-based model, where the states represent the status of the device and transition represents active action among states. The method used an extension of the labeled transition system which is able to describe the IoT system, and by using action flows, intrusions can be detected. This approach also built an event database and implemented an event analyzer to achieve better detection. For the implementation of the approach, the authors used Radius application and Raspberry Pi3 as the reduced function device. The proposed method can detect three kinds of IoT attacks such as false-attack, reply-attack, and jamming attack. However, the proposed approach does not provide a standardized solution. Wang et al. proposed a method which is based on support vector machine (SVM) with augmented features to design an effective IDS. The method implemented a logarithm marginal density ratio which is able to transform the original feature with improved version of features. This work used the NSL-KDD dataset to demonstrate empirical results, showing improved robustness, a high detection rate, a low false alarm rate, and a faster training speed. The consideration of binary cases of intrusion detection is one of the major drawbacks of the proposed system.

- *Knowledge-based Techniques*: In knowledge-based mechanism, some network analysis tools such as Tshark, and system call tracers such as strace, are used to capture the incoming and outgoing traffic of the IoT devices. The traffic features such as the IP address of source and destination, service address, port address, TTL value, etc. are the major components of the normal traffic. If there is any anomalous behavior of the network traffic based on previous knowledge, then some researchers suggest three kinds of solutions such as expert system, clustering, and finite-state-based approaches to detect the intrusion. Midi et al. proposed a self-adapting and knowledge-driven expert system, named Kalis, which is able to detect real-time intrusion in a wide variety of IoT devices. This system automatically collects the features information and monitored network activities and detects the dynamic changes. This system is also known as "security-in-a-box" which can be deployed in a standalone tool; it does not require any changes to the existing software and introduces no performance overhead. The system has the following components such as the communication system, data store, module manager, and knowledge base. The communication system provides an interface with the external environment using protocols. The module manager is able to coordinate all modules and collect alerts from detected incidents. Finally, the knowledge base component stores all the information about the features of the network traffic and detection module. Although Kalis is able to detect a wide range of IoT attacks, the deployment of Kalis is on tiny devices such as WSN nodes.

Liu et al. proposed an integrated method with suppressed fuzzy clustering (SFC) and principal component analysis (PCA) to improve the efficiency of botnet detection. Total data can be classified as high-risk data or low-risk data detected by high-frequency and low-frequency methods. The PCA algorithm is used to reduce the number of variables and functions without distortion in the original data. Reduced data is clustered and divided into high-risk and low-resistant data to achieve accuracy. It improves power index parameters, such as fake alarm speed, detection time, and accuracy speed. The system generates good simulation results, but if the system is implemented in a real-time environment, it can affect the performance of the system. We can also consider some new IoT features to increase the performance of the IDS model.

A Finite State-based IDS is implemented in each node to monitor the flow of the object. This model consists of a behavioral model that mainly has three components such as states (store the information of past behavior), transition (movement between the states), and actions (response of the transition to the state). The start state occurs when the object connects at the very first time, and the next state is the topology state which can detect the relationship for rank rule. The next two states are utilized for sending and receiving controls that are able to detect the control message with the object as sender or receiver. Each node must be covered by at least one monitoring node that can detect an attack on the order using a DIO message from a harmful node by comparing its value and superior node. If FSM detects any adjustment in the Endless message or order, it will move toward the state of the topological settings. Therefore, this process can increase the detection range from a large number of attacks, but there is a requirement for a more robust mechanism for ID-based mechanism. Arnes et al. proposed a Hidden Markov Model (HMM), which includes likelihood transitions among security states. The main advantage of the HMM approach is that it provides a well-established framework for the estimation of states. The main challenge is to determine hidden parameters with the help of observable parameters.

5.2.2 Programmed behavior-based approach

To detect all kinds of attacks in an IoT environment, the analysis of network traffic is not sufficient. So, to create an effective IDS, it requires agents either human (user) or artificial that can detect the intrusion. These kinds of IDSs are helpful to detect low-frequency attacks such as rootkits and abnormal behavior of the user. Programmed behavior-based approaches can be categorized as follows:

- *Static Behavior Approach*: The static behavior of the user can be detected passively using a behavioral profile without executing the program. Static analysis can be done by several researchers to identify privacy violating malware in an IoT environment. The static analysis can analyze the entire program passively. So, it needs less time and resources for the detection of intrusion in terms of behavior, features, and parameters. The results of static analysis provide call graphs, UML diagrams, and control flow graphs. Static behavior can be divided into two categories: specification based and profile based.

  Le et al. proposed a specification-based IDS which is able to detect intrusion if the attacker does not follow a specific behavior. These kinds of approaches are effective when the attacker node breaks the protocol rules. The authors proposed a prototype of RPL specification with a lack of verification and implementation rules. The procedure is divided into two parts. The first phase simulates the RPL network operations in the normal behavior to get the trace files. While in the second phase, they define all states with stability and analyze the transition among the states. The proposed module was improved by some experts by adding some verification modules for the detection. Although the simulated results were better, the IDS can be extended in terms of storage and computation to also detect internal threats. Specification-based approaches are a tedious and time-consuming process that needs to be maintained on a regular basis. Profile-based approach is one of the techniques of static analysis to analyze the program behavior. In this approach, first extract the features from the program and then apply some data mining algorithms to monitor the program behavior. If the extracted features match, then the behavior is normal; else, it may be anomalous. Lee et al. proposed a machine learning model to build an abnormal behavior profile of IoT devices, named ProFiOt. The model can integrate all kinds of abnormal behavior detection on all sensed data which are equipped with high computing power. The k-means and support vector machine (SVM) algorithms are used for supervised learning and detection of abnormal behavior, respectively. The proposed model can detect the behavior in two scenarios: first when the attacker hacks only one feature to mislead the system and second when actuators hack all features to compromise the whole system. To detect the abnormal behavior of the system, the proposed model continuously monitors the sensor activities using machine learning algorithms. The authors obtained the dataset of 32k samples from Intel Berkeley Research lab out of which 20k show normal operation. They discovered that the abnormal behavior accuracy rate dynamically decreased from 93.7% to 69.5% when they modify a single attribute instead of the whole dataset. The major problem of this approach is the selection of attributes that affect the results at most. Khan et al. proposed a reputation management-based intrusion detection method in an IoT environment which can monitor the behavior of the IoT network. A reputation can be built for all the nodes on behalf of their past interaction with their neighbors. If a node in the network is involved in dropping or selectively forwarding the packets, then its reputation may fall which may reach up to a threshold level. And if it goes down below a threshold level, then the node is labeled as anomalous or removed from the network by firewall. It results in less error rate or an increase in the trust-based attack if a node wrongly predicts the reputation. So, to optimize the error detection in reputation management, the solution can be combined with a honeypot. The honeypot will combine with possible maliciously behaving nodes and able to detect the behavior as it reduces the error rate but increase the cost in terms of extra energy and time consumption.

- *Dynamic Behavior Approach*: Dynamic behavior of a program may include system calls of the programs and generate a threshold profile for further analysis. There is no change in the dynamic behavior of a program after obfuscation of the code. Dynamic behavior models are explicit temporal variation models which can distinguish the abnormal behavior of the program from the normal behavioral users. Yeung et al. introduced an approach that was based on two models Hidden Markov Model (HMM) and the principal of likelihood. HMM is a stochastic model that has been used in several application areas such as knowledge discovery, pattern recognition, and state transition model. The expected maximization algorithm and maximum likelihood can be used for parameter estimation. The authors considered four parameters ps, named, login, and sendmail to formulate the detection problem and proved experimentally that dynamic behavior approaches are better than the static behavior detection model.

Nobakht et al. proposed an approach IoT-IDM which is a host-based IDS framework in smart devices. The proposed approach can monitor the network traffic to identify threats passing through the devices. Software Defined Network (SDN) architecture along with the Open-Flow communication protocol is used to detect compromised hosts and mitigate the attack by blocking the intruders. SDN segregates the control plane from the data plane and provides Security as a Service (SaaS). According to the authors, the solution is divided into five modules such as Device Manager (A Database to simplify the storage), Sensor Element (Inline Sensor to monitor the activity), Feature Extractor (Selection of features), Detection Unit (examine the captured network traffic), and Mitigation Unit (takes appropriate action to prevent from the identified threat). For the implementation of the setup, the authors used Open-vSwitch which supports OpenFlow. The system provides 94.25% accuracy rate; however, it is not able to detect all IoT threats due to a large volume of network traffic.

Breitenbacher et al. proposed an approach that provides proactive detection capabilities on a wide range of IoT threats. The main advantage of the proposed approach is low performance overheads, which can detect IoT threats such as VPNFilter and IoTReaper. The approach is a temper-proof lightweight approach which is used to monitor process spawning and to kill unauthorized programs before execution. A loadable kernel module of Linux OS allows detection of real-time attacks. There are two approaches for bootstrapping HADES-IoT. To build the profile, the authors create a whitelist through the profiling mode. The whitelisting approach is allowed to run known uninfected off-the-self devices. So, to create a whitelist for uninfected programs, profiling is a critical step once for each device. In the protection phase, device protection is enabled to detect IoT malware using a system call interception technique. It can locate the system call table and save the address with execve system calls. After that, the execve address is modified by the intercepting function and calculating a SHA256

Table 5.2 Anomaly-based IDS

IDS technique	Detection method	Botnet detected	Pros	Cons
MIDAS	Statistical anomaly detection	Unknown and zero-day botnets	Adaptable to evolving threats, minimal prior knowledge needed	May miss slow or stealthy attacks
iDetect	Clustering-based behavior analysis	Smart home botnets	Can detect novel attacks, protocol-agnostic	Requires high-quality training data, not real time in all cases
BotHunter	Correlation of network behavior over time	Botnet lifecycle stages	Good at identifying infection phases, behavior-based	Less effective against encrypted traffic
Kitsune	Lightweight online machine learning (autoencoders)	Mirai, Bashlite, Torii	Low overhead, suitable for resource-constrained IoT devices	Can produce false positives, requires training data
SVELTE	Anomaly detection in 6LoWPAN networks	RPL-based IoT botnets	Optimized for constrained IoT environments	Limited to specific IoT protocols and topologies

digest. So, using the digest, the intercepting function compares a value in the table for match. If a match is not found, then the ENOYSYS error code will be generated to stop the execution of the programs. Table 5.2 shows the recent research for anomaly-based IDS.

5.3 DNS-BASED ANALYSIS

The DNSs for IoT devices translate unique identifiers (URIs) of the physical objects with the network address which can help to extract the information of physical objects such as location, active state, etc. To generate and store a DNS name for IoT device, Internet Engineering Task Force (IETF) protocols are used. DNS name autoconfiguration is required for global DNS names and for local DNS names of IoT devices. Since an IoT environment can have a large number of devices, manual configuration of the IoT devices is not a good choice. There are some steps followed by an IoT device to provide a DNS name as follows: (i) first, a device connected to the network receives a message which include a DNS search list on the basis of the Ipv6 protocol, (ii) a redundancy check method for the domain name must be applied by the device on the basis of the neighbor discovery protocol, and (iii) if the domain name is not redundant, then DNS server registered the domain name and Ipv6 address for the device on the basis of the node information protocol. The DNS-based IDS pre-process the data and classify the botnet domains and legitimate botnet from the set of botnet domains (Figure 5.3). Sperling et al. proposed an IoT router or a software system which is able to verify DNS traffic generated by IoT devices and can detect the unauthorized DNS servers. The collected data is monitored by the analyzer which verifies the DNS protocol flows and detects DNS anomalies. The authors build an embedded system for the analyzer, which acts as a bridge between the IoT devices and the Internet. The hardware unit of the system is built using Raspberry pi 3B and small Wi-Fi EW-7811 and configured using access point with a DHCP server. And the software unit is written in Python using the DPKT library which is able to process the packets. Although the proposed middleware was able to classify the devices as trusted or not trusted devices, it was able to analyze DNS anomalies only.

Fast-Flux-based Technique: In this technique, an attacker assigns multiple IP addresses to the same domain name of an IoT device in the network. This technique is used by hackers for illegal activities such as spamming, spreading malware, or delivering ransomware. This approach is based on dynamic proxy, where attackers use some public IP addresses as a flux agent to hide the real server behind these flux agents. The IP address of the flux agent correlated with the domain name keeps changing continuously to provide the concealment. Passerini et al. introduced a system, named FluXOR, which was designed and used to detect the fast flux network. In this technique, hosts are assigned suspicious domain names that mimic victims, aiming to

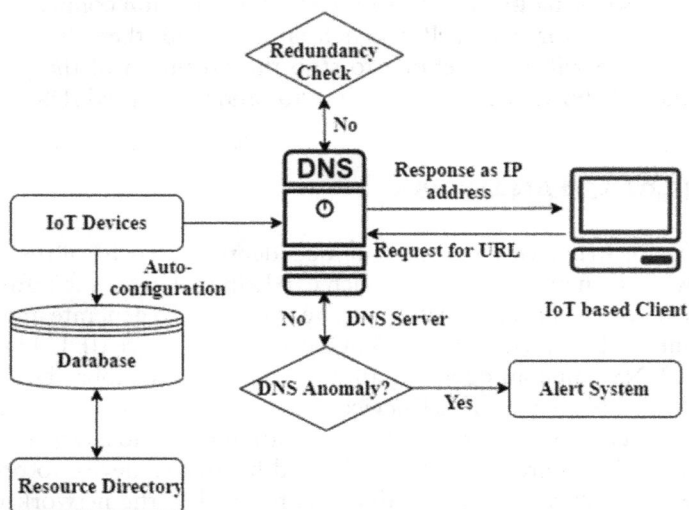

Figure 5.3 DNS-based IDS.

determine whether the host's name obscures the fast flow network in the domain. After this, the IP address is associated with a host that continuously monitors the activities of compromised IP addresses. Its detection is based on features that include three domain name properties, a network availability, and agent heterogeneity. The domain name has two domain age functions (F1: denotes the domain age and deactivates if it is created for a short period of time) and the domain register (F2: indicates when the domain is registered in the fast flow network). The network availability degree has assigned two functions such as the number of different DNS records (F3: denotes a set of active agents by returning multiple DNS records) and time to record DNS sources (F4: a malicious domain name indicates a very short time to record DNS sources). Agent heterogeneity contains five significant features such as the number of different networks (F5: malicious IP solved FQDN belongs to different networks), the number of different autonomous systems (F6: different networks can be connected to the Internet with the same autonomous system), (F7: network that can be recorded with network names), (F8: multiple domain names can be identified with the network name. A large group), and the number of different organizations (F9: a set of the same organization can be grouped). Although it shows better connectivity ratio, however, 80% accuracy does not work with the onion network.

Bilge et al. proposed a system EXPOSURE, passive DNS analyzer, which can detect malicious activity generated by the DNS server. The authors extracted 15 features from the DNS traffic and clustered them as time-based features, TTL-value-based features, domain-name-based features, and DNS-answer-based features. The whole system is divided into five components: (i) data collector—records the DNS traffic, (ii) feature attribution—attributing the domain and recorded with features, (iii) malicious and benign domain collector module—records malicious and benign domains and labels the output of feature attribution module, (iv) the learning module—trains the datasets and builds malicious domain detection module, and (v) classifier—it takes decision and classifies the domain as malicious or benign. One of the limitations of the system is an attacker who understands the working of the system and features can evade detection. Hu et al. developed a lightweight DNS probing engine, known as DIGGER, which works on single and double fast-flux domains. They collected DNS data for more than 3.5 months from a large set of domains and classified the behavioral features based on DNS-query results. The multi-level classifier can classify the domain type as malware or benign. The system can detect short TTLs, massive Ips, fast DNS, self-governing system numbers in DNS replies, etc.

Domain Generation Algorithm-based Technique: In the domain flow, the name of the C&C server domain is constantly modified to perform harmful operations in the IoT network. The domain flow algorithm can generate many C& C servers, and active C&C servers can combine robots by querying to the DNS server. In the past, Torpig, Conflicker and Newgosis are examples of DGA-based botnets. Botnets based on DGA is a hard to detect, and the most devastating botnet used the detection algorithm by generating domain names. In an DGA-based application, one independent domain can generate hundreds of pseudo-noisy domains dynamically and try to gradually connect with generated domains. If many domains are able to successfully survive and register Botmaster, they can be considered C&C server. In DGA-based detection technique, detection is made possible by differentiating malignant queries from normal in an algorithmically generated domain query. To evade the botnet detection, the botmaster program tries to connect with the bots with a domain for a small period of time and discarded thereafter. The main aim of the DGA-based approach is to detect algorithmically generated domains. Antonakakis et al. proposed a DGA-based detection approach without reverse engineering, known as Pleiades. The proposed approach is the combination of clustering and classification where clustering algorithms make a cluster of domains based on their similarity, and the classification algorithm is used to generate a model of known DGAs. If the cluster model does not fit to the known model, then a new model is produced with a new variant of the DGA family. To discover a DGA module, all non-existing domains can be discovered on the basis of statistical similarity such as length, frequency, etc. The authors built a prototype to implement the system over a large dataset by using four known DGA-based attacks. The major limitation of this technique was that it considers only a single character sequence.

Sharifnya et al. proposed a reputation-based approach which can assign a negative reputation to the suspicious node who is involved in the botnet activities. To build a reputation-based system, authors follow some steps.

First, they determine a DNS query after each time window on the basis of similar features. After that, they recognized the host which is a subset of a large group of suspicious domains. Statistical measure techniques such as Kull-back-Leibler (K-L) divergence and Spearman's rank correlation coefficient (SRCC) were used to recognize the host which is involved in suspicious activities. Third, they build a failure matrix which contains a list of hosts with highly failure DNS queries. Finally, the authors evaluate the negative reputation score for each host and assign a bot-infected label which has the highest negative score. Dwyer et al. designed a profiling mechanism based on DNS using a Mirai botnet data file. In this approach, the authors evaluated the real Honeypot data file and recognized activities similar to Notnet, undoubtedly different from benign activities. The authors used various machine learning algorithms to detect the botnet profile, but the random forest classifier provides the best accuracy of about 99%. The main limitation of this approach is that this technique can work with a single DNS question. Alazab et al. proposed a two-level frame for deep learning for

Table 5.3 DNS-based IDS

IDS technique	Detection method	Botnet detected	Pros	Cons
AnomDNS	Statistical DNS traffic analysis	Zero-day IoT botnets using DGA	Effective against evasion tactics using DNS	Susceptible to false positives with CDN or IoT firmware updates
IoT-Guard	Monitors DNS resolution patterns of IoT devices	Known and unknown IoT botnets	Designed for smart home environments, low resource consumption	Limited to DNS-based behaviors, can't detect payload-based threats
PIEChart	Anomalous DNS query detection (machine learning)	IoT botnets with DGA (Domain Generation Algorithms)	Real-time analysis, effective for fast-flux domains	May miss encrypted DNS (DoH/DoT), needs training phase
Khaos	DNS-based traffic anomaly detection using entropy	Mirai, Bashlite, IoT DDoS botnets	Lightweight, effective in detecting sudden traffic spikes	Less accurate with low-activity bots, not payload aware
BotMiner	Clustering of DNS traffic patterns	P2P and centralized IoT botnets	Detects unknown bots, protocol-independent	High computational cost, delayed detection

growing botnets and suspicious behavior in the DNS application layer. On the first level of the framework, DNS questions are evaluated using the most common DNS in the network. Second, deep learning architecture based on DGA for distinguishing between normal and abnormal domains was designed. The proposed framework was applied to two datasets and compared to some of the existing models of deep learning. The framework was used a self-learning method which enables detection of advanced persistent threats of the botnet. The main work of this research was applicable on raw domain names. Once a new DGA encountered that does not belong to the known threat, the classifiers can build a new family of the DGA and record it with feature engineering. The major limitation of this approach is hard to detect malware without additional contextual information. Table 5.3 shows the DNS-based IDS for the detection of IoT botnets.

5.4 EXPLAINABLE AI-BASED APPROACHES

Traditional ML models have been employed to detect IoT botnet activities; however, the "black-box" nature of these algorithms often impedes understanding and trust in the decision-making processes. To solve these challenges, the approaches of explainable artificial intelligence (XAI) were integrated into IoT detection systems, which increases transparency and interpretability. XAI techniques, such as **SHAP (SHapley Additive exPlanations) and LIME (Local Interpretable Model-agnostic Explanations)**, were used to clarify the internal functioning of the ML models, improving their reliability and facilitating better decision-making for shoe detection.

The development of models such as XG-BoT, which is based on a deep graph neural network, has shown their efficiency in detecting harmful botnet nodes on a large scale and provided automatic forensic by identifying suspicious network flows and related botnet knots. The XAI integration into Federate Learning Frameworks has been examined to increase the detection of botnets across the IoT distributed networks and to ensure data privacy while offering interpretable information about the model prediction. These advancements underscore the importance of incorporating explainability into AI-driven cybersecurity solutions, as they not only bolster the trustworthiness of detection systems but also empower security analysts to respond more effectively to emerging IoT botnet threats.

A comprehensive literature review by Al-Othman et al. (2020) delves into various ML-based detection techniques for IoT botnet attacks, emphasizing the necessity for models whose decisions can be understood and trusted by cybersecurity professionals. The study highlights that while ML models are effective in identifying botnet activities, their lack of interpretability poses challenges in practical applications. In response to these challenges, scientists explored the application of XAI methods to clarify the internal functioning of the ML models. A study published in scientific reports discusses the use of

SHAP and LIME to interpret the predictions of ML models in the detection of IoT botnets. The finding suggests that these XAI techniques can effectively increase the transparency of detection systems, thereby improving their reliability and facilitating better decision-making analysts. Further progress in this approach, Lo et al. (2022) introduced XG-Bot, a deep graph neural network designed for botnet detection and forensic analysis. XG-Bot not only detects harmful botnet nodes on a large scale, but also provides automatic forensic identification of suspicious network flows and related botnet knots. This model demonstrates the potential of integrating XAI into complex neural networks to enhance both detection accuracy and interpretability. The integration of XAI into IDS has also been explored in the context of IoT security. A study published in *Expert Systems with Applications* outlines the development of an IDS that leverages XAI to classify normal and attack traffic in IoT networks. The research emphasizes that incorporating explainability into IDS can significantly aid in understanding model decisions, thereby enhancing trust and facilitating the identification of false positives or negatives. Moreover, the application of XAI extends to active learning frameworks aimed at improving IoT botnet attack detection. Kalakoti et al. (2024) proposed an explainable active learning framework that enhances detection in Security Operations Centers (SOCs). This framework combines the strengths of active learning and XAI, enabling models to learn from limited labeled data while providing interpretable insights into their predictions, thus optimizing both efficiency and transparency in SOC environments.

The efficiency of the XAI method in improving the interpretability of ML botnet detection models was quantitatively evaluated in metric studies such as loyalty, consistency, complexity, and sensitivity. For example, research conducted at the North Arizona University has shown that applying LIME and SHAP to extreme gradient boosting models provides explanations with high fidelity and consistency while maintaining low complexity and sensitivity. Remarkably, it exceeds LIME in these metrics, indicating its excellent ability to increase the interpretability of the model. In addition to increasing interpretability, XAI techniques were used to improve the performance of detection models. A study published in *ICT Express* discusses the use of XAI to demystify ML models for massive IoT attack detection, highlighting that understanding model decisions can lead to better feature selection and model optimization, ultimately enhancing detection accuracy and efficiency. Furthermore, systematic reviews of ML and DL techniques for IoT security have underscored the importance of incorporating XAI to address the opacity of complex models. A review published in the *Journal of King Saud University* emphasizes the need for explainable models to ensure that IoT botnet detection systems are not only effective but also transparent and trustworthy, facilitating their adoption in real-world scenarios. The application of XAI in IoT botnet detection also involves the development of novel features and methodologies. For example, the introduction of PSI-rooted subgraphs as a novel feature for botnet detection has been explored,

Table 5.4 XAI-based IDSs

IDS technique	Detection method	Botnet detected	Pros	Cons
XAI4Botnet	Explainable deep learning with SHAP values	IoT botnets (e.g., Mirai, Gafgyt)	Provides model transparency, high accuracy	Computationally intensive, complex model interpretation
BotXAI	Hybrid ML with interpretable decision trees	Hybrid and zero-day IoT botnets	Balances accuracy with interpretability, good for compliance auditing	May oversimplify complex attack behavior
X-IDS	Neural networks with attention and visualization tools	Complex IoT botnet behavior	Visual explanation of detected anomalies, good for analyst feedback	Requires well-labeled training data, limited to supervised learning
Interpretable-SVM	Feature-based analysis using SVM with rule extraction	Lightweight IoT botnets	High interpretability, rule clarity	Lower detection rate for complex or obfuscated attacks
LIME-IDS	Local Interpretable Model-Agnostic Explanations (LIME)	General and unknown IoT botnets	Enhances trust in ML decisions, explains local predictions	May not scale well to large datasets, approximation errors

demonstrating how XAI can aid in identifying and utilizing meaningful patterns within network traffic data to improve detection capabilities. Table 5.4 shows the different XAI-based IDSs.

5.5 NETWORK TRAFFIC ANALYSIS AND BEHAVIORAL MONITORING

For the detection of IoT botnets, IoT network traffic analysis (NTA) and behavioral monitoring have emerged as critical methodologies. These approaches involve scrutinizing network data to identify patterns, anomalies, and behaviors indicative of malicious operations. NTA entails the systematic examination of data packets traversing a network to uncover insights into communication patterns and detect irregularities. By analyzing attributes such as packet size, flow duration, and protocol usage, NTA can identify deviations from normal traffic, signaling potential botnet activity. For example, the study has introduced a frame using a sequential closed graphical convolutional neural network (GGCN) designed specifically to detect botnets in the IoT network.

This approach represents network traffic as a complex graph structure, especially manipulation of time dynamics of its own botnet attacks, and reveals fine patterns critical to harmful behavior recognition. Behavior monitoring focuses on establishing a baseline of normal behavior and network behavior to detect anomalies that may indicate a compromise. It continuously monitors distinct metrics such as device communication frequencies, data transfer volumes, and typical interaction patterns, and deviations can signal unauthorized activities. A novel approach proposed modeling attacker behavior in IoT botnets using temporal convolution networks (TCNs). By analyzing heterogeneous events, including network traffic and command sequences input by attackers in compromised hosts, this method achieved a prediction accuracy of 85–97%, demonstrating the efficacy of behavioral analysis in identifying botnet activities.

The integration of ML and DL techniques has significantly enhanced the effectiveness of NTA and behavioral monitoring. The XGBoost algorithm has been employed to classify network traffic as normal or malicious based on extracted features, achieving high accuracy rates. For example, a study utilizing the CIC-IDS2017 dataset achieved an accuracy of 99.4% in detecting IoT botnet activities using XGBoost in conjunction with the CNN algorithm. To address the challenge of detecting botnet activities with minimal or no access to labeled malicious traffic, semi-supervised learning techniques have been explored. These methods focus on modeling benign network behavior to identify deviations that may indicate botnet presence. Research assessing the feasibility of semi-supervised techniques demonstrated their potential in detecting a wide range of bot types by identifying deviations from established network traffic patterns. Furthermore, hybrid models combining different ML architectures have been developed to enhance detection capabilities. The intelligent detection framework integrates an improved network of deep faith (IDBN) with RNN, which increases traditional correlation analysis by weighing data points based on proximity. This approach has improved the detection of complex relationships essential to identify the behavior of botnets. In addition to ML-based approaches, the utilization of communication graphs has proven effective in representing device behavior within IoT networks. By constructing communication graphs that encapsulate interactions between devices, it becomes possible to better characterize behavior than traditional traffic analysis, facilitating the detection of botnet attacks. Simulations using the IoT-23 dataset have validated the efficacy of this method. Despite these advancements, challenges persist in IoT botnet detection through NTA and behavioral monitoring. The heterogeneity of

IoT devices, each with distinct communication patterns and resource constraints, complicates the establishment of universal detection models. Additionally, the dynamic nature of botnets, which continuously evolve to evade detection, necessitates the development of adaptive and robust detection mechanisms. Moreover, the vast volume of network data generated by IoT ecosystems poses scalability challenges for real-time analysis.

5.6 CHALLENGES IN DETECTING IoT BOTNETS

IoT botnet detection is a multilateral challenge due to the unique characteristics of the IoT device and sophisticated tactics used by cyber opponents. One primary difficulty stems from the IoT heterogeneity, which varies greatly in hardware capabilities, operating systems, and communication protocols. This diversity complicates the development of universal detection mechanisms, as the solution effective for one type of device can be ineffective for the other. Many IoT devices are limited to resources and have limited power of processing, memory, and energy sources that reduce the implementation of robust safety measures and real-time monitoring tools. The widespread deployment of IoT devices in various environments, often with minimal security oversight, further exacerbates the challenge, creating a vast and dynamic attack surface that is difficult to monitor comprehensively. Compounding these issues is the prevalent use of default or hard-coded credentials, making devices susceptible to unauthorized access and subsequent recruitment into botnets.

The lack of standardized security protocols across IoT devices leads to inconsistent security postures, hindering the establishment of uniform detection strategies. Furthermore, IoT devices often have long lifecycles with infrequent firmware updates, resulting in outdated systems with unpatched vulnerabilities that attackers can exploit. The evolution of botnet architectures adds another layer of complexity; modern botnets employ decentralized command-and-control structures, such as peer-to-peer networks, which enhance resilience against traditional detection and takedown efforts. The sheer volume of network traffic generated by IoT ecosystems poses significant challenges for anomaly detection systems, as distinguishing between legitimate and malicious traffic requires sophisticated analysis amidst vast data flows. Attackers increasingly utilize encryption to conceal malicious communications, rendering content-based inspection techniques less effective and necessitating the development of advanced detection methods capable of analyzing encrypted traffic without compromising privacy. The adaptive nature of botnets, characterized by rapid evolution and the ability to modify behavior to evade detection, demands continuous updating of detection models to remain effective.

In addition, the integration of AI opponents allows the creation of botnets driven by AI capable of autonomously identifying and using vulnerability and further complicating detection efforts. The solution of these challenges requires a multilateral approach, including the development of light safety solutions adapted to resources limited, creating standardized security protocols, regular firmware updates and implementing advanced machine learning techniques capable of detecting anomalous behavior of anomalous behavior. Cooperation between manufacturers, scientists, and politicians is essential to increase the attitude of the security of equipment and networks of IoT, ensuring the resistance of IoT ecosystems to the evolving threat of botnets.

Chapter 6

Mitigation and prevention strategies

6.1 BEST PRACTICES FOR SECURING IoT DEVICES

The proliferation of IoT devices has transformed industries, enabling smart homes, connected healthcare, intelligent transportation, and more. However, their rapid deployment, often with inadequate security measures, has introduced significant vulnerabilities. Securing IoT devices is critical to protect personal privacy, organizational data, and broader network integrity. There are several practices to ensure that IoT ecosystems remain resilient to cyberattacks. Secure device configuration is one of the most critical steps in securing IoT devices, as it ensures proper functionality. Many devices are shipped with default settings, including weak or generic passwords that attackers can exploit. The modification of default passwords to strong, unique ones and disabling unnecessary services or ports reduces the attack surface. The IoT devices should be configured to use the principle of least privilege, granting only minimum permissions necessary for operation.

Strong authentication and authorization mechanisms: Implementation of multi-factor authentication (MFA) ensures that even if one credential is endangered, another layer of security is introduced. Password principles should order complexity, which ensures that passwords are difficult to guess or brutal force. Employment of role-based access control (RBAC) limits access to the device based on user roles and ensures that only authorized individuals or applications can interact with the equipment. The firmware and software often contain vulnerabilities that attackers use to obtain unauthorized access. Device manufacturers and users should prefer timely space updates in security. Automatic update mechanisms help ensure that the device remains up-to-date without requiring a manual intervention. However, the update process itself should be safe using a cryptographic firmware to avoid attackers in the injection of malicious updates. Data encryption during data transmitted between IoT devices and servers should be used to be protect the information. TLS implementation ensures that data in transit remains safe. For data stored on devices, encryption algorithms should be used to ensure sensitive information. End-to-end encryption further increases security by ensuring that data remains inaccessible for unauthorized entities during their journey. While the secure network forms the backbone of the IoT device, the IoT network segmentation from critical systems in the network using VLAN or firewall reduces the impact of potential violations. Enabling secure communication protocols such as HTTPS, while deactivating unsecured protocols such as Telnet or FTP, strengthens the network's defense.

Regularly update and patch devices: Implementation of secure protection against boot and hardware ensures that the device introduces only credible firmware. It prevents attackers from replacing legitimate firmware by harmful versions. Hardware-based hardware security modules, such as trusted platform modules (TPMs) or hardware security modules (HSM), provide additional layers of protection by storing cryptographic keys and certificates. These modules can also facilitate the identity of the device. It is necessary to maintain the reserves of all IoT devices connected to the network for efficient security management. Asset management tools can help monitor the device's activity, identify unauthorized devices, and ensure that security principles are constantly used. The device supplies should contain details such as firmware versions, device location, and associated users to allow a quick response in the case of a security incident.

Secure APIs: Ensured API and cloud integration play a key role in allowing communication between IoT devices and cloud services. Ensuring these APIs is necessary to prevent unauthorized access and data leakage. Critical steps include using secure API authentication methods such as OAuth and implementing rate limits to prevent abuse. In addition, cloud integration should adhere to proven procedures, such as encryption of data stored in the cloud, monitoring unusual activities and ensuring compliance with industrial regulations. Management tools can also be used to monitor IoT deviations from normal behavior, which could indicate a compromise. Anomalous activities, such as unexpected data transfers or unusual communication formulas, can cause notifications for further examination. These tools often use machine learning to create basic behavior and identify threats that might be missed by traditional signature-based methods.

Secure communication channels: The detection of IoT botnets is significantly complicated by the widespread use of secure communication channels, particularly those employing encryption protocols such as TLS. While TLS is essential for protecting legitimate data exchanges by ensuring confidentiality and integrity, it also provides a cloak for malicious activities, enabling botnets to conceal their C&C communications within encrypted traffic. This encryption hampers traditional detection mechanisms that rely on inspecting packet contents, as the payload is no longer accessible for analysis. These methods face challenges due to the vast diversity of legitimate TLS implementations and the potential for sophisticated attackers to mimic benign fingerprints. The resource constraints inherent in many IoT devices limit the feasibility of deploying advanced detection algorithms directly on the devices, necessitating reliance on network-level monitoring solutions.

The dynamic nature of botnet behaviors and the continuous evolution of encryption standards require detection systems to be perpetually updated, posing operational challenges. Balancing the imperative for secure communications with the need for effective botnet detection remains a complex endeavor, demanding ongoing research and the development of innovative approaches that can adapt to the evolving cybersecurity landscape.

Monitor and Log Device Activity: The behavior of the IoT device and maintaining detailed protocols of their activities can identify anomalies that may indicate security violations or the presence of malicious software. Effective monitoring includes analysis of network traffic formulas, such as unexpected tips when transferring data or communication with unknown external servers, which often testifies the botnet activity. Implementation of ID in an IoT environment can recognize these suspicious formulas and provoke alerts for further examination. The activity of the logging device provides a historical record that is invaluable during the forensic analysis, allowing security teams to monitor the origin and method of attacking, informing about future prevention strategies. However, restricting the sources of many IoT devices presents challenges for monitoring of devices, which requires the use of a network level or light monitoring. The huge number of devices and the volume of data they generate requires scalable and efficient data processing techniques, often using ml algorithms to detect significant deviations from normal behavior. Regular revisions and updates and monitoring protocols are necessary to adapt to the evolving tactics of cyber opponents. In addition, ensuring that the protocols are safely stored and protected from handling is essential for maintaining their integrity and usefulness in the investigation. Incorporating these practices into the complex IoT security framework increases the ability to detect, respond, and prevent infections of botnets, thus protecting critical infrastructure and data.

Conducting penetration testing and security audits: The safety audit is a comprehensive evaluation method that evaluates the organization's information systems according to set standards, proven procedures, and regulatory requirements to ensure the effectiveness of security controls and compliance with the relevant principles. This process involves investigating security policies, control, and risk management procedures and provides a holistic view of the security holding of the organization. In contrast, penetration testing includes authorized simulated cyberattacks on systems, networks, or applications to identify the vulnerability. By imitating the real-world attack scenarios, penetration tests evaluate the resistance of security defense and reveal weaknesses that may not be obvious through standard audit procedures. The integration of both security audits and penetration testing into a regular security strategy offers a comprehensive risk management approach. Security audits provide structured assessment of policies and controls, ensure the alignment of industrial standards and regulatory mandates, while penetration testing offers practical knowledge of how defense is done in the attack. This dual approach allows organizations to actively identify and solve security gaps, increase readiness to response to incidents, and take informed decisions on investment in security. To maximize the efficiency of these practices, organizations should follow proven procedures, such as clearly defining the scope and objectives of evaluation, selection of qualified experts or reputable companies with relevant expertise and regularly perform evaluations to adapt to threatening threats and changes in IT environments. In addition, the immediate solution of identified vulnerability and integration into the process of constant improvement is essential for maintaining robust security holding.

Resilience planning: It encompasses proactive strategies aimed at preventing, detecting, responding to, and recovering from botnet infections within IoT ecosystems. A foundational element involves conducting comprehensive risk assessments on all IoT devices prior to their deployment. This process evaluates potential vulnerabilities, including outdated operating systems, insecure communication protocols, and inadequate vendor support, thereby enabling organizations to make informed decisions about device integration and implement necessary security measures. The continuous monitoring of network traffic and endpoints is vital for the early detection of anomalous behaviors indicative of botnet activity. The implementation of adaptive detection models that evolve alongside emerging botnet tactics enhances the effectiveness of monitoring efforts. This collective approach enables organizations to stay ahead of adversaries and refine their detection capabilities accordingly. With the integration of these strategies into a comprehensive resilience plan, organizations can significantly enhance their defenses against IoT botnet threats, ensuring the security and integrity of their networks and devices.

Secure decommissioning of devices: As IoT devices reach the end of their operational life or are phased out, it is imperative to ensure that all sensitive data is irreversibly removed and that the devices are properly retired to maintain the integrity and security of the broader network. The decommissioning process should commence with a comprehensive inventory assessment to identify all devices slated for retirement, ensuring none are overlooked. The identification of stored sensitive information, such as network credentials, personal user data, and device-specific configurations, is essential for such devices. Implementing secure data erasure techniques is paramount. These techniques involve overwriting the device's memory with random data or utilizing data scrubbing algorithms to ensure complete data removal. It is crucial to recognize that merely reflashing the device's firmware is insufficient, as it may not eliminate all residual data. After data erasure, validating the process through forensic tools to confirm the absence of recoverable information is advisable. Proper disposal or recycling of hardware, therefore, in accordance with environmental regulations, ensures that the device excluded from operation does not pose ecological risks. The implementation of these practices can effectively alleviate the risk that IoT retirement devices are co-opted into botnets, protecting their networks and data from potential cyberthreats. The best procedure for securing the IoT device requires a comprehensive and integrated approach that combines technical measures, organizational policies, and users' awareness. By complying with proven procedures such as robust verification, regular updates, encryption, and threat monitoring, organizations can mitigate risks and protect their IoT ecosystems. Cooperation between parties, compliance with industrial standards, and obligations to security principles of the proposal are necessary for building the trust and ensuring the long-term success of IoT technologies. As the IoT landscape continues to evolve, proactive and adaptive security strategy will remain critical in defense against emerging threats.

6.2 FIRMWARE UPDATES AND PATCH MANAGEMENT

Firmware updates and patch management are critical components of maintaining the security, functionality, and reliability of IoT devices. As IoT devices proliferate across industries and homes, their security vulnerabilities become a significant target for cyberattacks. Firmware, the embedded software that controls hardware functions, often contains vulnerabilities due to outdated code, limited design foresight, or new exploit discoveries. Without regular updates and patches, these vulnerabilities can be exploited, leading to devastating consequences such as data breaches, device malfunction, or botnet formation. Effective firmware updates and patch management begin with a secure delivery mechanism. IoT manufacturers must ensure updates are cryptographically signed to prevent tampering and should leverage secure channels for their distribution. Automatic update systems reduce reliance on users to manually apply updates, ensuring that critical patches are applied promptly. However, the process must be carefully implemented to avoid unintended disruptions or bricking devices during updates. Manufacturers should also prioritize transparency by communicating the purpose and impact of updates to users. Firmware update policies must include version control and rollback mechanisms to recover from failed updates.

Another vital aspect is timely patch development. As new vulnerabilities are discovered, manufacturers must swiftly analyze, develop, test, and deploy patches. A delay in this process provides attackers with a window to exploit devices. Adopting a proactive approach to vulnerability management through bug bounty programs or collaborative threat intelligence-sharing mechanisms allows vulnerabilities to be identified early. Additionally, firmware updates should be lightweight and resource-efficient, as many IoT devices operate with limited processing power, memory, and bandwidth. Organizations deploying IoT devices must implement robust patch management policies, including an inventory of devices, their firmware versions, and update schedules. Regular audits and penetration testing can help identify devices requiring patches, while real-time monitoring systems can detect abnormal behavior that might indicate exploitation of unpatched vulnerabilities.

Despite these measures, challenges persist. The heterogeneity of IoT ecosystems, involving devices from various manufacturers with differing update policies and support timelines, complicates patch management. End-of-life devices, which no longer receive updates, are particularly vulnerable and require additional compensatory controls, such as network isolation. Educating users and administrators about the importance of firmware updates is equally essential. Many users neglect updates due to concerns about device downtime or lack of awareness, leaving devices exposed. Manufacturers must address these concerns by designing seamless, non-disruptive update processes and promoting user-friendly interfaces that highlight the necessity of updates. Regulatory frameworks and industry standards also play a significant role in enforcing patch management practices. For instance, regulations such as the EU's Cybersecurity Act and standards such as ISO/IEC 27001 encourage manufacturers to integrate security into the lifecycle of IoT devices, including firmware update processes.

The importance of patch management extends beyond security; it also enhances device performance and introduces new features, extending device lifecycles and improving user satisfaction. As IoT ecosystems grow increasingly interconnected, a single unpatched device can become a weak link, jeopardizing entire networks. Thus, firmware updates and patch management represent not only a technical necessity but also a critical aspect of building trust in IoT technology. In conclusion, a comprehensive firmware update and patch management strategy involves timely and secure updates, transparency with users, proactive vulnerability management, and adherence to regulatory standards. Only through collaborative efforts among manufacturers, users, and regulators can the challenges of IoT security be addressed effectively, ensuring resilient and reliable IoT ecosystems.

6.3 STRONG ENCRYPTION AND AUTHENTICATION TECHNIQUE

Strong mechanisms of authentication and encryption are the cornerstone of IoT ecosystems against the ever-increasing range of cyberthreats. With IoT devices increasingly put into critical applications, from healthcare and transport to intelligent houses and industrial automation, the importance of robust authentication and encryption cannot be overcome. Verification ensures that only legitimate users or devices have access to the system, while encryption protects the confidentiality and integrity of data when transmission or storage. Weak or absent authentication mechanisms are left by IoT vulnerable to unauthorized access, which can lead to data theft, manipulation of the system or kidnapping of the device. Similarly, unencrypted, or poorly encrypted data are an easy goal for eavesdropping and handling and exposing sensitive information to harmful actors.

Implementation of strong authentication and encryption mechanisms requires a multilateral approach, combining technological innovations, users' awareness, and adherence to established safety standards. Strong verification begins with enforcing identity verification for each user. Traditional methods of verification, such as passwords, are insufficient in the IoT environment due to their susceptibility to attacks of gross strength, theft of credentials, and reuse. MFA offers a safer alternative which requires at least two verification factors such as something the user knows (password), something they have (security token), and something that is (biometric data). For IoT devices, certificates based on public key infrastructure (PKI) are highly efficient. PKI assigns to each device a unique digital certificate that allows mutual verification between devices and servers. This ensures that only verified devices can participate in the network and prevent unauthorized access. The device certificate that includes the verification of the integrity of the hardware and the device software may further strengthen the verification by ensuring that the device has not been manipulated. Another emerging approach is the use of hardware-based verification, such as trusted platform modules (TPMs) or hardware security modules (HSMs) that safely store cryptographic keys and provide manipulation-resistant processes.

Encryption mechanisms are equally vital for securing data in IoT environments. Data encryption ensures data protection during network transmissions and storage of information across the Internet and devices and cloud servers. Advanced Encryption Standard (AES) functions as a common symmetric encryption algorithm for IoT applications because of its efficiency which works well with restricted IoT devices. A secure key management system becomes essential since one key handles all aspects of encryption and decryption during symmetric encryption operations. Security key management becomes possible through asymmetric encryption because it utilizes two different keys called public and private keys which facilitates safe key transfers. This approach commonly works together with symmetric encryption to secure end-to-end data transmissions. The public protocol Transport Layer Security (TLS) uses asymmetric encryption to protect digital channels through encryption and prevention of both interception and tampering.

IoT-specific encryption challenges include the diversity of devices, limited computational resources, and varying communication protocols. Lightweight encryption algorithms, such as SPECK or PRESENT, have been developed to address these constraints, enabling robust encryption even on low-power devices. End-to-end encryption (E2EE) is another critical strategy that ensures that data remains encrypted from the point of origin to the target. This eliminates the risk of exposure to medium nodes such as gates or cloud servers. The secure key management is the basic aspect of encryption. IoT must safely generate, store, and exchange cryptographic keys to avoid unauthorized access. Techniques such as key rotation where keys are regularly exchanged, and key diversification, where unique keys for each device or session are generated increase the security of the key compromise.

In addition to data encryption in transit and at rest, the encryption of the data used is becoming more important, especially in applications including sensitive information such as healthcare or finance. Homomorphic encryption and secure calculation of multiple pages are technologies that allow data processing in everlasting and maintain confidentiality during their life cycle. In order to ensure extensive acceptance of strong verification and encryption mechanisms, IoT manufacturers must design devices with regard to security from the beginning. Security by design principles, including the integration of hardware-based encryption and authentication modules, can mitigate vulnerabilities and simplify implementation. Over-the-air (OTA) update capabilities should be included to enable timely deployment of security patches and upgrades.

User awareness and education also play a crucial role. Users must understand the importance of enabling security features, such as strong passwords and firmware updates, and the risks of neglecting them. Simplifying the user experience, such as by automating certificate installation or offering intuitive interfaces for configuring encryption settings, can encourage adoption. Regulatory frameworks and industry standards are essential for ensuring consistent and effective implementation of authentication and encryption. Standards such as ISO/IEC 29192 for lightweight cryptography, FIDO Alliance specifications for authentication, and NIST guidelines for IoT security provide clear benchmarks for manufacturers and developers. Compliance with these standards not only enhances security but also fosters trust among users and stakeholders.

The dynamic nature of IoT ecosystems presents ongoing challenges for authentication and encryption. Devices may operate in environments with intermittent connectivity, requiring offline authentication methods or caching of cryptographic keys. Mobility and scalability, such as in vehicular networks or industrial IoT, demand robust and efficient mechanisms that can adapt to changing network topologies and high device densities. Interoperability between devices from different manufacturers further complicates implementation, necessitating the development of universal protocols and frameworks. Emerging technologies, such as blockchain, offer innovative solutions for authentication and encryption in IoT. Blockchain's decentralized and tamper-proof nature makes it well-suited for verifying device identities, managing cryptographic keys, and securing data transactions. Integration of blockchain with IoT can enable thrustless authentication and immutable audit trails, enhancing overall security.

The advancements made have not yielded solutions to all original challenges. Circumstances involving resource restrictions in IoT devices restrict encryption algorithms to remain simple, thereby making the systems vulnerable to brute-force attacks or future quantum computing developments. The development of post-quantum cryptography receives emphasis from researchers because they seek to create encryption techniques which quantum attacks cannot breach. Specific authentication methods together with robust encryption form essential components for defending Internet of Things devices while securing their corresponding networks. The first barrier against unauthorized access and data breaches appears in the form of strong authentication systems which protect the confidentiality as well as integrity and availability of information. Through technological advancement and education programs and regulatory frameworks, stakeholders establish resilient Internet of Things ecosystems which resist developing cyberthreats. Manufacturers together with developers and regulators need to work in partnership to tackle present IoT problems and predict forthcoming security dangers to enable a successful and sustainable integration of IoT technology.

6.4 NETWORK ISOLATION AND SEGMENTATION

Network segmentation together with isolation functions as essential cybersecurity methods which help networks succeed in both security and performance alongside management capabilities especially within setups requiring substantial numbers of IoT devices. The main idea behind these methods involves splitting networks into separate distinct portions followed by regulating and tracking their communication abilities. The method defends entire networks from threat expansion while simultaneously securing important information while strengthening the capability of systems to endure cyberattacks. The booming number of IoT devices results in higher importance of network segmentation and isolation techniques because security measures built into these devices remain weak which makes them vulnerable attack entry points. The dedicated segregation of IoT devices creates separate security boundaries which helps organizations to restrict vulnerability impact so that an attack on one device stays limited to its allocated segment.

The benefits of network segmentation and isolation extend beyond cybersecurity. From a performance perspective, segmenting a network reduces congestion by optimizing data flow within each segment, ensuring that critical applications receive adequate bandwidth. This is particularly crucial in environments with high data traffic, such as industrial IoT systems or smart city infrastructures, where latency or network overload could lead to operational failures. Furthermore, segmentation aids in regulatory compliance, as it allows organizations to isolate sensitive data, such as personally identifiable information (PII) or financial records, within specific network zones. This simplifies adherence to data protection regulations, such as GDPR, HIPAA, or PCI-DSS, by ensuring that access to sensitive data is tightly controlled and monitored.

In practice, implementing network segmentation and isolation involves a combination of architectural design, policy enforcement, and technological tools. Virtual LANs (VLANs) are a widely used method to create logical segments within a physical network. VLANs enable administrators to assign devices to different broadcast domains, effectively isolating their communication even when connected to the same network infrastructure. Similarly, SDN provides dynamic and granular control over network traffic, allowing administrators to create, modify, and enforce segmentation policies through centralized controllers. Firewalls and access control lists (ACLs) further enhance segmentation by defining specific rules for traffic flow between segments. For instance, IoT devices responsible for non-critical functions, such as environmental monitoring, can be restricted from accessing sensitive data or critical systems.

Another key technology in network segmentation is micro-segmentation, which takes the concept a step further by isolating workloads or applications at the granular level. Unlike traditional segmentation, which focuses on network zones, micro-segmentation applies security controls directly to individual workloads, ensuring that only authorized interactions occur between applications, devices, and users. This approach is particularly effective in cloud environments or data centers, where workloads are highly dynamic and interconnected. In addition to these tools, network isolation can be achieved through air-gapped networks, which physically separate critical systems from external networks or the Internet. Air-gapping is often employed in highly sensitive environments, such as defense or critical infrastructure, to eliminate the risk of remote cyberattacks.

Despite its advantages, network segmentation and isolation present challenges, particularly in complex and evolving environments. The heterogeneity of IoT ecosystems, with devices from different manufacturers using diverse protocols and communication standards, complicates the design and enforcement of segmentation policies. Additionally, the dynamic nature of modern networks, where devices frequently join, leave, or move across segments, requires automated and adaptive solutions to maintain effective segmentation without manual intervention. Misconfigurations in segmentation policies can also create vulnerabilities or disrupt legitimate operations, underscoring the importance of thorough planning, continuous monitoring, and regular audits.

Organizations must take a methodical approach to network isolation and segmentation in order to overcome these obstacles. A thorough inventory of all network assets, such as devices, apps, and data flows, is the first step in the process. Administrators can create segmentation policies that are suited to the unique requirements and risk profile of the company by comprehending the network's architecture and recognizing its most important assets. IoT sensors, user workstations, and payment systems are a few examples of devices that can be divided into distinct segments based on their shared security needs or capabilities. The least privilege concept should also be taken into account by segmentation policies to guarantee that users and devices have access to only the resources required for their jobs.

Automation plays a vital role in managing network segmentation in dynamic environments. Tools such as network access control (NAC) systems can automatically assign devices to appropriate segments based on predefined criteria, such as device type, security posture, or user identity. ML and AI can further enhance segmentation by analyzing network traffic patterns and detecting anomalies that may indicate misconfigurations or security threats. Continuous monitoring and real-time analytics are essential for maintaining segmentation integrity and responding to potential breaches. In addition to technological measures, user education and organizational policies are critical for successful network segmentation and isolation. Employees must be aware of the importance of adhering to access controls and reporting suspicious activity. Organizations should establish clear protocols for onboarding new devices, including security assessments and proper segmentation assignments. Regular training sessions can help employees understand their roles in maintaining network security.

Network segmentation and isolation are not standalone solutions but part of a broader cybersecurity strategy. They must be complemented by other measures, such as strong authentication, encryption, endpoint protection, and threat intelligence, to provide a comprehensive defense against cyberthreats. As organizations embrace digital transformation and integrate IoT into their operations, the need for robust network security will continue to grow. Network segmentation and isolation offer a scalable and effective approach to managing this complexity, reducing attack surfaces, and ensuring the resilience of critical systems.

The implementation of network segmentation and isolation receives additional benefits from emerging technologies and standards. The implementation of zero-trust architecture (ZTA) matches the operational principles of segmentation through its approach that requires untrustworthy device and user defaults. The combination of zero-trust architecture enforcement with continuous trust verification produces stronger network security which supports the efforts of segmentation. The incorporation of NFV with SDN technology will create adaptive network segmentation architecture that adjusts to operational requirements or threat situations quickly. Network segmentation with isolation stands as an essential protection strategy that enhances IoT-rich network security in modern technological environments. These security techniques enhance digital systems by minimizing threat spread and data protection which results in improved reliability and resilience. The successful use of network segmentation and isolation depends on prepared planning with strong tools and continuous management for dealing with obstacles and achieving effectiveness. Sectored networks along with isolated systems will maintain their status as essential defense mechanisms as cyberthreats mature because they allow organizations to securely operate in interconnected domains. Companies will maintain sustainable digital operations in our modern technological age by using innovation and strategic policy frameworks together with collective security initiatives to maximize the protections that segmentation and isolation bring to their networks.

6.5 INCIDENT RESPONSE AND RECOVERY MECHANISMS

Organizations require incident response and recovery strategies as essential components to protect their resilience against cyberthreats. The strategies establish systematic methods which handle the impact of cybersecurity incidents using detection and containment and eradication and recovery and post-incident analysis processes. Reliable incident response procedures represent a mandatory organizational element for every business, government institution, and organization as cyberattacks have become sophisticated in our modern, connected world. A properly designed incident response strategy alongside recovery methods helps businesses achieve minimal downtime and decreases liability damages and saves their reputation and satisfies regulatory standards and boosts their overall security measures.

A strategic incident response approach depends on an established proactive incident response plan (IRP). The incident response plan includes the responsibility of each personnel, along with procedural frameworks and established procedures for security events. Any organization should base its IRP on industry standards through the inclusion of NIST Cybersecurity Framework or ISO/IEC 27001, thus maintaining alignment with industrial best practices. The process typically begins with preparation, which involves equipping the organization with the tools, skills, and resources needed to address incidents effectively. Preparation includes defining an incident response team (IRT) comprising technical, legal, public relations, and management personnel, conducting regular training, and maintaining updated documentation. The team should have access to the necessary resources, such as intrusion detection systems, endpoint detection and response (EDR) tools, and threat intelligence feeds, to monitor and respond to potential threats.

After incident detection and analysis takes place, organizations need to identify and evaluate potential threats. A strong monitoring system needs to exist to detect irregularities that include atypical network traffic patterns together with unauthorized access trials and data theft activities. SIEM systems as well as behavioral analysis tools and artificial intelligence-analytics identify malicious patterns through advanced detection technology during incident detection phases. After incident detection, operational teams need to analyze it to identify what parts were affected as well as the degree of impact and study the fundamental cause of the incident. Forensic technicians must gather logs and network traffic data and forensic evidence to decipher attack nature and attack implications. Prioritizing incident responses depends heavily on incident classification because it enables authorities to identify critical incidents during this phase.

The third step of incident response called Containment enables authorities to block further spread of the incident across systems. Totally essential for this phase is its focus on prevention of further harm alongside the preservation of evidence needed for forensic examination. Long-term and short-term containment plans depend on how complex the active incident proves to be. Short-temporary containment includes severing damaged systems from the network to block questionable IP addresses and suspend compromised user access. Utilizing deployed patches together with enhanced security measures and network reconfiguration forms part of long-term containment procedures. Organizations need to achieve a balance between risk mitigation and operational continuity during containment procedures because sudden actions might negatively impact essential business operations.

The next phase is eradication, where the root cause of the incident is addressed to eliminate any residual threat. This phase often involves removing malware, closing vulnerabilities, and cleaning up affected systems. Root cause analysis plays a vital role here, as it identifies the exact entry points or weaknesses exploited by attackers, allowing organizations to take corrective actions. For instance, if the incident was caused by an unpatched software vulnerability, the organization must ensure that all systems are updated to prevent recurrence. Similarly, compromised credentials must be reset, and additional authentication mechanisms such as MFA should be implemented to bolster security.

Recovery is the penultimate phase, where affected systems are restored to normal operations while ensuring that they are free from vulnerabilities or malicious remnants. This phase requires meticulous planning and testing to avoid reintroducing risks during the restoration process. Recovery strategies include restoring data from secure backups, rebuilding compromised systems, and conducting thorough testing to verify the integrity of restored systems. Organizations should also ensure that all security measures, such as firewalls, antivirus solutions, and endpoint protections, are fully operational and updated. A phased approach to recovery can be beneficial, starting with critical systems to minimize downtime and gradually restoring less essential systems.

The final phase, post-incident analysis, is essential for continuous improvement and learning. This phase involves a detailed review of the incident, including the response efforts, challenges faced, and lessons learned. A post-incident report should document the timeline of events, root causes, impact assessment, and recommendations for strengthening defenses. This analysis helps organizations refine their incident response plans, update their security policies, and train staff to better handle future incidents. Regularly conducting incident response drills or tabletop exercises can also help identify gaps in preparedness and ensure that the team is well-practiced in executing the IRP.

The primary focus of incident response is on mitigating and recovering from individual incidents, while its recovery strategies extend beyond the immediate aftermath to support long-term organizational resilience. In order to ensure that vital operations can continue both during and after an incident, business continuity and disaster recovery strategies are essential to this endeavor. For these strategies to guarantee operational continuity in the event of disruptions, redundancy mechanisms such backup systems, cloud-based recovery solutions, and alternate communication channels should be included. Businesses must also consider the human part of recovery, offering assistance and open communication to impacted stakeholders, consumers, and workers to restore confidence. In both event response and recovery plans, communication is essential. Clear and prompt communication during an incident guarantee that all parties involved are aware of the circumstances and know their responsibilities during the response. Both external and internal communication with partners, consumers, regulators, and the media are included in this. Organizations should have predefined communication templates and protocols to avoid delays and ensure consistency. Transparency is particularly important in maintaining trust, as withholding information or providing inaccurate updates can exacerbate reputational damage.

Incident response and recovery plans also need to take legal and regulatory factors into account. Organizations must report particular incidents, such data breaches, within a given time range in many jurisdictions. Maintaining client trust and avoiding legal repercussions depend on compliance with these rules. Legal counsel should be extensively consulted by organizations to fully comprehend their responsibilities and make sure that crisis response procedures comply with legal requirements. Cooperation with cybersecurity and law enforcement organizations can also help with the investigation and prosecution of cybercriminals, supporting larger initiatives to counteract cyberthreats. Strategies for effective incident response and recovery must constantly change to stay up with the ever-evolving threat landscape. For organizations to keep ahead of new dangers, they should make continuous investments in threat intelligence, technology improvements, and training. Sharing insights, best practices, and threat data with government agencies, cybersecurity groups, and industry counterparts can also improve readiness. In addition to lessening the effects of cyber disasters, firms can create a solid basis for future expansion and innovation by using a proactive and all-encompassing approach to incident response and recovery.

To protect an organization's operations, assets, and reputation from cyberattacks, incident response and recovery plans are essential. By using a systematic approach that includes planning, identifying, containing, eliminating, recovering, and analyzing the aftermath of security incidents, companies may successfully manage and lessen their effects. These strategies require an integration of technological tools, skilled personnel, clear communication, and continuous improvement to remain effective. As the digital landscape continues to evolve, organizations must prioritize incident response and recovery as part of their broader cybersecurity framework, ensuring resilience and readiness to face the challenges of an increasingly interconnected world.

6.6 CONCLUSION

This chapter highlights the critical importance of proactive measures in securing IoT ecosystems and mitigating the risks posed by evolving cyberthreats. As IoT devices become integral to daily life, industries, and infrastructure, the vulnerabilities inherent in their architecture, connectivity, and deployment demand robust and multidimensional security frameworks. Effective mitigation and prevention strategies require a combination of technological innovation, regulatory enforcement, organizational preparedness, and collaborative efforts across stakeholders. The central point of this effort is the implementation of strong verification mechanisms such as MFA, robust password, and biometry policy that prevent unauthorized access to networks and IoT. Encryption technology, both for rest and transit data, ensures the confidentiality and integrity of sensitive information, and protects it from eavesdropping and unauthorized publication. In addition, regular firmware updates and repair management are necessary to close security gaps, vulnerability solutions, and contradictory threats.

Network and insulation segmentation further increases safety by limiting the surface of the attack and containing potential violations, preventing lateral movement of malware in interconnected systems. The deployment of tool protection tools, firewall gate, and detection and prevention systems (IDP) strengthen peripheral defense and offer real-time threat detection and alleviation. Behavioral analysis, supported by artificial intelligence and machine learning, provides an advanced layer of protection of identification of anomalies and formulas to indicate harmful activity. Organizations must also prefer DNS security to protect against spooling and phishing attacks by domain in implementing safety measures to protect critical interfaces. A well-defined response plan to incidents ensures fast and coordinated measures during security violations, minimization of downtime, data loss, and reputation damage.

Beyond technical measures, organizational policies and processes play a pivotal role in mitigation and prevention. Regular security audits, employee training, and awareness campaigns foster a culture of cybersecurity, empowering staff to recognize and respond to threats. Regulatory compliance with standards such as GDPR, HIPAA, or ISO/IEC 27001 ensures accountability and adherence to best practices. Collaboration with threat intelligence networks, law enforcement, and industry consortia enhances situational awareness, enabling organizations to stay ahead of adversaries. The chapter also underscores the importance of addressing persistent challenges, such as ensuring device interoperability, maintaining energy efficiency, and managing the cost of security measures, which can otherwise hinder the adoption of robust defenses.

Ultimately, the chapter emphasizes that securing IoT ecosystems is an ongoing endeavor requiring adaptability, innovation, and vigilance. As cybercriminals employ increasingly sophisticated tactics, such as botnets, ransomware, and stealthy communication channels, organizations must stay ahead through continuous improvement and investment in advanced security solutions. A layered approach to security, combining preventive, detective, and corrective controls, remains the most effective strategy to safeguard IoT systems. By integrating mitigation and prevention strategies into the design, deployment, and operation of IoT devices and networks, stakeholders can reduce risks, ensure business continuity, and foster trust in IoT technology. This chapter serves as a comprehensive guide to navigating the complex security landscape of IoT, empowering organizations to build resilient systems capable of withstanding the challenges of an increasingly connected world.

Chapter 7

The role of IoT manufacturers and developers

7.1 SECURE SOFTWARE DEVELOPMENT LIFE CYCLE FOR IoT

The software development life cycle (SDLC) for IoT is a comprehensive approach to integrating security practices into every phase of the software development process, tailored to meet the unique challenges of IoT ecosystems. Given the expansive attack surface and the critical role IoT devices play across industries, ensuring software security throughout the lifecycle is paramount. IoT devices often operate in distributed environments, rely on limited resources, and handle sensitive data, making them particularly susceptible to cyberattacks. A well-implemented secure SDLC focuses on building robust, secure, and reliable IoT applications and firmware while mitigating risks and vulnerabilities from inception to deployment and beyond. The first phase of a secure SDLC involves identifying the functional, performance, and security requirements of the IoT system. Security considerations must align with the intended use of the IoT application, regulatory requirements, and organizational policies. Threat modeling is utilized to identify the potential threats specific to IoT devices, such as physical tampering, unauthorized access, or data breaches. This is followed by setting standards for encryption, authentication, data integrity, and secure communication protocols. Finally, compliance requirements for standards such as GDPR, HIPAA, PCI DSS, or IoT-specific frameworks such as ETSI EN 303 645 are addressed. This phase lays the foundation for embedding security into the design and development process, ensuring that security is not treated as an afterthought. The second phase, named design phase, translates requirements into architectural components and workflows, integrating security mechanisms to safeguard the IoT system. A secure architecture design is implementing a layered security model to protect different components of the IoT ecosystem, including devices, networks, and cloud infrastructure. Several techniques such as minimizing open ports, disable unused features, and avoiding hardcoded credentials to minimize the attack surface are used. Industry-standard protocols such as MQTT with TLS, CoAP with DTLS, or HTTPS for data encryption and secure communication are also used. This

DOI: 10.1201/9781003631460-7

phase incorporates features such as data minimization, pseudonymization, and encryption during design to safeguard sensitive data. A secure design sets the stage for resilient software, reducing vulnerabilities in subsequent stages.

Implementation Phase: The implementation phase in the SDLC for IoT is where the theoretical designs, plans, and security strategies materialize into functioning software or systems. It involves coding the application, configuring the hardware components, integrating IoT devices, and implementing the security measures that were meticulously planned in earlier phases. This phase is critical, as it translates the conceptual design into a tangible and operational IoT ecosystem. The emphasis is on adhering to secure coding practices, maintaining the integrity of the architecture, and ensuring compliance with the security requirements established in the design and requirement phases. Given the complexity and interconnectivity of IoT systems, the implementation phase requires careful coordination between developers, engineers, and cybersecurity specialists to build a solution that is both functional and secure.

One of the central aspects of the implementation phase is secure coding. Developers follow established guidelines and best practices, such as those outlined by OWASP or ISO/IEC standards, to minimize vulnerabilities such as buffer overflows, injection attacks, or cross-site scripting (XSS). This includes input validation, error handling, and avoiding hardcoded credentials or cryptographic keys within the code. Secure coding is particularly important in IoT because many devices operate with constrained resources, making them less capable of running robust security software or monitoring tools after deployment. By embedding security at the code level, IoT systems can defend against common attack vectors from the outset. Developers often use automated tools to perform static code analysis during this phase to identify and rectify vulnerabilities before they evolve into critical flaws.

Another crucial component is the integration of hardware and software. IoT systems typically consist of multiple hardware devices such as sensors, microcontrollers, and actuators that must seamlessly interact with the software. During the implementation phase, developers ensure that these integrations are both functional and secure. For instance, firmware is loaded onto IoT devices with secure boot mechanisms to prevent unauthorized modifications. At the same time, encryption protocols such as TLS or DTLS are implemented to secure communication between devices. Additionally, security measures such as ACLs and certificate-based authentication are configured to ensure that only authorized entities can interact with the devices. The implementation phase also involves configuring the networking components of the IoT ecosystem. IoT systems rely heavily on networks for D2D and device-to-cloud (D2C) communications, making network configuration a critical aspect of implementation. Developers set up secure communication channels using protocols such as MQTT, CoAP, or HTTPS, ensuring that data in transit is encrypted and protected from eavesdropping or tampering. Network segmentation is implemented to isolate IoT devices from critical infrastructure, reducing the attack surface. For example, creating VLANs for IoT devices prevents an attacker from accessing sensitive systems in case one device is compromised. Firewalls and intrusion detection systems are also configured to monitor and block suspicious traffic, further enhancing the network's security posture.

Authentication and authorization mechanisms are implemented during this phase to control access to IoT devices and systems. This includes setting up multi-factor authentication (MFA), enforcing strong password policies, and implementing RBAC. Developers configure APIs to require secure tokens or certificates for authentication, ensuring that only verified requests are processed. This is particularly important for IoT systems that interact with third-party applications or cloud services, where the potential for unauthorized access is heightened. Additionally, default credentials on IoT devices are changed during implementation to mitigate the risk of brute force or credential-stuffing attacks. The implementation of encryption mechanisms is another key focus. Developers ensure that data stored on devices, transmitted over networks, or processed in cloud environments is encrypted using industry-standard algorithms such as AES-256 or RSA. Secure key management practices are followed to ensure encryption keys are stored and transmitted securely. This includes leveraging hardware security modules (HSMs) or trusted platform modules (TPMs) for key storage, and using protocols such as PKCS (Public Key Cryptography Standards) for secure key exchange.

During the implementation phase, logging and monitoring capabilities are also established. Developers integrate logging frameworks to capture critical events such as authentication attempts, firmware updates, or abnormal device behavior. These logs are securely stored and formatted to facilitate analysis during audits or incident investigations. Monitoring tools are configured to provide real-time insights into the system's performance and security, enabling rapid detection of anomalies. This proactive approach is essential in IoT environments, where delayed detection of a threat can led to widespread compromise.

Testing within the implementation phase serves as a bridge between development and deployment. Unit tests, integration tests, and system tests are performed to validate that the implemented system functions as intended and meets security requirements. Developers use automated testing tools to verify the integrity of the software and hardware components, while manual testing is conducted to assess usability and resilience against edge cases. Penetration testing and vulnerability scanning are also carried out during this phase to identify and mitigate potential weaknesses. Any issues discovered during testing are addressed promptly to ensure the system's readiness for deployment. The implementation phase includes preparing the system for deployment. This involves packaging the software for installation, configuring deployment scripts, and setting up mechanisms for OTA updates.

OTA updates are particularly important for IoT devices, as they allow developers to patch vulnerabilities and enhance features post-deployment without requiring physical access to the devices. Developers also ensure that rollback mechanisms are in place, allowing systems to revert to a stable state in case an update introduces issues.

Testing Phase: The testing phase of the SDLC is a pivotal stage where the robustness, reliability, and security of IoT software, devices, and systems are rigorously evaluated before deployment. Given the unique challenges and vulnerabilities associated with IoT ecosystems, ranging from constrained hardware resources and distributed architecture to a wide array of communication protocols, the testing phase ensures that potential flaws and weaknesses are identified and addressed early. Comprehensive testing is crucial to mitigating risks such as unauthorized access, data breaches, and device malfunction, which could compromise the overall security and functionality of the IoT system. The phase encompasses various testing methodologies and tools, each tailored to address the specific demands of IoT environments. One of the core aspects of the testing phase is functional testing, which verifies that the IoT system behaves as expected under normal operational conditions. This involves assessing the functionality of sensors, actuators, communication modules, and data processing components. Functional testing ensures that devices perform their intended tasks accurately and reliably, forming the foundation for evaluating higher-level security and performance requirements. This type of testing is complemented by performance testing, which examines how IoT systems respond under varying workloads, including stress testing to identify bottlenecks and limits in processing, memory, and network capacity. For IoT systems that operate in real time, performance testing is vital to guarantee that latency, throughput, and data transmission rates remain within acceptable parameters even under heavy loads.

Penetration testing simulates real-world cyberattacks to identify vulnerabilities that could be exploited by malicious actors. For IoT devices, this involves examining firmware, APIs, network communications, and hardware interfaces for weaknesses such as default credentials, unsecured ports, or improper input validation. By adopting the perspective of an attacker, penetration testing uncovers both known and unknown vulnerabilities that may not be apparent during routine development. This is often paired with static and dynamic application security testing (SAST/DAST). SAST tools analyze source code for vulnerabilities such as buffer overflows, SQL injection, or insecure API usage, while DAST tools evaluate the runtime behavior of applications to detect security flaws that arise during execution. Fuzz testing is another specialized technique frequently employed during the testing phase for IoT systems. This method involves providing unexpected, malformed, or random inputs to the IoT device or application to evaluate its robustness and identify vulnerabilities such as crashes, memory leaks, or improper error handling. Fuzz testing is particularly useful for IoT environments where devices interact with diverse and unpredictable data inputs, such as those from external sensors or third-party integrations. Coupled with fuzz testing, regression testing is used to ensure that newly introduced fixes or updates do not inadvertently create new issues. This practice is essential in iterative development environments where security patches and feature enhancements are continually deployed.

Due to hardware-dependent nature of IoT, hardware security testing plays a significant role in the testing phase. This involves analyzing physical components such as sensors, microcontrollers, and communication modules for vulnerabilities that could be exploited through physical tampering or reverse engineering. Hardware security testing often includes examining debug interfaces (e.g., JTAG, UART), testing the effectiveness of secure boot mechanisms, and assessing resistance to side-channel attacks. This level of testing is critical in environments where IoT devices are deployed in exposed or hostile locations, making them vulnerable to physical access by attackers.

Another essential focus during the testing phase is network security testing, which evaluates the security of communication channels and protocols used by IoT devices. This includes ensuring that data transmitted between devices and servers is encrypted using industry-standard protocols such as TLS/SSL, analyzing network traffic for signs of unauthorized access or data exfiltration, and testing the implementation of secure protocols like MQTT with authentication and CoAP with DTLS. Network security testing also involves identifying and mitigating potential risks such as MITM attacks, packet sniffing, and DoS attacks, which can disrupt the availability and integrity of IoT systems. Usability and UI testing are essential for ensuring that IoT systems are not only secure but also user-friendly. IoT devices often rely on companion applications or web interfaces for configuration and monitoring, making it crucial to test these interfaces for intuitive design, proper error handling, and secure user interactions. For example, UI testing ensures that error messages do not disclose sensitive information and that user authentication mechanisms, such as password strength enforcement and two-factor authentication, are easy to understand and implement. Compliance testing is another important aspect of the testing phase, particularly for IoT systems that must adhere to regulatory standards and industry certifications. This involves verifying that the system complies with frameworks such as GDPR for data privacy, HIPAA for healthcare-related devices, or ISO/IEC 27001 for information security management. Compliance testing not only ensures legal and regulatory alignment but also builds trust with customers and stakeholders. Finally, logging and monitoring enablement testing is conducted to verify that the IoT system has robust mechanisms for tracking and reporting security events. This includes ensuring that logs are securely stored, that they provide sufficient detail for forensic analysis, and that monitoring systems can detect and alert on anomalous behaviors in real time. This aspect of testing is crucial for post-deployment security, as it facilitates incident detection, response, and recovery. By integration of functional, performance, penetration, fuzz, and compliance testing, developers can identify and mitigate vulnerabilities before deployment. This phase not only validates the effectiveness of security mechanisms but also builds confidence in the system's ability to withstand real-world threats. Through comprehensive and iterative testing, organizations can deliver IoT solutions that meet the highest standards of quality and security, ensuring the long-term success and safety of their IoT deployments.

Deployment Phase: The deployment phase in SDLC for IoT is crucial as it marks the transition from development to actual use in a production environment. During this phase, the software or system that has undergone various stages of design, testing, and validation is finally made available to the end-users or devices. However, deploying IoT systems involves more than just installing software; it requires careful planning to ensure security, reliability, and scalability in a connected, often distributed environment. One of the first steps in this phase is the deployment of the IoT software or firmware on the devices themselves. This process must be handled securely to prevent any tampering or unauthorized access during installation. Often, IoT devices are vulnerable due to limited computational resources, making security at this stage particularly critical. For instance, ensuring that the software is signed and verified before installation is essential for preventing man-in-the-middle attacks. Similarly, firmware updates must be securely transmitted and applied, using cryptographic techniques to ensure integrity and authenticity. The deployment phase must include configuring secure communication channels such as TLS or VPNs to ensure that data transmitted between IoT devices and central servers or cloud systems is encrypted and protected from interception. A key consideration is managing the IoT devices' identities and ensuring that secure authentication mechanisms are in place to prevent unauthorized access to both devices and data. Strong authentication protocols, such as mutual TLS or device-specific credentials, are often used to enhance security during the deployment process.

The deployment phase also involves ensuring that the IoT system is scalable and capable of handling the expected data loads and traffic. IoT systems often generate massive volumes of data, and the underlying infrastructure must be able to store, process, and manage this data efficiently while maintaining the desired level of security and performance. In this phase, testing in the real-world environment becomes crucial to identify potential vulnerabilities that may have been overlooked in earlier testing phases, particularly those related to network performance, device failure, or system overload. Any identified vulnerabilities must be mitigated swiftly, often by issuing patches or updates to the deployed software. During deployment, security considerations should not end with the initial setup. Continuous monitoring of the deployed IoT devices and software is necessary to detect any signs of intrusion, malicious activity, or system malfunctions. Implementing robust logging and monitoring tools enables the detection of anomalies in real time. Additionally, a comprehensive update and patch management strategy must be in place to address any new vulnerabilities that might emerge post-deployment. Given the dynamic nature of IoT environments, where new devices and software components can be integrated into the network, maintaining an ongoing security posture is essential to safeguard against evolving threats. Finally, the deployment phase must also address compliance with relevant regulatory and industry standards. For IoT systems, this could involve ensuring adherence to laws related to data privacy, such as the GDPR for systems handling personal data, or industry-specific standards such as ISO/IEC 27001 for information security management. Ensuring compliance helps mitigate legal risks and build trust with users. In summary, the deployment phase for IoT in the Secure SDLC is about ensuring a seamless, secure transition from development to operation, focusing on secure installation, communication, scalability, continuous monitoring, and compliance with regulatory requirements.

Maintenance and Monitoring phase: The maintenance and monitoring phase in the SDLC for IoT is a critical stage that ensures the ongoing security, reliability, and performance of IoT systems after they have been deployed. This phase requires continuous attention to maintain the integrity and functionality of the system throughout its operational life. The first key aspect of this phase is the continuous monitoring of the IoT devices and network. Since IoT systems are often deployed in environments with numerous devices, each potentially handling sensitive data, it is essential to implement robust monitoring tools that can track the performance, health, and security status of both individual devices and the overall system. Real-time monitoring helps detect anomalies, failures, or performance degradation, allowing for timely intervention before minor issues escalate into major problems. Security monitoring is particularly important, as IoT devices are frequently targeted by cyberattacks such as DDoS or malware infections. To mitigate these threats, security events must be tracked through logging and alerting systems that identify unusual behavior, unauthorized access attempts, or signs of data breaches. In addition to monitoring, maintaining an IoT system involves routine updates and patching to address vulnerabilities or fix bugs. Over time, new security threats may emerge, or flaws in the system's software may be discovered, necessitating prompt patching to prevent exploitation. Since many IoT devices are often deployed in remote locations with limited access for physical intervention, implementing an automated update mechanism is crucial for ensuring that devices stay up to date without requiring manual intervention. Secure, encrypted OTA updates are commonly used to deliver patches and updates to IoT devices, ensuring the integrity and authenticity of the updates and minimizing the risk of man-in-the-middle attacks during the update process. Furthermore, testing updates in a controlled environment before rolling them out across the entire system is important to ensure that they do not introduce new issues or security vulnerabilities. Another critical element of maintenance is scalability. IoT systems often grow over time as new devices are added to the network, increasing the demand on the infrastructure. Ensuring that the system can scale without compromising performance or security is vital. This includes evaluating the cloud infrastructure or edge computing systems that handle data processing and storage to ensure they can handle growing workloads. Load balancing, efficient data storage strategies, and ensuring network capacity are important considerations for maintaining optimal system performance. Data privacy and integrity must also be consistently ensured throughout the system's lifecycle. Regular audits and reviews of data storage and handling processes help ensure that sensitive data, such as personal information, is adequately protected and that access controls are functioning properly. Continuous monitoring also includes assessing user access controls to ensure that only authorized entities are allowed to interact with the IoT network. It involves proactive monitoring of device performance and security, regular updates and patches, scalability management, and ensuring ongoing compliance with regulations and standards. This phase ensures that the IoT system remains resilient to evolving threats and continues to deliver reliable, secure service over time.

End-of-life (EOL) management focuses on properly retiring and decommissioning IoT devices and systems when they are no longer useful, functional, or secure. As IoT devices have limited lifespans, whether due to hardware obsolescence, security vulnerabilities, or changing user needs, EOL management ensures that the devices and systems are securely phased out without compromising data privacy, security, or compliance with regulatory requirements. One of the first steps in EOL management is to identify when a device or system has reached its end of life. This might be triggered by the device no longer receiving vendor support, the discovery of critical security vulnerabilities that cannot be patched, or the emergence of more efficient or secure alternatives. Once this stage is identified, a structured plan must be put in place to decommission the device or system in a manner that prevents any potential risks or breaches. Many IoT devices handle sensitive data, and the improper disposal or decommissioning of these devices can expose private information or create opportunities for exploitation by malicious actors. Therefore, one of the most important steps is to securely erase all data stored on the device. This can involve wiping local storage, deleting personal data, and ensuring that encryption keys or credentials stored in the device are properly deactivated or destroyed. Furthermore, it is essential to decommission devices from the network to prevent unauthorized access. This includes disabling remote management capabilities and removing the device from any monitoring or control systems that could allow external actors to interact with it after it has been retired.

EOL management also includes addressing the physical disposal of IoT devices. IoT devices often contain hazardous materials or components that must be disposed of according to environmental and regulatory standards. Manufacturers and organizations must ensure that the proper recycling processes are followed, in compliance with regulations such as WEEE (Waste Electrical and Electronic Equipment) and RoHS (Restriction of Hazardous

Substances). In addition, there may be legal considerations related to the disposal of devices that contain personally identifiable information (PII) or other sensitive data. Organizations must ensure that all data protection regulations, such as GDPR, are adhered to when managing EOL devices, especially when it comes to data destruction and recycling practices. From a software standpoint, EOL management also involves ensuring that any associated software or services supporting the IoT device are properly terminated. This includes ensuring that APIs, cloud services, or network infrastructure related to the device are also decommissioned or repurposed to avoid unnecessary resource consumption or security risks. The final step in the EOL phase is to update inventory and documentation, ensuring that the organization keeps accurate records of which devices have been decommissioned and how they were securely disposed of. This documentation helps with audit trails and compliance verification, ensuring that the entire EOL process has been handled correctly and securely. This phase involves securely erasing data, disabling network access, complying with environmental and legal disposal requirements, and ensuring that all associated software and services are terminated. Proper EOL management not only mitigates security risks but also ensures compliance with regulations, contributing to a more sustainable and secure IoT ecosystem.

Implementing the SDLC for IoT systems presents a variety of challenges and considerations due to the unique nature of IoT technologies, their distributed environments, and their complex security and scalability requirements. One of the primary challenges is the integration of diverse hardware, software, and networking components that make up an IoT ecosystem. Unlike traditional software systems, IoT systems often include a wide range of devices with varying capabilities, from simple sensors to advanced, multifunctional devices. This heterogeneity can complicate the development and testing processes as each type of device may require specific handling in terms of software compatibility, power management, and performance optimization. The variability in device capabilities also means that solutions need to be adaptable to different resource constraints, such as limited processing power, memory, and battery life, which can significantly impact the overall design and implementation of an IoT system.

Security is another critical challenge when implementing SDLC for IoT. IoT devices are often deployed in environments that are physically accessible, and once compromised, they can be used as entry points into broader networks. These devices can be targets for various cyberattacks, including data breaches, DDoS attacks, and MITM attacks. Securing the entire IoT ecosystem, which includes not only the devices themselves but also the networks and cloud infrastructure that connect them, requires careful attention to encryption, authentication, access control, and continuous monitoring. The need for robust security practices throughout the SDLC from design and development to deployment and maintenance adds complexity to the implementation of IoT systems.

Scalability and performance are additional concerns when developing IoT systems, as the number of devices and data generated in an IoT ecosystem can grow exponentially. This creates significant demands on the network infrastructure, data storage, and processing capabilities. Efficient data management becomes a key challenge, as IoT systems often generate vast amounts of real-time data that must be processed and analyzed quickly to provide useful insights. Handling this volume of data requires scalable cloud or edge computing infrastructure, which can introduce additional costs and complexities in terms of resource allocation, load balancing, and ensuring that the system remains performant as it scales. Achieving this balance between scalability, performance, and cost-effectiveness is one of the key challenges in implementing SDLC for IoT systems.

The IoT ecosystem is diverse, with various manufacturers, platforms, and communication protocols in use. Devices from different vendors may not be compatible with each other, making it difficult to integrate them into a cohesive system. The lack of standardized protocols and interfaces can also lead to difficulties in system maintenance and upgrades, as different components may require different approaches to software updates, security patches, and troubleshooting. This lack of standardization can result in vendor lock-in, where users are dependent on a single vendor for updates and support, limiting flexibility and increasing long-term costs. To address these issues, it is important for IoT system developers to choose widely accepted standards and ensure that their solutions are designed with interoperability in mind, allowing for easier integration and future-proofing of the system. In addition to these technical challenges, regulatory and compliance issues present a significant consideration. IoT devices, especially those handling personal data, must comply with data protection laws such as the GDPR or industry-specific standards such as the Health Insurance Portability and Accountability Act (HIPAA) in the healthcare sector. Ensuring that IoT systems adhere to these regulations throughout their lifecycle requires continuous attention to data privacy, secure storage, user consent management, and audit trails. Implementing SDLC for IoT also means addressing compliance in all phases, including development, deployment, and maintenance. Given the global nature of IoT systems, navigating the complexities of different regional laws and regulations adds an additional layer of difficulty.

7.2 IMPLEMENTING SECURITY BY DESIGN

Implementing security by design is a comprehensive approach to ensuring that security considerations are embedded into every stage of the development process, rather than being added as an afterthought. This proactive methodology ensures that systems, software, and devices are built with robust defenses against current and emerging threats. The interconnected IoT devices operate in a dynamic and vulnerable ecosystem, making security by design crucial to addressing the unique challenges posed by these technologies. This principle involves integrating security requirements from the outset, encompassing architecture, design, development, testing, deployment, and maintenance phases. By prioritizing security from the beginning, organizations can mitigate risks, prevent vulnerabilities, and foster user trust while reducing long-term costs associated with breaches or retrofitting security measures post-deployment.

The foundation of implementing security by design lies in risk assessment and threat modeling during the initial phase. The assessment guides the design process, ensuring that security features are tailored to the specific needs of the system. Threat modeling tools such as STRIDE (Spoofing, Tampering, Repudiation, Information Disclosure, Denial of Service, Elevation of Privilege) or PASTA (Process for Attack Simulation and Threat Analysis) are often used to predict and counteract potential attack vectors. These models enable designers to prioritize risks and allocate resources effectively, ensuring that critical security concerns are addressed early in the lifecycle. The next step in implementing security by design is creating a secure architecture and design that aligns with identified risks. This includes principles such as least privilege, secure defaults, and defense in depth. Least privilege ensures that users, applications, and devices have access only to the resources necessary for their tasks, reducing the potential impact of a compromised component. Secure defaults involve configuring systems to be secure out of the box, requiring users to opt-in for less secure settings rather than opt-out. Defense in depth involves layering multiple security mechanisms to create redundancies, ensuring that if one layer fails, others remain intact to protect the system. For example, an IoT system could employ secure boot to prevent unauthorized firmware, use encrypted communication protocols such as TLS to protect data in transit, and implement intrusion detection systems to monitor anomalous behavior. A secure architecture also considers scalability and interoperability, ensuring that new devices or services can be integrated without compromising the system's security.

Secure coding practices are another cornerstone of security by design. Developers must adhere to guidelines and frameworks that prioritize security during the coding phase. This includes input validation to prevent injection attacks, secure handling of sensitive data to avoid leakage, and rigorous error handling to ensure that vulnerabilities are not exposed through system responses. Automated tools for static and dynamic code analysis are often employed to detect vulnerabilities during the development phase. For instance, static analysis tools can identify hardcoded credentials or unvalidated input in the code, while dynamic analysis tools test the software in runtime environments to uncover vulnerabilities like buffer overflows or race conditions. Secure coding practices also emphasize the importance of avoiding deprecated or insecure functions, using libraries and frameworks with proven security records, and conducting regular code reviews to identify potential issues.

Authentication and authorization mechanisms play a critical role in ensuring only legitimate users and devices can access the system. By design, these mechanisms should incorporate strong MFA and RBAC. MFA combines multiple authentication factors, such as passwords, biometrics, and hardware tokens, making it significantly harder for attackers to gain access. RBAC ensures that users or devices have access only to the resources required for their role, minimizing the impact of a compromised account. In an IoT context, this could involve device certificates for authentication and token-based mechanisms for API access. Additionally, secure session management techniques, such as the use of short-lived session tokens and automatic session termination, can further enhance system security.

A key aspect of security by design is data protection and encryption. All sensitive data, whether at rest, in transit, or in use, must be encrypted using strong, industry-standard algorithms such as AES-256 or RSA-2048. Encryption ensures that even if data is intercepted or accessed by unauthorized entities, it remains unreadable without the proper decryption key. Secure key management practices are integral to this process, involving the use of HSMs or secure key storage systems to protect encryption keys. Furthermore, data minimization principles should be implemented to collect, process, and store only the data necessary for the system's functionality, reducing the risk associated with data breaches. Testing and validation are essential components of security by design. Comprehensive testing ensures that security measures function as intended and that vulnerabilities are identified and mitigated before deployment. This includes unit testing, integration testing, system testing, and penetration testing. Automated tools can simulate attacks to identify weaknesses, while manual testing can uncover subtle vulnerabilities that automated tools might miss. Vulnerability scanning tools, fuzz testing, and ethical hacking practices are frequently employed during this phase. Additionally, security tests should be repeated periodically throughout the development lifecycle to ensure that new changes or additions do not introduce vulnerabilities. During deployment, secure configuration and monitoring practices ensure that the system remains secure in real-world environments. Systems should be configured with secure defaults, with unnecessary services and ports disabled to reduce the attack surface. Continuous monitoring tools provide real-time insights into system behavior, allowing administrators to detect and respond to potential threats promptly. Logging mechanisms are configured to capture security-relevant events, such as failed authentication attempts or unusual traffic patterns, and these logs are securely stored for analysis and compliance purposes.

Regular updates and patch management are vital to maintaining security after deployment. By design, systems should support OTA updates to ensure that vulnerabilities can be patched without requiring physical access to devices; secure update mechanisms, including cryptographic signing and verification of update files; and prevent unauthorized or malicious updates from being installed. Automated update systems can ensure that patches are deployed promptly, reducing the window of opportunity for attackers. Another important consideration in security by design is user education and awareness. Users often represent the weakest link in a security chain, and designing systems that guide them toward secure behavior is critical. This includes implementing user-friendly security features, providing clear instructions for secure configuration, and educating users on recognizing phishing attempts or other social engineering attacks. Finally, security by design emphasizes compliance with industry standards and regulations. Adhering to standards such as ISO/IEC 27001, NIST Cybersecurity Framework, or GDPR ensures that the system meets established security benchmarks and regulatory requirements. Compliance not only reduces legal and financial risks but also fosters trust among users and stakeholders. By prioritizing security from the outset, organizations can build systems that are not only functional but also capable of withstanding the evolving threat landscape, ensuring the safety and trust of users and stakeholders. There are several stages included for the security design in IoT botnets.

Risk Assessment and Threat Modeling: Begin with a comprehensive risk assessment to identify potential vulnerabilities in IoT devices and networks. Use threat modeling frameworks such as STRIDE (Spoofing, Tampering, Repudiation, Information Disclosure, Denial of Service, Elevation of Privilege) or MITRE ATT&CK to anticipate attack scenarios. Prioritize high-risk areas, such as insecure communication, weak credentials, and unpatched software, and allocate resources accordingly.

Secure Device Design and Architecture: Incorporate principles such as least privilege and defense in depth into the architecture. Implement secure boot mechanisms to ensure only authenticated firmware can run on devices. Design devices with tamper-proof hardware, including Trusted Platform Modules (TPMs) and secure enclaves, to protect critical data and processes.

Strong Authentication and Authorization: Use MFA for both users and devices to prevent unauthorized access. Implement device-specific certificates for mutual authentication between IoT devices and networks. Enforce role-based access control (RBAC) to limit permissions based on user or device roles, reducing the potential impact of a compromised node.

End-to-End Data Encryption: Encrypt all data in transit using secure protocols such as TLS or DTLS to prevent interception by attackers. Ensure data at rest is encrypted with strong algorithms, such as AES-256, to protect sensitive information from unauthorized access. Adopt secure key management practices, including hardware-based key storage, to prevent attackers from accessing encryption keys.

Secure Software Development Practices: Follow secure coding standards to prevent vulnerabilities such as buffer overflows and SQL injections. Conduct regular code reviews and use static and dynamic analysis tools to identify and address vulnerabilities during development. Avoid hardcoding sensitive information like credentials in software.

Firmware Updates and Patch Management: Design devices to support over-the-air (OTA) updates, allowing rapid deployment of security patches. Ensure updates are cryptographically signed and verified to prevent malicious updates. Automate patch management to address vulnerabilities promptly.

Network Segmentation and Isolation: Segregate IoT devices into separate network segments to limit the spread of botnet malware. Use firewalls and intrusion detection systems (IDS) to monitor and block malicious traffic. Implement VLANs or other isolation techniques to contain compromised devices.

Behavioral Monitoring and Anomaly Detection: Deploy behavioral monitoring systems to detect unusual device activities that may indicate botnet infections. Use AI and machine learning algorithms to analyze traffic patterns and identify anomalies. Regularly update detection models to account for evolving botnet tactics.

Secure APIs and Communication Protocols: Secure APIs with strong authentication, rate limiting, and input validation to prevent exploitation. Use lightweight, secure communication protocols like MQTT with authentication and encryption extensions. Regularly test APIs for vulnerabilities that could be exploited by botnets.

Physical Security Measures: Design devices to resist physical tampering, such as using secure casings and tamper-evident seals. Store critical credentials and encryption keys in hardware-based secure storage, like TPMs. Disable unused physical interfaces, such as USB ports, to prevent unauthorized access.

Device Identity and Lifecycle Management: Assign unique, immutable identities to IoT devices for tracking and authentication. Implement device attestation mechanisms to verify the integrity of devices before connecting them to the network. Enforce secure device decommissioning practices, such as wiping data and revoking credentials.

DNS and Traffic Filtering: Use DNS filtering to block access to known malicious domains used by botnets. Implement traffic analysis tools to identify command-and-control (C&C) communication and block it. Employ fast-flux detection mechanisms to mitigate advanced botnet tactics.

User Awareness and Training: Educate users about secure practices, such as changing default passwords and avoiding suspicious links. Provide intuitive interfaces and alerts to guide users toward secure configurations. Encourage reporting of anomalies or security concerns.

Redundancy and Resilience: Design systems with fail-safe mechanisms to ensure functionality during an attack. Use redundant communication paths and backup servers to maintain availability. Implement automatic failover mechanisms to ensure continuity during disruptions.

Collaboration and Information Sharing: Collaborate with industry groups and threat intelligence platforms to stay informed about emerging botnet threats. Share insights and threat data with the wider community to strengthen collective defenses. Participate in coordinated takedown efforts against botnets.

Regular Security Audits and Penetration Testing: Conduct regular security audits to identify and address vulnerabilities. Use penetration testing to simulate botnet attacks and evaluate system resilience. Document findings and implement corrective actions promptly.

Zero Trust Architecture: Implement a zero-trust model where no device or user is automatically trusted. Continuously verify identities and enforce strict access controls. Use micro-segmentation to protect critical resources from compromised devices.

Incident Response Planning: Develop comprehensive incident response plans to address botnet infections. Include procedures for isolating infected devices, mitigating the spread, and restoring functionality. Regularly test and update response plans to ensure effectiveness.

By implementing these security-by-design methods, IoT ecosystems can significantly enhance their resilience against botnet threats, ensuring a safer and more secure environment for users and devices.

7.3 THE IMPORTANCE OF USER EDUCATION AND AWARENESS

User education and awareness are critical components of any effective cybersecurity strategy, especially in the context of rapidly evolving technologies like the IoT. As devices become more interconnected and digital ecosystems grow more complex, the role of users as a frontline defense against cyberthreats has never been more significant. Educating users and building awareness ensures they understand the risks associated with their online behaviors, the technology they use, and how they can proactively mitigate vulnerabilities. Cybersecurity threats, including phishing, malware, botnets, and data breaches, often succeed due to human error or ignorance. For example, IoT devices frequently suffer from weak passwords, misconfigurations, or unpatched software vulnerabilities—issues that stem largely from user negligence or a lack of knowledge. Educating users empowers them to recognize risks, take appropriate security measures, and ultimately play an active role in protecting personal, organizational, and global networks.

One of the most prominent aspects of user education is fostering an understanding of password hygiene. Weak or reused passwords remain a top vulnerability exploited by attackers, making it imperative for users to create strong, unique passwords for each account and device. Educating users on the importance of using password managers and enabling MFA can significantly reduce unauthorized access. Similarly, raising awareness about phishing schemes—where attackers trick users into revealing sensitive information—can dramatically limit the success of such tactics. Teaching users how to identify suspicious emails, verify the authenticity of senders, and avoid clicking on untrusted links or downloading suspicious attachments is fundamental to cybersecurity. Awareness campaigns should also address emerging threats, such as credential stuffing and cryptojacking, ensuring users are equipped to recognize and respond to these challenges. User education must emphasize the unique risks posed by interconnected systems. IoT users are often unaware of how a compromised smart device—such as a thermostat, security camera, or voice assistant—can serve as an entry point for attackers to infiltrate a broader network. Training should highlight the importance of changing default credentials, regularly updating device firmware, and disabling unnecessary features that could expose vulnerabilities. Furthermore, users must understand the significance of secure configurations, such as enabling encryption for data transmission and implementing strong access controls for devices. Awareness of these practices ensures users maintain secure IoT environments and reduce the likelihood of their devices being co-opted into botnets or other malicious activities.

The importance of user education extends beyond individuals to organizations, where employees often represent a critical vulnerability in cybersecurity frameworks. Organizations should invest in comprehensive training programs that cover a wide range of topics, from recognizing social engineering attacks to safeguarding sensitive data. These programs should be tailored to various roles within the organization, ensuring that every employee understands their specific responsibilities in maintaining cybersecurity. For example, IT staff should receive advanced training on network security and incident response, while non-technical employees should focus on recognizing phishing attempts, securing workstations, and protecting sensitive documents. Simulated phishing campaigns and regular assessments can help organizations measure the effectiveness of training and reinforce best practices.

Building user awareness also requires addressing psychological factors that influence behavior. Many users exhibit a false sense of security, believing they are unlikely to be targeted by cybercriminals. Awareness campaigns must debunk these misconceptions and emphasize that every user, regardless of their role or level of technical expertise, is a potential target. Additionally, educational initiatives should focus on reducing complacency and encouraging proactive behaviors, such as reporting suspicious activities and adhering to organizational security policies. By fostering a culture of accountability and vigilance, organizations can significantly reduce human error and enhance overall security.

User education is not a one-time effort but an ongoing process that must evolve with the changing threat landscape. As new vulnerabilities and attack vectors emerge, users need continuous updates and guidance to stay ahead of cybercriminals. This is particularly important in the era of IoT, where the rapid proliferation of devices introduces new challenges. Governments, industry leaders, and educational institutions must collaborate to develop standardized training materials and awareness campaigns that reach a broad audience. Public awareness initiatives, such as National Cybersecurity Awareness Month, play a crucial role in promoting best practices and encouraging a collective commitment to security. In addition to formal training programs, organizations and communities can leverage technology to enhance user education. Gamified learning platforms, interactive simulations, and real-world case studies make cybersecurity training engaging and memorable. For instance, simulated attacks can help users experience the consequences of phishing or ransomware attacks in a controlled environment, reinforcing the importance of vigilance and proper response protocols. Leveraging tools like AI-driven training platforms can also provide personalized education tailored to individual users' needs and knowledge gaps, maximizing the effectiveness of awareness efforts.

Parents and educators also play a vital role in fostering cybersecurity awareness from an early age. With children growing up in a digital-first world, teaching them about online safety, data privacy, and responsible technology use is essential. Lessons on identifying fake websites, protecting personal information, and recognizing cyberbullying can instill lifelong habits that contribute to a safer online environment. Schools should integrate cybersecurity into their curricula, ensuring that students develop a solid understanding of the risks and responsibilities associated with technology use. Another critical aspect of user education is empowering users to make informed decisions about the technology they adopt. Consumers should be encouraged to research devices and services, prioritize products with robust security features, and advocate for greater transparency from manufacturers. Raising awareness about security certifications and standards, such as ISO/IEC 27001 or the OWASP IoT Top Ten, helps users evaluate the security of products before purchase. Educated consumers can drive demand for secure technologies, incentivizing manufacturers to prioritize security in their designs.

User education also contributes to broader societal resilience against cyberthreats. As individuals and organizations adopt best practices, they create ripple effects that enhance the security of interconnected systems. For example, secure configurations on a single IoT device reduce its potential to serve as a launchpad for botnet attacks, benefiting the entire network. Similarly, widespread adoption of MFA and encryption makes it more challenging for attackers to achieve their goals, reducing the overall prevalence of successful cyberattacks. In this way, user education serves as a cornerstone of collective cybersecurity defense.

User education and awareness are indispensable for securing the digital landscape, particularly in the context of IoT and emerging technologies. By empowering users with the knowledge and tools to recognize and mitigate risks, organizations and communities can create a culture of cybersecurity that extends from individual behaviors to global networks. Continuous education, tailored training, and public awareness campaigns are essential to ensuring users remain vigilant and proactive in the face of evolving threats. As the complexity of the digital ecosystem grows, the importance of user education will only increase, making it a fundamental pillar of cybersecurity in the modern world.

7.4 INDUSTRY STANDARDS AND CERTIFICATIONS

Industry standards and certifications play a pivotal role in ensuring the security, reliability, and interoperability of technology systems, particularly in domains such as the IoT, cybersecurity, and IT infrastructure. As digital ecosystems grow increasingly complex and interconnected, adherence to well-defined standards and the acquisition of relevant certifications become essential for organizations, manufacturers, developers, and end-users alike. These standards and certifications serve as benchmarks that define best practices, enforce minimum security requirements, and foster trust among stakeholders by ensuring compliance with globally recognized protocols and frameworks. They provide a unified language and approach to addressing critical issues such as data security, privacy, interoperability, and quality assurance, thereby reducing vulnerabilities and facilitating smooth integration across diverse systems and platforms. By aligning with industry standards, organizations can demonstrate their commitment to excellence, regulatory compliance, and customer satisfaction, which is crucial in highly competitive and risk-laden environments.

One of the foundational benefits of industry standards is their ability to establish a baseline for security in an era where cyberattacks are increasingly sophisticated and pervasive. Standards such as the ISO/IEC 27001, which focuses on information security management systems (ISMS) and NIST's Cybersecurity Framework (CSF), provide organizations with structured guidelines to identify, assess, and mitigate risks. These frameworks emphasize crucial elements such as risk assessment, access control, incident response, and continuous monitoring. For IoT devices, the OWASP IoT Top Ten and ETSI EN 303 645 outline specific security measures to counter vulnerabilities, such as weak authentication, unpatched firmware, and insecure communication channels. Adopting these standards helps organizations prevent common exploits and reduce the attack surface, thus safeguarding critical infrastructure and sensitive data from breaches, ransomware, and botnet attacks. Moreover, compliance with such standards is often a prerequisite for doing business with governments, enterprises, or other entities that mandate a high level of security assurance.

Certifications further reinforce adherence to industry standards by validating that an organization, product, or individual has met predefined criteria of competency, security, or quality. For organizations, certifications like ISO/IEC 27001 and SOC 2 Type II provide third-party assurance that their processes and systems meet rigorous standards for information security, risk management, and operational control. These certifications instill confidence among customers, partners, and regulators, serving as tangible proof of the organization's commitment to protecting data and assets. Similarly, individual certifications such as Certified Information Systems Security Professional (CISSP), Certified Ethical Hacker (CEH), and CompTIA Security+ validate the expertise of professionals in areas such as cybersecurity, ethical hacking, and network defense. By earning these credentials, individuals enhance their career prospects and contribute to the organization's overall security posture.

Interoperability is another critical area where industry standards and certifications have a transformative impact. As IoT devices, cloud platforms, and legacy systems must coexist within the same ecosystems, ensuring seamless communication and compatibility is paramount. Protocols such as MQTT, Zigbee, LoRaWAN, and BLE are industry-standard frameworks that enable diverse IoT devices to connect and share data efficiently. Certification programs, such as those offered by the Wi-Fi Alliance or the Zigbee Alliance, validate that devices comply with these protocols, guaranteeing interoperability across products from different manufacturers. This ensures a consistent user experience while reducing technical hurdles during deployment. Furthermore, adherence to interoperability standards accelerates innovation by allowing developers to build on existing technologies without being constrained by proprietary limitations or compatibility issues.

In addition to security and interoperability, privacy is a growing concern that industry standards and certifications address comprehensively. Regulations such as the GDPR in Europe and the CCPA in the United States set strict guidelines for handling personal data. Standards such as ISO/IEC 27701, which extends ISO/IEC 27001 to include privacy information management, help organizations align with these regulations. Certifications like GDPR certification demonstrate that an organization has implemented measures to protect user data, respect individual rights, and ensure transparency in data processing activities. These certifications not only mitigate the risk of legal penalties but also build trust with customers who increasingly prioritize privacy in their interactions with businesses.

The global adoption of industry standards and certifications also fosters greater accountability and governance within organizations. Standards like COBIT (Control Objectives for Information and Related Technologies) and ITIL (Information Technology Infrastructure Library) provide frameworks for IT governance, service management, and business alignment. By adopting these frameworks, organizations can streamline their operations, optimize resource allocation, and ensure that IT initiatives align with broader business goals. Certifications such as COBIT 5 Foundation or ITIL certifications validate that individuals and organizations have the necessary knowledge and skills to implement these frameworks effectively, resulting in better decision-making, reduced operational risks, and improved overall performance.

The key advantage of industry standards and certifications is their role in supporting regulatory compliance. Governments and regulatory bodies often rely on established standards to define minimum requirements for sectors such as healthcare, finance, energy, and transportation. For instance, the Payment Card Industry Data Security Standard (PCI DSS) governs the secure handling of credit card data, while the Health Insurance Portability and Accountability Act (HIPAA) defines standards for protecting healthcare information. Organizations that achieve compliance certifications demonstrate their adherence to these regulations, reducing legal and financial risks. In highly regulated industries, non-compliance can result in severe penalties, reputational damage, and loss of customer trust, making certifications an indispensable part of risk management strategies. Standards and certifications also play a crucial role in ensuring the safety and reliability of emerging technologies such as autonomous vehicles, industrial IoT, and AI. For example, ISO 21434 addresses cybersecurity for road vehicles, ensuring that manufacturers implement robust security measures during the design, development, and production of connected cars. Similarly, AI-focused standards such as ISO/IEC TR 24028 provide guidelines for ensuring the ethical use, transparency, and accountability of AI systems. By adhering to these standards, organizations can mitigate potential risks, foster public confidence, and pave the way for broader adoption of innovative technologies. Despite their numerous benefits, implementing industry standards and certifications comes with challenges. Achieving certification often requires significant time, effort, and financial investment, which can be a barrier for SMEs. Additionally, the rapid pace of technological advancements can render some standards outdated, necessitating frequent updates and revisions. Organizations must also navigate the complexity of multiple overlapping standards and certifications, which can create confusion and inefficiencies. To address these challenges, industry bodies, governments, and stakeholders must collaborate to streamline certification processes, provide financial support or incentives for SMEs, and ensure that standards remain relevant in a fast-changing landscape. Industry standards and certifications are indispensable for ensuring the security, interoperability, privacy, and reliability of modern technological systems. They provide a structured framework for addressing complex challenges, foster trust among stakeholders, and drive innovation by enabling seamless integration across diverse ecosystems. By adhering to established standards and achieving relevant certifications, organizations can enhance their competitive edge, comply with regulatory requirements, and build a resilient foundation for long-term success. As the digital landscape continues to evolve, the importance of standards and certifications will only grow, making them a cornerstone of sustainable and secure technological progress.

7.5 CONCLUSION

The current chapter highlights the indispensable role these stakeholders play in shaping the security, reliability, and functionality of the IoT ecosystem. As the creators of devices, systems, and platforms that underpin modern IoT networks, manufacturers and developers hold the primary responsibility for embedding robust security measures and ensuring seamless performance. This chapter explored how their decisions during design, development, deployment, and maintenance stages significantly impact the resilience of IoT systems to vulnerabilities and cyberthreats. By adopting proactive strategies such as security-by-design principles, adherence to secure SDLC, and rigorous testing protocols, manufacturers and developers can pre-emptively address weaknesses, laying a strong foundation for safer IoT deployments. Their commitment to innovation, coupled with accountability and ethical practices, is crucial to the long-term success and trustworthiness of IoT technology. It includes designing devices with built-in safeguards, such as secure boot processes, encryption protocols, and authentication mechanisms, while also ensuring that software and firmware are regularly updated to address emerging threats. The chapter emphasized that security cannot be an afterthought or a cost-cutting casualty; instead, it must be a fundamental aspect of product design and development. Developers also need to engage in rigorous testing, employing penetration tests, vulnerability scans, and automated tools to identify potential flaws. Furthermore, the importance of providing clear, actionable documentation and user guidance was stressed, as these resources enable end-users to configure and maintain their devices securely.

Another critical aspect explored in the chapter is the need for IoT manufacturers and developers to embrace regulatory compliance and align with industry standards. Frameworks such as ISO/IEC 27001, GDPR, and NIST Cybersecurity Guidelines offer structured approaches to security that not only safeguard devices but also build consumer confidence. By adhering to such standards, manufacturers demonstrate their commitment to transparency and accountability, fostering a culture of trust. Additionally, certifications such as UL 2900 or IoT Security Foundation badges provide external validation of a product's security posture, giving consumers a tangible way to assess the safety of devices they purchase. Developers, on the other hand, must ensure that their applications, APIs, and integrations meet these same rigorous standards to create a cohesive and secure IoT ecosystem. This chapter also underscored the importance of ongoing support and lifecycle management. IoT devices often remain operational for years, making long-term firmware and software support essential to addressing new vulnerabilities that arise over time. Manufacturers must establish clear update mechanisms that deliver patches efficiently without compromising device performance. This requires investment in secure update delivery systems, such as OTA updates, which ensure that fixes are applied seamlessly and promptly. Similarly, end-of-life planning is critical, with manufacturers needing to communicate support timelines clearly and provide guidance for securely decommissioning obsolete devices.

In addition to technical measures, the chapter highlighted the ethical obligations of manufacturers and developers to consider user privacy and data protection as fundamental priorities. The integration of privacy-by-design principles ensures that devices collect only necessary data, with clear consent mechanisms and strong encryption to safeguard personal information. Developers must create transparent and secure systems for data processing, storage, and sharing, adhering to legal and ethical guidelines. Moreover, manufacturers have a responsibility to educate users about best practices, providing intuitive interfaces and resources that empower individuals to take an active role in securing their devices. Finally, it emphasized the role of collaboration among manufacturers, developers, regulators, and industry bodies to create a unified front against cyberthreats. Shared threat intelligence, open-source tools, and collaborative frameworks help accelerate the development of innovative security solutions and establish industry-wide benchmarks. This collective effort fosters a resilient and trustworthy IoT ecosystem that benefits all stakeholders, from consumers to enterprises. Their commitment to innovation, security, and ethical practices determines the trajectory of IoT's evolution and its ability to deliver transformative benefits while mitigating risks. By prioritizing security-by-design, adhering to standards, providing ongoing support, and fostering collaboration, manufacturers and developers can ensure that IoT remains a trusted and impactful enabler of the connected future. The responsibility they bear is significant, but so too is their potential to shape a secure, ethical, and user-centric IoT ecosystem that enhances lives and drives global progress.

Chapter 8

Global perspectives on IoT security

8.1 INTERNATIONAL STANDARDS AND FRAMEWORKS

International standards and frameworks serve as critical pillars for ensuring the security, functionality, interoperability, and reliability of IoT ecosystems in a globally connected environment. With IoT devices proliferating across diverse industries—from healthcare and transportation to smart cities and industrial automation—these standards are essential to address the challenges of security, scalability, privacy, and performance. By establishing consistent guidelines and best practices, international frameworks provide a foundation for manufacturers, developers, regulators, and enterprises to design, deploy, and maintain IoT systems that meet global expectations. These standards not only promote seamless integration and compatibility but also play a pivotal role in fostering consumer trust and regulatory compliance. This unified approach helps stakeholders mitigate risks, manage complexity, and ensure that IoT solutions are robust, scalable, and adaptable to the ever-evolving threat landscape.

IoT international standards are organizations such as International Organization for Standardization (ISO), Institute of Electrical and Electronic Engineers (IEEE), International Business Union (ITU), and Regional Authorities such as the European Telecommunications Standard Institute (ETSI). These organizations are developing protocols and frames that deal with different aspects of IoT, including communication, data protection, device security, and interoperability. For example, ISO/IEC 27001 provides a comprehensive framework for information security management systems (ISMS) and offers the IoT parties a systematic approach to protecting sensitive data and alleviating cyberthreats. Similarly, ISO/IEC 27017 and 27018 focus on cloud and privacy security and solve specific challenges associated with storing and processing IoT data in cloud environments.

By complying with these standards, organizations can strengthen their safety holding and prove liability to regulatory bodies and consumers. IEEE standards also play an important role in forming IoT technologies, especially wireless communication and network creation. Standards such as

DOI: 10.1201/9781003631460-8

IEEE 802.11 (Wi-Fi) and IEEE 802.15.4 (used in ZigBee) ensure reliable and efficient communication between IoT devices while maintaining compatibility of different manufacturers. These standards are helpful in allowing IoT systems to function smoothly in a heterogeneous environment such as intelligent houses, industrial automation, and vehicles. Additionally, IEEE 2413 provides an architectural framework for IoT, offering guidance on system design, scalability, and security considerations. This framework helps developers and manufacturers align their solutions with industry best practices, ensuring that IoT systems are resilient and future-proof.

The ITU also contributes significantly to the development of IoT standards, particularly in areas related to telecommunications and connectivity. ITU-T Y.2060, for example, defines the overall IoT framework, including fundamental concepts, reference models, and enabling technologies. This standard serves as a foundation for designing interoperable IoT systems that can integrate seamlessly across various networks and domains. Similarly, ITU-T SG20 focuses on IoT and smart city standards, addressing challenges such as resource optimization, data sharing, and sustainable development. These standards are crucial for governments and enterprises looking to implement large-scale IoT deployments, such as smart grids, intelligent transportation systems, and urban infrastructure management.

The role of regional standards bodies, such as ETSI, cannot be overlooked. ETSI develops standards that address specific regional requirements while maintaining alignment with global frameworks. For example, ETSI standards for Low-Power Wide-Area Network (LPWAN) are widely accepted in IoT applications that require long-distance communication and low energy consumption such as intelligent agriculture and asset monitoring. ETSI also contributes to the development of cyber safety standards for IoT, including ETSI EN 303 645, which provides basic safety requirements for IoT equipment for consumers. This standard emphasizes policy, such as secure password management, software updates, and vulnerability, helping manufacturers to improve their products and protect end-users from cyberthreats.

Another critical aspect of international standards is their focus on privacy and data protection, which are primary in IoT ecosystems, where a huge amount of personal and sensitive data is collected and processed. Frameworks such as GDPR in Europe and CCPA in the United States provide statutory data protection requirements and user rights. Although these regulations are not specific to IoT, they significantly affect the design and operation of IoT systems, which requires the organization to implement privacy principles according to the design, to minimize data, and provide transparent consent mechanisms. Compliance with these regulations is facilitated by international standards such as ISO/IEC 27701, which extends ISO/IEC 27001 to include information on personal data protection (PIMS). These standards help organizations navigate the complex regulatory landscape while ensuring that user privacy is prioritized.

Interoperability is another critical focus of international standards, as IoT systems often involve devices, platforms, and applications from different manufacturers. Standards such as the Open Connectivity Foundation (OCF) specifications and the oneM2M framework address interoperability challenges by providing common protocols and APIs for device communication and management. These frames allow smooth integration of IoT devices and systems, reducing complexity and support innovations. Standards of interoperability also play a key role in ensuring that IoT systems are scalable and adaptable, allowing organizations to expand their deployment without encountering compatibility problems.

In addition to technical standards, the international framework also emphasizes the importance of risk management and IoT resistance. For example, the cybersecurity framework for the National Institute for Standards and Technology (NIST) provides a comprehensive approach to identifying, protection, detection, response to cybersecurity incidents. This framework is widely accepted by organizations to increase their safety holding of IoT and harmonization with proven procedures in the field. NIST also offers IoT-specific guidance, such as NISTIR 8259, which outlines core cybersecurity capabilities for IoT devices. These guidelines help manufacturers and developers design products that are resilient to cyberthreats while providing organizations with the tools to assess and mitigate risks.

Collaboration and harmonization are key to the success of international standards and frameworks. Organizations such as the Internet Engineering Task Force (IETF) and the World Wide Web Consortium (W3C) work collaboratively to develop standards that address specific technical challenges in IoT, such as communication protocols (e.g., MQTT, CoAP) and data representation (e.g., JSON-LD). These collaborative efforts ensure that IoT systems are built on a foundation of widely accepted principles, reducing fragmentation and enabling global interoperability. Moreover, the involvement of stakeholders from various sectors—such as academia, industry, and government—ensures that the standards address diverse perspectives and requirements, fostering innovation and inclusivity.

The international standards and frameworks are indispensable for the secure, efficient, and interoperable operation of IoT systems. They provide a structured approach to addressing the technical, regulatory, and ethical challenges associated with IoT, enabling stakeholders to build solutions that are resilient, scalable, and user-centric. By aligning with these standards, manufacturers, developers, and organizations can enhance the security and reliability of their products, foster consumer trust, and contribute to the sustainable growth of the IoT ecosystem. As IoT continues to evolve and expand, the role of international standards and frameworks will remain pivotal in shaping a connected world that is both innovative and secure.

8.2 THE ROLE OF GOVERNMENTS AND REGULATORY BODIES

Governments and regulatory bodies play a pivotal role in shaping the IoT landscape, ensuring its secure, ethical, and sustainable development. As IoT devices become integral to critical infrastructure, industries, and daily lives, the responsibility of these entities extends across various domains, including security, privacy, interoperability, and innovation. Governments and regulators must establish frameworks and policies that mitigate risks, protect users, and foster technological advancement. Their role is multifaceted, encompassing policymaking, standard-setting, enforcement, international collaboration, and capacity-building, which collectively create an ecosystem where IoT can thrive while addressing societal, economic, and security challenges.

A primary responsibility of governments is to enact legislation that addresses the inherent security and privacy risks associated with IoT. IoT devices, often characterized by their weak security measures, are highly susceptible to cyberattacks such as botnets, data breaches, and ransomware. To counter these risks, governments worldwide have introduced laws and regulations mandating baseline security requirements for IoT manufacturers. For instance, the United Kingdom's "Product Security and Telecommunications Infrastructure (PSTI) Act" outlines specific security standards for consumer IoT devices, such as banning default passwords and requiring vulnerability disclosure mechanisms. Similarly, the European Union's Cybersecurity Act empowers the European Union Agency for Cybersecurity (ENISA) to establish certification frameworks for IoT devices, ensuring that products meet stringent security criteria before entering the market. These regulatory measures compel manufacturers to prioritize security during the design phase, reducing vulnerabilities and enhancing consumer trust.

Privacy is another critical area where governments and regulators play a key role. IoT devices collect a huge amount of personal and sensitive data, from metrics to information to placement, increasing significant concerns about personal data protection. Regulatory frameworks, such as GDPR in Europe and CCPA in the United States, have set benchmarks for data protection and user rights. These regulations require that the IoT parties involved implement privacy policies according to the proposal, obtain users' consent for data collection, and provide transparency in data processing practices. By promoting these standards, the government ensures that IoT ecosystems respect the user's privacy and follow ethical data procedures. In addition, they encourage organizations to accept advanced privacy technologies such as differential privacy and secure more parties to minimize exposure and data abuse.

In addition to security and privacy, governments and regulators are helpful in promoting interoperability and standardization in IoT systems. Lack of standardized protocols and interfaces often lead to fragmented ecosystems, preventing trouble-free integration of equipment and platforms. In order to resolve this, the Government cooperates with international standards, such as the International Trade Union Telecommunications (ITU), International Organization for Standardization (ISO), and the Institute of Electrical and Electronic Engineers (IEEE), for the purpose of IoT universal standards. These standards ensure that devices from different manufacturers can communicate and function, and support innovations and scalability. In addition, governments support open-source initiative and industrial consortium, such as the Open Connectivity Foundation (OCF) and OneM2M, which controls the development of interoperable IoT solutions. The support of government standardization enables various industries, from healthcare to intelligent cities, to effectively use IoT technologies.

Another significant role of governments is to incentivize and support research and development (R&D) in IoT technologies. Through grants, tax incentives, and partnership of the public and private government sector, innovations such as Edge Computing, artificial intelligence, and IoT energy-efficient devices support. For example, initiatives such as interdisciplinary research of the interdisciplinary research of "intelligent and connected communities" of the US National Science Foundation (NSF) for the development of IoT solutions for social challenges. Similarly, the European Commission's Horizon Europe program allocates significant sources to IoT research and emphasizes sustainable and inclusive digital transformation.

By strengthening the environment, contributing to the innovation not only develops technological abilities, but also increases economic growth and creation of jobs in the IoT sector. Regulatory bodies also play a decisive role in ensuring the ethical use of IoT technologies. IoT application, such as facial recognition and predictive analysts, increases ethical dilemmas related to supervision, discrimination, and autonomy. Governments deal with these concerns by determining ethical instructions and mechanisms of responsibility for the deployment of IoT. For example, the European Union for artificial intelligence has developed ethical principles for AI and IoT, emphasized by justice, transparency, and design focused on humans. Similarly, the International Telecommunication Union (ITU) of the UN for IoT ethical practices in areas such as intelligent cities and digital healthcare is held. By inserting ethical considerations into IoT policies, governments ensure that technological progress is in accordance with social values and human rights.

The role of governments extends to protecting critical infrastructure and national security from IoT-related threats. IoT devices integrated into power grids, transportation systems, and healthcare facilities are prime targets for cyberattacks, which can disrupt essential services and jeopardize public safety. To address this, governments implement stringent cybersecurity policies and frameworks, such as the US National Institute of Standards and Technology (NIST) Cybersecurity Framework and the European Union's Network and Information Systems (NIS) Directive. These frameworks guide organizations in identifying, protecting, detecting, responding to, and recovering from IoT-related cyberincidents. Additionally, governments establish cybersecurity agencies and task forces, such as the US Cybersecurity and Infrastructure Security Agency (CISA), to coordinate responses to IoT threats and enhance resilience in critical sectors.

International collaboration is another vital aspect of governments' roles in the IoT domain. IoT ecosystems are inherently global, with devices, data, and networks transcending national borders. To address cross-border challenges, governments participate in international forums and initiatives, such as the G20 Digital Economy Task Force and the International IoT Council. These platforms facilitate knowledge sharing, policy harmonization, and coordinated responses to global IoT challenges, such as botnets and supply chain vulnerabilities. Furthermore, governments negotiate bilateral and multilateral agreements to enhance cooperation in IoT-related research, standards development, and cybersecurity efforts. By fostering international collaboration, governments contribute to a cohesive and secure global IoT ecosystem.

Capacity-building is another critical responsibility of governments and regulatory bodies. As IoT adoption accelerates, there is a growing need for skilled professionals who can develop, deploy, and manage IoT systems securely. Governments address this need by investing in education and training programs, such as coding bootcamps, IoT certifications, and university courses. Additionally, governments support initiatives that promote digital literacy and raise awareness about IoT security and privacy among consumers. Public awareness campaigns, such as the United Kingdom's "Cyber Aware" initiative, educate users on best practices for securing IoT devices, such as changing default passwords and enabling automatic updates. By building a skilled workforce and informed user base, governments empower stakeholders to maximize the benefits of IoT while minimizing risks.

Finally, enforcement is a critical aspect of governments' roles in IoT regulation. Regulatory bodies monitor compliance with IoT-related laws and standards, conducting audits, investigations, and penalties for non-compliance. For example, the Federal Trade Commission (FTC) in the United States has taken action against companies for failing to implement adequate security measures in their IoT products. Similarly, the European Data Protection Board (EDPB) enforces GDPR compliance in IoT deployments, ensuring that organizations uphold user privacy rights. Effective enforcement not only deters malpractice but also establishes a level playing field for ethical and responsible IoT stakeholders.

The governments and regulatory bodies are central to the development and governance of IoT ecosystems. Through legislation, standard-setting, R&D support, ethical oversight, international collaboration, capacity-building, and enforcement, they create a framework that balances innovation with security, privacy, and societal well-being. As IoT continues to evolve, the role of these entities will remain crucial in addressing emerging challenges, fostering trust, and ensuring that IoT technologies contribute positively to a connected and sustainable future. Their proactive and adaptive approach is essential to unlocking the full potential of IoT while safeguarding individuals, businesses, and nations.

8.3 COLLABORATIVE EFFORTS IN COMBATTING IoT BOTNETS

Collaborative efforts are essential to combat the ever-evolving threat of IoT botnets, which leverage vulnerabilities in interconnected devices to execute large-scale cyberattacks such as DDoS attack, data theft, cryptojacking, and spam campaigns. The interconnected nature of IoT devices and the globalized Internet infrastructure necessitates a unified approach involving stakeholders from diverse sectors, including governments, private organizations, academia, cybersecurity firms, and end-users. These collaborations focus on information sharing, policy development, technical innovation, education, and enforcement to mitigate the risks posed by IoT botnets. By associating resources, expertise, and news, this effort seeks to disrupt the operations of botnets, increase the safety of IoT ecosystems, and protect the critical infrastructure and individuals from cyberthreats.

The cornerstone of cooperation effort is sharing information between governments, cybersecurity organizations, and private entities. Initiatives, such as Global Forum for Cyber Expertise (GFCE), European Union Agency for Cybersecurity (ENISA), and the Program of Sharing and Cooperation within the US Ministry of Internal Security (CISCP), facilitate intelligence, vulnerability data, and proven procedures. These programs enable the identification of threats to stakeholders, analyze attack formulas, and implement proactive measures to neutralize botnets. Cybersecurity companies such as Kaspersky, Palo Alto Networks, and Cisco also contribute by providing intelligence channels and detailed reports on the activity of botnets, allowing organizations to strengthen their defense against familiar and unknown threats. The partnership of the public and private sector plays a decisive role here and spans the abyss between government supervision and technical expertise of the private sector. Governments around the world have acknowledged the importance of the creation of policy of cooperation in solving the global nature of IoT botnets.

Regulatory frameworks, such as GDPR in Europe and the Act on Cyber Security in the United States, determine the basic safety requirements for IoT equipment, including secure authentication, encryption, and vulnerability procedures. Co-initiatives, such as Paris, require confidence and security in cyberspace, combine governments, industry, and civil society to support international cooperation in the fight against cyberthreats, including botnets. This effort emphasizes the need for coordinated global reactions because botnets often use devices and networks across different jurisdictions. International organizations, such as the International Telecommunication

Union of the UN (ITU) and the organization for economic cooperation and development (OECD), also play a key role in supporting dialogue and determining IoT security guards on a global scale.

Technical innovation and research are crucial to combating IoT botnets, and collaboration between academia, industry, and government is driving advancements in this field. Research institutions and universities contribute to developing new techniques for botnet detection, mitigation, and prevention. For example, machine learning and artificial intelligence (AI) are being leveraged to analyze network traffic and identify anomalous behavior indicative of botnet activity. Collaborative research projects such as the European Commission-funded IoT-A (Internet of Things Architecture) and the National Science Foundation's Secure and Trustworthy Cyberspace (SaTC) program bring together multidisciplinary teams to address IoT security challenges. Industry players, including major tech companies such as Microsoft, Google, and Amazon, also invest heavily in R&D to enhance the security of their IoT platforms and services. By sharing the outcomes of these initiatives, stakeholders can collectively raise the bar for IoT security and resilience.

Another critical aspect of collaborative efforts is capacity-building and awareness campaigns aimed at educating stakeholders about the risks and best practices for IoT security. Governments, non-governmental organizations (NGOs), and industry groups organize workshops, webinars, and training programs to equip developers, manufacturers, and end-users with the knowledge to secure IoT devices. For instance, the Internet Society (ISOC) runs initiatives to promote IoT security awareness among consumers and small businesses, emphasizing the importance of changing default passwords, enabling automatic updates, and using secure networks. Collaborative campaigns such as the US CISA's "Stop. Think. Connect." initiative raise public awareness about cyberthreats, including botnets, and encourage responsible online behavior. These efforts highlight the shared responsibility of all stakeholders in securing IoT ecosystems and mitigating botnet risks.

Industry-wide collaboration is also vital in addressing the fragmented nature of IoT device security. Manufacturers, services, and standards cooperate on the development and reception of security standards and certificates that provide basic protection for IoT equipment. For example, IoT Security Foundation (IOTSF) provides instructions and proven procedures for ensuring IoT equipment, while international standardization organizations (ISO) and institutes of electrical engineers and electronic engineers (IEEE) create technical standards that promote interoperability and security. Certification programs, such as the UL 2900 series for cyber safety in connected devices and the iOXT Alliance certification program, confirm that IoT products meet the safety reference values. By compliance with these standards, manufacturers can reduce vulnerability in their devices, while consumers gain more confidence in the security of the products they use.

Cooperation is equally important in the operational aspects of the fight against IoT botnets, especially in an effort to disable the botnet. Cybersecurity companies, Internet service providers (ISP), and coercive agencies often cooperate on the dismantling of botnets and control infrastructure (C&C). Remarkable examples include disabling the Mirai botnet and its variants, which were responsible for some of the greatest DDoS attacks in history. These operations require coordination across different jurisdictions and include activities such as C&C identification and seizure, disturbance of communication channels, and arrests of individuals involved in botnet operations. Cooperation platforms, such as the European Center for Computer Crime led by Europol (EC3) and the Center of Complaints about the FBI (IC3) Internet crime, facilitate cross-border cooperation in monitoring and dismantling the network of botnets. Such effort emphasizes the importance of unified action in alleviating the impact of botnets on the global network.

International cooperation is another critical element of combating IoT botnets, as these threats often transcend national boundaries. Governments, regulatory bodies, and industry stakeholders collaborate through multilateral agreements and international forums to address IoT security challenges collectively. The Budapest Convention on Cybercrime and the United Nations' Open-ended Working Group on developments in the field of information and telecommunications in the context of international security (OEWG) are examples of platforms that promote international dialogue and cooperation. These initiatives focus on harmonizing laws, sharing intelligence, and coordinating responses to cyberthreats. Moreover, regional alliances such as the European Union's Cybersecurity Strategy and the Asia-Pacific Economic Cooperation's (APEC) Cross-Border Privacy Rules System facilitate cooperation among member states to address IoT botnets and related challenges.

The role of public–private partnerships (PPPs) in combating IoT botnets cannot be overstated. These partnerships leverage the strengths of both sectors to develop innovative solutions, share resources, and implement effective strategies. For example, the Cyber Threat Alliance (CTA), comprising leading cybersecurity firms, shares threat intelligence and collaborates on research to combat cyberthreats, including botnets. Similarly, the Global Cyber Alliance (GCA) brings together public and private stakeholders to develop tools and frameworks that enhance IoT security. By fostering trust and collaboration between the public and private sectors, PPPs enable a more coordinated and effective response to botnet threats.

The combating IoT botnets requires a comprehensive and collaborative approach involving governments, private organizations, academia, cybersecurity firms, and end-users. By sharing information, developing policies, advancing technical innovation, raising awareness, and coordinating operational efforts, stakeholders can collectively address the complex and evolving challenges posed by IoT botnets. International cooperation, standardization, and PPPs further strengthen these efforts, creating a unified front against cyberthreats. As IoT adoption continues to grow, these collaborative initiatives will be critical in ensuring the security, resilience, and sustainability of interconnected ecosystems, safeguarding individuals, organizations, and nations from the adverse impacts of botnets.

8.4 THE FUTURE OF GLOBAL IoT SECURITY

The rapid proliferation of IoT devices has revolutionized industries, economies, and everyday life, yet it has also introduced unprecedented security challenges that demand a comprehensive, forward-looking approach. As IoT adoption accelerates, the future of global IoT security will hinge on the ability of governments, industries, and individuals to proactively address emerging threats while fostering innovation and trust in connected ecosystems. The future landscape of IoT security will involve advancements in technology, evolving regulatory frameworks, widespread adoption of best practices, global collaboration, and continuous education to address the risks associated with billions of interconnected devices. This evolution will reflect the integration of AI, blockchain, ML, zero-trust architecture, and quantum computing to bolster security, alongside increasing consumer awareness and government intervention to mitigate vulnerabilities.

In the coming years, artificial intelligence and machine learning will play an increasingly central role in IoT security. These technologies will be used to analyze massive amounts of data generated by IoT devices, identifying anomalies, detecting threats, and predicting attacks before they occur. AI-driven solutions will enhance intrusion detection systems (IDS) and endpoint protection platforms (EPP), enabling real-time responses to cyberthreats. For example, self-learning algorithms will monitor network traffic patterns to identify and isolate malicious activity, reducing the time between detection and mitigation. Additionally, AI will support more sophisticated behavioral analysis, allowing systems to differentiate between legitimate and malicious activity, even in the absence of known attack signatures. This predictive capability will be essential for addressing zero-day vulnerabilities and advanced persistent threats (APTs) targeting IoT ecosystems.

Blockchain technology is also expected to become a cornerstone of IoT security in the future. By providing decentralized, immutable, and transparent ledgers, blockchain can ensure data integrity, prevent unauthorized access, and enable secure communication between IoT devices. Blockchain-based identity management systems will allow devices to authenticate and interact with one another without relying on centralized authorities, reducing the risk of single points of failure. Smart contracts, powered by blockchain, can automate security protocols, ensuring that devices comply with predefined rules and policies. Furthermore, blockchain will facilitate secure software updates and patch management by providing verifiable records of firmware versions and update processes, reducing the risk of tampering or supply chain attacks.

The integration of quantum computing into the IoT security landscape will also have profound implications. While quantum computers have the potential to break traditional cryptographic algorithms, they will also drive the development of quantum-resistant encryption methods. Post-quantum cryptography will become a critical focus for securing IoT devices and networks against future quantum-enabled cyberattacks. Researchers and organizations are already working on quantum-safe encryption protocols that can protect sensitive data and communications in a post-quantum era. The adoption of quantum key distribution (QKD) and other advanced cryptographic techniques will ensure that IoT ecosystems remain resilient against evolving threats.

Another significant trend shaping the future of IoT security is the widespread adoption of zero-trust architecture. This security model assumes that no device, user, or application can be trusted by default, regardless of whether they are inside or outside the network perimeter. Zero-trust principles, such as continuous authentication, micro-segmentation, and least-privilege access, will be applied to IoT ecosystems to minimize the attack surface and limit the lateral movement of threats. By implementing zero-trust strategies, organizations can enhance their ability to prevent, detect, and respond to IoT-related cyberattacks. Regulatory frameworks and international standards will continue to evolve to address the unique security challenges posed by IoT devices. Governments and regulatory bodies will play a pivotal role in establishing mandatory security requirements for IoT manufacturers and service providers. These requirements may include secure authentication mechanisms, encryption standards, and vulnerability disclosure policies. For example, the European Union's Cyber Resilience Act and the United States' IoT Cybersecurity Improvement Act are early examples of regulatory efforts aimed at improving IoT security. As these frameworks mature, they will provide a foundation for global cooperation and harmonization of IoT security practices. Industry-driven initiatives, such as the IoTSF and the ioXt Alliance, will complement regulatory efforts by developing best practices, certification programs, and compliance guidelines that ensure the security and reliability of IoT products.

Global collaboration will be essential for addressing the transnational nature of IoT security threats. Governments, industry stakeholders, academia, and NGOs will need to work together to share threat intelligence, coordinate responses, and develop innovative solutions. PPPs will play a critical role in bridging the gap between regulatory oversight and technical expertise. Collaborative platforms, such as the Global Forum on Cyber Expertise (GFCE) and the World Economic Forum's (WEF) Centre for Cybersecurity, will facilitate dialogue and cooperation among diverse stakeholders. Additionally, regional initiatives, such as the European Union's Cybersecurity Strategy and the APEC's Cross-Border Privacy Rules, will foster collaboration and capacity-building among member states.

Consumer awareness and education will also be a key factor in the future of IoT security. As the number of connected devices in homes, workplaces, and public spaces continues to grow, end-users must become more vigilant about securing their devices. Awareness campaigns, training programs, and user-friendly security tools will empower individuals to adopt best practices, such as changing default passwords, enabling automatic updates, and using secure networks. Manufacturers will need to prioritize usability and transparency in their security features, ensuring that consumers can easily understand and implement them. Additionally, educational institutions will play a crucial role in developing a cybersecurity-savvy workforce capable of addressing the complex challenges of IoT security.

IoT security will also benefit from advancements in hardware-based protections. Secure boot processes, trusted platform modules (TPMs), and hardware security modules (HSMs) will become standard features in IoT devices, ensuring that only trusted firmware and software can execute on the device. These hardware-based solutions will provide a robust foundation for protecting sensitive data and preventing unauthorized access. Furthermore, innovations in chip design and manufacturing will enhance the physical security of IoT devices, making them more resilient against tampering, reverse engineering, and side-channel attacks.

The future of IoT security will also prioritize sustainability and energy efficiency. As the number of connected devices grows, the energy consumption of IoT ecosystems will become a significant concern. Security solutions will need to be designed with energy efficiency in mind, ensuring that they do not compromise the performance or battery life of IoT devices. Emerging technologies, such as energy-harvesting sensors and low-power communication protocols, will support the development of sustainable IoT security solutions that align with global environmental goals.

Despite these advancements, the future of IoT security will not be without challenges. The complexity and diversity of IoT ecosystems will continue to pose significant hurdles for standardization, interoperability, and scalability. The growing sophistication of cyberthreats, including AI-driven attacks and quantum-enabled exploits, will require constant innovation and vigilance. Additionally, the ethical and societal implications of IoT security, such as privacy concerns and surveillance risks, will demand careful consideration and balanced approaches. The future of global IoT security will be shaped by a combination of technological innovation, regulatory evolution, collaborative efforts, and user education. By leveraging AI, blockchain, quantum computing, and zero-trust architecture, stakeholders can enhance the resilience and trustworthiness of IoT ecosystems. Governments, industry leaders, and academia must work together to establish comprehensive security frameworks and standards that address the unique challenges of IoT devices. At the same time, empowering end-users with knowledge and tools to secure their devices will be critical for building a culture of cybersecurity. As the IoT landscape continues to evolve, a proactive and unified approach will be essential for ensuring the security, privacy, and sustainability of interconnected systems worldwide. Through these collective efforts, the vision of a secure and thriving IoT ecosystem can become a reality.

8.5 CONCLUSION

The current chapter highlights the complexities, challenges, and opportunities associated with securing the rapidly expanding IoT ecosystem. As IoT devices become deeply integrated into industries, governments, and households worldwide, ensuring their security has evolved into a critical global concern. The chapter underscores how the interconnected nature of IoT amplifies vulnerabilities that transcend geographic borders, requiring unified, collaborative approaches. It emphasizes that no single entity—whether a nation-state, organization, or individual—can address IoT security challenges alone. Instead, a combination of technological innovation, robust policy frameworks, global cooperation, and heightened user awareness is essential. Regulatory efforts, such as the development of international standards and compliance frameworks, demonstrate the increasing recognition of IoT security as a global priority. These efforts are complemented by advancements in technology, including blockchain, artificial intelligence, machine learning, and quantum-resistant cryptography, which provide robust tools for mitigating risks and enhancing the resilience of IoT systems. The chapter also highlights the role of collaborative platforms, PPPs, and cross-border initiatives in fostering the exchange of threat intelligence and best practices. Furthermore, it stresses the importance of ethical considerations, as the misuse of IoT data or unchecked surveillance can undermine trust in IoT technologies. While the chapter acknowledges the challenges posed by the diversity and complexity of IoT devices, it also offers hope by showcasing success stories where multistakeholder efforts have led to substantial progress in securing IoT environments. Looking ahead, the chapter concludes that a sustainable and secure IoT future requires continuous adaptation, innovation, and vigilance. Governments, manufacturers, developers, and users must work collectively to address evolving threats while ensuring that IoT technologies remain a force for progress and connectivity. By fostering global cooperation and prioritizing security from the design phase to implementation, the world can build an IoT ecosystem that upholds privacy, security, and trust across all sectors.

Chapter 9

Future trends in IoT botnets and security

9.1 EMERGING THREATS IN IoT ECOSYSTEMS

Emerging threats in IoT ecosystems represent a growing concern as the IoT continues to expand, connecting billions of devices across industries, homes, cities, and critical infrastructures. The interconnected nature of IoT creates a fertile ground for new and sophisticated cyberthreats, magnifying the attack surface and exposing vulnerabilities that malicious actors are quick to exploit. Among the most pressing threats is the rise of IoT botnets, where compromised devices are harnessed to launch DDoS attacks, crippling networks and disrupting essential services. These botnets leverage the often-weak security measures in IoT devices, such as default passwords and outdated firmware, to proliferate rapidly and operate undetected. Furthermore, ransomware attacks have evolved to target IoT devices, holding essential systems such as smart homes, healthcare equipment, or industrial controls hostage, with potentially life-threatening consequences. The integration of IoT into critical infrastructure, such as energy grids, transportation systems, and water supplies, has also introduced risks of nation-state-sponsored cyberattacks aimed at causing widespread disruption or espionage.

Another significant emerging threat is data privacy breaches, as IoT devices collect vast amounts of sensitive information, including health data, location, and behavioral patterns. Inadequate encryption, insecure data storage, or vulnerabilities in cloud services can lead to massive data leaks or unauthorized access, fueling identity theft, financial fraud, or corporate espionage. Moreover, advancements in AI have enabled attackers to conduct more precise and automated attacks on IoT ecosystems. AI-driven malware can learn and adapt to bypass traditional security measures, while adversarial AI attacks can manipulate IoT systems such as autonomous vehicles or industrial robots, causing physical harm or operational failure. The proliferation of edge computing in IoT ecosystems has also introduced new risks, as attackers target edge devices to compromise local networks, inject malicious code, or disrupt real-time analytics.

 DOI: 10.1201/9781003631460-9

Supply chain vulnerabilities further exacerbate the threat landscape, as many IoT devices rely on components or software sourced from third-party vendors. Compromised supply chains can result in the distribution of devices with pre-installed malware or backdoors, providing attackers with a direct entry point into networks. The advent of 5G networks, while enhancing IoT connectivity, also brings its own set of challenges, including increased attack vectors due to the sheer volume of connected devices and the complexity of managing secure communication channels. In addition, the lack of standardized security protocols across IoT ecosystems leaves devices from different manufacturers prone to interoperability vulnerabilities, which attackers can exploit to infiltrate multidevice environments.

Physical security threats are also a growing concern, as IoT devices often reside in unprotected or publicly accessible areas, making them susceptible to tampering, theft, or physical attacks that can compromise their functionality or integrity. Side-channel attacks, where attackers exploit physical signals like electromagnetic emissions or power consumption patterns, represent another emerging risk for IoT systems, particularly in industrial or military applications. Furthermore, the rise of deepfake technology poses unique threats to IoT ecosystems, as attackers can manipulate audio-visual inputs to deceive surveillance systems, voice assistants, or biometric authentication mechanisms.

The growing reliance on IoT in healthcare, through devices such as smart implants, remote monitoring tools, or connected medical equipment, introduces risks that directly impact patient safety. Cyberattacks on these systems can lead to altered diagnoses, tampered medication dosages, or even life-threatening device malfunctions. Similarly, the adoption of IoT in smart cities, including connected traffic systems, energy grids, or public safety networks, creates vulnerabilities that could result in widespread disruption or public safety hazards if exploited. Emerging threats in IoT ecosystems also include the exploitation of IoT APIs (Application Programming Interfaces), which often lack robust security measures, enabling attackers to hijack communications, manipulate data, or execute malicious commands. The convergence of IoT with blockchain technology, while promising enhanced security, has also introduced new attack surfaces, as vulnerabilities in smart contracts or blockchain networks can undermine trust and integrity in IoT applications. Furthermore, the increasing use of IoT devices in industrial environments has given rise to threats targeting Operational Technology (OT), where cyberattacks can disrupt manufacturing processes, cause equipment damage, or compromise worker safety.

Social engineering attacks have also evolved to exploit IoT vulnerabilities, where attackers manipulate users into granting unauthorized access to devices or networks. Phishing campaigns targeting IoT device credentials, QR code scams for connected devices, or deceptive firmware update notifications are becoming more prevalent. The integration of IoT with augmented and virtual reality (AR/VR) systems adds another layer of risk, as attackers can exploit AR/VR devices to manipulate perceptions, steal sensitive data, or launch denial-of-service attacks in immersive environments. The environmental implications of IoT security breaches are an emerging area of concern, particularly in the context of smart agriculture, where compromised IoT systems could disrupt food production, irrigation systems, or pest control mechanisms, potentially leading to economic and ecological consequences. In addition, geopolitical tensions have increased the risk of IoT devices being weaponized for cyberwarfare, where nation-state actors exploit IoT vulnerabilities to target adversaries' critical infrastructures, disrupt communication networks, or conduct espionage campaigns.

Addressing these emerging threats requires a multifaceted approach that combines technological advancements, regulatory measures, and user awareness. Strengthening device authentication, implementing robust encryption, and adopting secure-by-design principles are crucial to mitigating risks. Governments and industry stakeholders must collaborate to establish and enforce international IoT security standards, while manufacturers should prioritize transparency and accountability in their supply chains. The adoption of AI-driven threat detection systems, real-time network monitoring, and behavioral analysis can enhance the ability to identify and respond to emerging threats proactively. Additionally, educating users on the importance of secure configurations, regular updates, and cautious interaction with IoT devices is vital to reducing human-related vulnerabilities.

The rapidly evolving IoT ecosystem is accompanied by a parallel evolution of threats that challenge traditional security paradigms. From IoT botnets and ransomware to AI-driven malware and supply chain vulnerabilities, the threat landscape continues to expand in complexity and scale. As IoT becomes increasingly integral to daily life and critical systems, addressing these threats requires a global, collaborative effort that encompasses technological innovation, regulatory oversight, and user education. Only through a comprehensive and proactive approach can the potential of IoT be harnessed safely and securely, ensuring its benefits outweigh the risks.

9.2 THE ROLE OF AI AND MACHINE LEARNING IN FUTURE BOTNETS

The role of AI and ML in the evolution of botnets represents a transformative shift in the landscape of cybersecurity threats. Botnets, traditional networks of compromised devices under the control of malicious actors, have relied on relatively static and predictable methods of operation. However, the integration of AI and ML is set to redefine the capabilities of these networks, making them more adaptive, efficient, stealthy, and dangerous than ever before. By leveraging AI and ML, future botnets will exhibit enhanced automation, decision-making, and resilience, significantly amplifying their potential impact on systems, organizations, and individuals. This discussion explores the profound implications of AI and ML in the development, operation, and mitigation of future botnets.

Enhanced Automation and Self-Learning: AI and ML provide botnets with the ability to automate tasks that previously required manual intervention by attackers. For instance, AI-driven botnets can autonomously identify and exploit vulnerabilities in target systems, significantly reducing the time required for reconnaissance and attack. Machine learning algorithms can analyze vast datasets, such as network traffic patterns, device configurations, and system logs, to identify weak points in real time. This enables botnets to adapt their strategies dynamically, choosing the most effective methods of infiltration and propagation based on current conditions. Self-learning capabilities further enhance botnet operations. ML models trained on historical attack data can predict the success of specific attack vectors, enabling botnets to optimize their efforts. Over time, these models refine their accuracy, making botnets increasingly effective at evading detection and compromising targets. For example, an AI-driven botnet could monitor the response of a network's IDS and modify its behavior to bypass the system's defenses.

Stealth and Evasion Techniques: AI and ML are particularly effective in enhancing the stealth capabilities of botnets. Traditional botnets often rely on predictable patterns of communication and behavior, which make them susceptible to detection by security systems. In contrast, AI-driven botnets can use ML algorithms to analyze the detection mechanisms employed by security tools and adapt their behavior to avoid triggering alerts. For example, they can mimic legitimate network traffic patterns, making it difficult for network administrators to distinguish malicious activity from normal operations. One notable advancement is the use of AI in generating polymorphic malware. Polymorphic malware changes its code structure with each iteration, rendering traditional signature-based detection methods ineffective. By integrating AI, botnets can create highly sophisticated polymorphic malware that adapts in real time, evading even the most advanced detection systems. Additionally, botnets can leverage adversarial ML techniques to attack AI-based security tools directly. This involves generating adversarial inputs designed to fool ML models into misclassifying malicious activity as benign, further complicating detection efforts.

Intelligent C&C: The C&C infrastructure of botnets is critical for coordinating the activities of compromised devices. AI and ML enhance the efficiency and resilience of C&C systems by enabling decentralized and adaptive communication. For instance, botnets can use AI-driven algorithms to establish P2P communication networks that are resilient to takedown attempts. These networks can dynamically reconfigure themselves to maintain connectivity even if a significant portion of the botnet is disrupted. Moreover, AI enables the implementation of stealthy communication techniques, such as steganography, where malicious commands are hidden within innocuous data transmissions. ML models can analyze the network environment and select the most inconspicuous channels for communication, reducing the likelihood of detection. Additionally, AI can optimize the timing and frequency of communication, ensuring that C&C traffic blends seamlessly with legitimate network activity.

Advanced Attack Strategies: AI and ML empower botnets to execute more sophisticated and targeted attacks. For example, AI-driven botnets can use ML algorithms to analyze social engineering opportunities, crafting highly personalized phishing campaigns that are far more convincing than traditional methods. By mining social media profiles, emails, and other data sources, these botnets can tailor their messages to exploit individual vulnerabilities, increasing the likelihood of success. In DDoS attacks, AI can optimize the distribution of attack traffic across multiple devices and network routes, maximizing the impact while minimizing the likelihood of detection. ML models can identify the most critical components of a target's infrastructure and focus the attack on those points, causing maximum disruption with minimal effort. Furthermore, AI-driven botnets can use real-time analytics to adjust their attack strategies based on the target's response, making them highly adaptive and effective.

Resilience and Survivability: One of the most significant challenges for botnet operators is maintaining the longevity and effectiveness of their networks in the face of active defense measures. AI and ML enhance the resilience of botnets by enabling them to detect and respond to attempts at mitigation. For instance, AI-driven botnets can monitor the status of their infected devices and redistribute tasks as needed to compensate for losses. They can also use ML algorithms to identify and exploit new vulnerabilities, ensuring a constant supply of new recruits to the botnet. Decentralized architectures, supported by AI, further enhance botnet survivability. By distributing control functions across multiple nodes, AI-driven botnets can continue operating even if key components are neutralized. Additionally, AI can facilitate the development of "smart" botnets that can self-heal by identifying and removing compromised or underperforming nodes from the network.

Challenges in Combating AI-Driven Botnets: The integration of AI and ML into botnets presents significant challenges for cybersecurity professionals. Traditional detection and mitigation strategies are often ill-equipped to handle the dynamic and adaptive nature of AI-driven threats. For example, signature-based detection methods are ineffective against polymorphic malware, while rule-based systems struggle to keep up with the rapid evolution of attack patterns. To combat AI-driven botnets, defenders must adopt equally advanced techniques. AI-powered threat detection systems can analyze network traffic, device behavior, and other indicators to identify anomalies that may indicate the presence of a botnet. Behavioral analysis, supported by ML, can detect subtle deviations from normal activity that traditional methods might overlook. Additionally, collaborative efforts between organizations, governments, and industry stakeholders are essential to share intelligence and develop standardized defenses against AI-driven threats. The increasing availability of AI tools and frameworks lowers the barrier to entry for attackers, enabling even less-experienced cybercriminals to create sophisticated botnets. Furthermore, the convergence of AI with other emerging technologies, such as 5G and edge computing, will create new opportunities for botnet operators to exploit. While AI-driven botnets pose a significant threat, they also highlight the importance of innovation in cybersecurity. By staying ahead of the curve and adopting proactive defense measures, organizations can mitigate the risks posed by these advanced threats and protect their networks, systems, and users.

AI and ML are poised to revolutionize the capabilities of botnets, transforming them into highly adaptive, intelligent, and resilient networks capable of executing sophisticated attacks. From enhanced automation and stealth to advanced attack strategies and resilience, the integration of AI and ML will significantly amplify the impact of botnets on the global cybersecurity landscape. Addressing this emerging threat requires a concerted effort from cybersecurity professionals, organizations, and policymakers to develop innovative detection and mitigation strategies, invest in AI-driven defense systems, and promote collaboration and information sharing. As the role of AI in botnet development continues to evolve, the stakes for cybersecurity will rise, making it imperative to stay vigilant and proactive in the fight against these advanced threats.

9.3 PREDICTING AND PREPARING FOR THE NEXT WAVE OF ATTACKS

Predicting and preparing for the next wave of cyberattacks, especially in the context of evolving threats such as IoT botnets and AI-driven malware, requires a strategic approach that combines advanced technology, proactive risk management, and collaboration among stakeholders. The rapid evolution of cyberthreats, driven by advances in technology, global connectivity, and increased reliance on IoT devices, demands forward-thinking strategies that address both current and emerging risks. This discussion outlines the importance of prediction in cybersecurity, methods to anticipate new attack vectors, and actionable steps to prepare for and mitigate the impact of future attacks. The cybersecurity landscape is continuously shifting, with attackers adopting more sophisticated techniques to exploit vulnerabilities. Traditional reactive approaches are no longer sufficient to address the dynamic and adaptive nature of modern threats. Predicting attacks before they occur allows organizations to build stronger defenses, mitigate risks, and reduce downtime or financial loss. By analyzing past trends and leveraging predictive technologies such as AI and ML, security teams can anticipate new attack methods and understand attackers' potential motivations and targets. For example, with the proliferation of IoT devices, there has been a significant rise in IoT botnets that exploit weak authentication, outdated firmware, and insufficient encryption. Predicting the evolution of such threats involves identifying patterns in device vulnerabilities, understanding advancements in attack methods like C&C infrastructures, and recognizing societal or technological changes that could increase attack opportunities.

By processing vast amounts of data, AI and ML can identify patterns and anomalies that indicate potential threats. ML algorithms can analyze network traffic, user behavior, and system logs to detect deviations from normal activity, signaling an impending attack. For example, early detection of unusual login attempts or high-volume traffic targeting a specific port can indicate an impending DDoS attack. Predictive models can also simulate potential attack scenarios. By feeding these models with data from previous attacks, security teams can determine the likelihood of similar attacks occurring in the future and prioritize defenses accordingly. For instance, a predictive model might identify that ransomware attacks tend to target healthcare organizations during crises, allowing these entities to strengthen their defenses during vulnerable periods.

Threat Intelligence and Attack Forecasting: Threat intelligence is a cornerstone of predicting and preparing for future attacks. It involves collecting, analyzing, and sharing information about potential threats, including attackers' methods, tools, and motivations. Threat intelligence feeds, powered by global data collection and AI analysis, help organizations identify emerging trends and weak points in their infrastructure. For instance, if intelligence reports indicate a rise in phishing campaigns targeting financial institutions, those organizations can proactively train employees, implement stronger email filters, and introduce two-factor authentication to mitigate the risk. Similarly, monitoring hacker forums and the dark web can provide insights into planned attacks or newly developed malware, enabling organizations to prepare in advance. To predict and prepare for the next wave of attacks, organizations must understand the evolving threat landscape. Attackers are increasingly integrating AI into malware to enhance its capabilities. AI-driven malware can adapt in real time, evade detection systems, and identify high-value targets more effectively. The number of IoT devices is projected to continue growing, providing attackers with a vast pool of vulnerable endpoints. IoT botnets can be used for large-scale DDoS attacks, data theft, and infrastructure disruption. Ransomware attacks are becoming more targeted and sophisticated, with attackers employing double extortion tactics that not only encrypt data but also threaten to release it publicly.

Preparing for the Next Wave of Attacks: Preparation is key to mitigating the impact of future cyberattacks. Organizations must adopt a multifaceted approach that includes technological, procedural, and cultural changes.

Strengthening Infrastructure and Networks:

- Implement advanced firewalls, intrusion detection systems (IDS), and endpoint protection tools to monitor and block malicious activity.
- Use network segmentation to isolate critical systems from less-secure environments, limiting the spread of malware.

- Ensure IoT devices are deployed with proper security configurations, such as strong passwords, firmware updates, and secure boot mechanisms.

Improving Software Development Practices:

- Adopt Secure Software Development Life Cycle (SDLC) practices to minimize vulnerabilities in software and firmware.
- Conduct regular vulnerability assessments and penetration testing to identify and fix security gaps.
- Ensure that third-party software and libraries are thoroughly vetted for security before integration.

Enhancing Employee Awareness:

- Conduct regular training sessions to educate employees about phishing, social engineering, and other common attack methods.
- Encourage a culture of cybersecurity awareness, where employees feel empowered to report suspicious activity without fear of repercussions.
- Implement access controls and enforce the principle of least privilege to minimize the impact of compromised accounts.

Developing Incident Response Plans:

- Establish a clear incident response plan that outlines roles, responsibilities, and procedures for handling security breaches.
- Conduct regular tabletop exercises and simulations to ensure teams are prepared to respond effectively to various attack scenarios.
- Maintain backups of critical data and test recovery procedures to ensure business continuity in the event of a ransomware attack.

Leveraging Threat Intelligence:

- Subscribe to threat intelligence feeds to stay informed about emerging threats and vulnerabilities.
- Collaborate with industry peers, government agencies, and cybersecurity organizations to share intelligence and best practices.
- Use threat intelligence platforms to automate the analysis and prioritization of threats.

Investing in Advanced Technologies:

- Deploy AI-powered security tools to detect and respond to threats in real time.
- Use blockchain technology to secure supply chains, verify data integrity, and protect sensitive information.

- Explore quantum-resistant encryption algorithms for future-proof data protection.

Implementing Regulatory Compliance:

- Adhere to industry standards and regulations, such as GDPR, HIPAA, and ISO 27001, to ensure robust security practices.
- Conduct regular audits to verify compliance and identify areas for improvement.

9.4 INNOVATIONS IN DETECTION AND PREVENTION TECHNOLOGIES

In today's rapidly evolving cybersecurity landscape, the need for innovative detection and prevention technologies has never been more critical. With the proliferation of sophisticated threats, including IoT botnets, ransomware, and AI-driven malware, traditional methods of securing networks and systems are no longer adequate. To counter these emerging threats, the cybersecurity industry has embraced new technologies and approaches that leverage AI, ML, blockchain, behavioral analysis, and more. These innovations aim to enhance the speed, accuracy, and effectiveness of threat detection and prevention while reducing false positives and enabling more proactive responses to attacks.

AI and Machine Learning for Cybersecurity: AI and ML are transforming the cybersecurity landscape by enhancing the ability to detect, prevent, and respond to threats with greater speed and precision. These technologies empower organizations to address the growing volume and complexity of cyberattacks by analyzing massive datasets, identifying patterns, and adapting to evolving threats in real time. AI and ML excel in threat detection by automating the analysis of network traffic, system logs, and user behavior to identify anomalies that may indicate malicious activity. Traditional methods, such as signature-based detection, struggle to keep pace with advanced threats such as zero-day exploits, polymorphic malware, and sophisticated phishing schemes. However, AI and ML models can recognize subtle deviations and emerging attack vectors, even those previously unseen, by learning from historical and real-time data. Behavioral analysis is a cornerstone of AI-driven cybersecurity. By establishing baselines for normal user and device activity, ML algorithms can detect irregularities, such as unusual login locations, abnormal file access patterns, or spikes in network usage. These insights enable organizations to act swiftly to mitigate risks, preventing attackers from gaining a foothold. AI-powered tools are also effective in identifying insider threats, a growing concern as employees or contractors with legitimate access may misuse it intentionally or accidentally.

Another critical application of AI and ML is automated threat hunting. These technologies sift through vast amounts of data to uncover hidden threats that human analysts might overlook. By automating repetitive tasks, AI frees up cybersecurity professionals to focus on strategic decision-making and incident response. AI also enhances endpoint protection by identifying and mitigating malware, ransomware, and other threats targeting devices such as laptops, servers, and IoT devices. Machine learning models can detect suspicious file behaviors, block malicious processes, and quarantine compromised endpoints to prevent the spread of infections. AI-driven systems are instrumental in detecting and responding to phishing attacks, which often rely on human error. By analyzing email content, sender reputation, and user interaction patterns, AI can flag potential phishing attempts and protect users from fraudulent links or malicious attachments. In addition to detection, AI plays a significant role in incident response. Automated playbooks powered by AI can execute predefined actions, such as isolating affected systems, blocking IP addresses, or resetting compromised accounts, reducing the time it takes to contain threats. AI-driven analytics also support forensic investigations by providing detailed insights into attack timelines, entry points, and methods used by attackers. Machine learning models can predict future attack scenarios by analyzing historical data and threat intelligence, enabling organizations to proactively strengthen their defenses. One of the most promising applications of AI is its ability to counteract adversarial AI—cyberattacks that leverage AI to evade detection or craft highly targeted attacks. AI-based defenses adapt to these challenges by continuously updating algorithms to counteract attackers' evolving tactics. However, implementing AI and ML in cybersecurity is not without challenges. Models require large datasets for training, which must be free from bias and representative of diverse threat scenarios. Additionally, adversaries may attempt to manipulate ML models by introducing false data, known as poisoning attacks.

To mitigate such risks, organizations must adopt robust model validation, monitoring, and updating practices. The integration of AI and ML into cybersecurity also requires skilled professionals who can interpret AI-driven insights, refine algorithms, and address ethical concerns. Transparency in AI decision-making is crucial to building trust, as organizations need to understand how and why AI flags certain activities as threats. Collaboration between organizations, governments, and academia is vital for advancing AI-driven cybersecurity. Sharing threat intelligence and research findings accelerates the development of more effective defenses. AI and ML are already proving invaluable in addressing IoT security challenges, where the sheer number and diversity of devices create significant vulnerabilities. AI-powered systems can monitor IoT ecosystems, detect compromised devices, and enforce security policies to ensure resilience. Looking ahead, AI and ML will continue to evolve, incorporating technologies such as quantum computing and federated learning to tackle increasingly complex threats. Their role in cybersecurity is indispensable, providing organizations with the tools to stay ahead of adversaries, secure their networks, and protect sensitive data in an era of ever-growing digital threats. AI and ML have revolutionized threat detection by providing systems with the ability to learn from data and adapt to new threats. These technologies analyze vast amounts of data in real time, identifying patterns and anomalies that could indicate malicious activity.

- Behavioral Analytics: AI-powered systems monitor user behavior and detect deviations from established norms. For example, if an employee's account suddenly initiates a large data transfer at an unusual time, the system can flag this as suspicious.
- Automated Threat Hunting: Machine learning models sift through network logs, system activity, and metadata to identify threats that might otherwise go unnoticed by traditional security tools.
- Adaptive Defenses: ML algorithms evolve with the threat landscape, learning from each attempted breach to strengthen defenses against similar attacks in the future.

Behavioral-Based Threat Detection: This threat detection is a modern approach to identifying and mitigating cyberthreats by analyzing the behavior of users, systems, and devices in real time. Unlike traditional signature-based methods, which rely on predefined patterns or known threat signatures, behavioral detection focuses on spotting deviations from established norms to uncover malicious activities, even if the specific threat is previously unknown. This technique utilized ML, AI, and advanced analytics to create baselines for normal behavior within a network, application, or endpoint. By monitoring patterns such as login attempts, file access, system processes, and network traffic, it identifies irregularities that could signal potential threats, such as unauthorized access, malware infections, insider threats, or lateral movement by attackers. For example, a sudden spike in file downloads, unexpected data exfiltration, or login attempts from unusual geographic locations might trigger alerts for further investigation. One of the primary strengths of behavioral-based detection is its ability to combat APTs, zero-day exploits, and polymorphic malware—threats that are not easily detectable by traditional systems. APTs, for instance, often rely on subtle and stealthy tactics, avoiding immediate detection by acting within legitimate workflows.

Behavioral analysis detects these by flagging unusual patterns or activity anomalies over time, such as a user's account being used to access data outside of their job function. Additionally, behavioral-based systems are particularly effective against insider threats, which pose significant risks because they originate from individuals with legitimate access. By monitoring atypical behaviors, such as accessing sensitive files during unusual hours or transferring data to external devices, these systems can identify and mitigate potential security breaches early. Another advantage of behavioral-based detection is its adaptability. As attackers continuously evolve their techniques to bypass traditional defenses, behavioral systems dynamically adjust to detect new forms of attack. Machine learning models learn and refine their understanding of "normal" behaviors over time, ensuring resilience against emerging threats. For IoT environments, where devices often lack robust security features, behavioral analysis is indispensable. It helps monitor devices for unexpected communication patterns, unusual commands, or unauthorized firmware updates, ensuring the integrity and security of connected systems. Despite its strengths, behavioral-based detection is not without challenges. One of the most significant issues is the potential for false positives. Since the system flags deviations from normal behavior, legitimate but uncommon activities—such as an employee working unusual hours during a deadline—may trigger alerts, leading to "alert fatigue" among cybersecurity teams.

To mitigate this, behavioral detection systems require fine-tuning and contextual awareness, ensuring that they distinguish between benign anomalies and actual threats. Privacy concerns also arise, as behavioral-based systems often rely on extensive monitoring of user activities, raising questions about data collection, storage, and compliance with privacy regulations like GDPR. Organizations must strike a balance between effective threat detection and respecting user privacy by implementing strong governance, encryption, and anonymization practices. Another consideration is the computational demand of behavioral-based systems. Real-time monitoring and analysis of massive data volumes require significant processing power and robust infrastructure. To address this, many organizations employ cloud-based solutions or hybrid models to balance scalability and performance. Integrating behavioral detection with other security layers, such as endpoint protection, network traffic analysis, and threat intelligence, creates a holistic cybersecurity framework. By correlating insights across multiple sources, organizations can enhance accuracy, reduce false positives, and streamline incident response. For example, a behavioral-based system might detect unusual login attempts, while threat intelligence correlates them with known indicators of compromise (IOCs) to confirm the threat's validity. Automation and orchestration further enhance the effectiveness of behavioral-based detection.

AI-powered playbooks can execute predefined responses to detected threats, such as isolating affected systems, blocking IP addresses, or escalating alerts to security analysts. This reduces response times and minimizes the potential damage caused by attacks. Behavioral-based detection is increasingly critical in sectors like finance, healthcare, and government, where the stakes for data breaches are high. For instance, in the financial sector, monitoring for unusual transaction patterns helps detect and prevent fraud. In healthcare, it ensures the security of patient records and medical devices, while in government, it protects sensitive data and critical infrastructure from nation-state actors. Looking ahead, behavioral-based threat detection will continue to evolve alongside advancements in AI and ML. Future systems may incorporate federated learning to enhance collaboration across organizations without compromising data privacy, as well as quantum computing to analyze data at unprecedented speeds. Behavioral-based detection will also play a pivotal role in securing emerging technologies, such as 5G networks, autonomous vehicles, and smart cities. As cyberthreats become increasingly sophisticated, behavioral-based threat detection offers a proactive and dynamic defense mechanism, enabling organizations to identify and respond to threats before they escalate. By combining advanced analytics, machine learning, and contextual awareness, this approach provides a robust layer of security in an ever-changing threat landscape. Behavioral analysis goes beyond static rules and signatures by focusing on the actions and behaviors of users, applications, and devices. By establishing a baseline of normal activity, behavioral detection systems can identify anomalies that indicate potential security incidents.

- Insider Threat Detection: Behavioral tools can detect unusual actions by employees or contractors, such as unauthorized access to sensitive files.
- Device Anomaly Detection: In IoT ecosystems, behavioral analytics monitor device communication patterns and flag deviations, such as a thermostat suddenly attempting to access the corporate database.
- Attack Chain Disruption: By identifying early-stage behaviors in an attack, such as reconnaissance or privilege escalation, behavioral detection can disrupt the attack before significant damage occurs.

Endpoint Detection and Response (EDR): It is a comprehensive cybersecurity solution designed to provide continuous monitoring, detection, and response capabilities at the endpoint level, such as computers, servers, mobile devices, and IoT devices. As cyberthreats evolve in sophistication, endpoints have become prime targets for attackers, making EDR a critical component of modern security frameworks. Unlike traditional antivirus software, which primarily relies on signature-based detection, EDR solutions incorporate advanced behavioral analysis, threat intelligence, and machine learning to identify known and unknown threats. The key advantage of EDR lies in its ability to provide real-time visibility into endpoint activities, allowing organizations to detect suspicious behaviors, investigate potential threats, and respond quickly to mitigate damage. This approach is vital in combating APTs, fileless malware, ransomware, and zero-day exploits, which often bypass conventional security defenses.

One of the core functions of EDR is endpoint telemetry, which involves the continuous collection of data from endpoints, including file execution, network connections, process behaviors, and user actions. This data is analyzed in real time using AI and ML algorithms to establish baselines of normal activity and identify deviations that could indicate malicious activity.

For instance, an EDR system may flag an unexpected process attempting to access sensitive files or a device communicating with a known malicious IP address. This granular visibility enables security teams to detect subtle threats that may go unnoticed by traditional methods. In addition to detection, EDR solutions provide robust response capabilities, such as isolating compromised endpoints, terminating malicious processes, quarantining infected files, and rolling back systems to a pre-attack state. These features enable organizations to contain threats swiftly and reduce the risk of lateral movement within the network, where attackers attempt to escalate privileges or exfiltrate sensitive data. Another significant feature of EDR is its ability to provide detailed forensic data for threat investigation and analysis. By maintaining historical records of endpoint activity, EDR platforms enable security teams to trace the timeline of an attack, identify its origin, and understand its impact. This forensic capability is invaluable for incident response, helping organizations develop targeted remediation strategies and prevent future attacks. EDR also integrates with Security Information and Event Management (SIEM) systems and other threat intelligence platforms to enhance detection accuracy and streamline incident response workflows. For example, threat intelligence feeds can provide indicators of compromise (IOCs) to an EDR platform, enabling it to identify threats more efficiently and correlate them with global attack trends.

In addition to addressing external threats, EDR is instrumental in combating insider threats, where employees or contractors misuse their access privileges to harm an organization. By monitoring endpoint activities, EDR can detect unusual patterns, such as an employee accessing unauthorized data or transferring files to external devices, and alert security teams to act. This capability is particularly crucial in industries with high regulatory compliance requirements, such as finance, healthcare, and government. Despite its benefits, implementing EDR poses several challenges. One of the primary issues is managing the volume of data generated by endpoint telemetry, which can overwhelm security teams with alerts and lead to "alert fatigue." To address this, organizations must configure EDR solutions to prioritize high-risk threats and reduce false positives through fine-tuned algorithms and contextual analysis. Scalability is another concern, especially for organizations with many endpoints distributed across various geographies. Cloud-based EDR solutions offer a scalable alternative, enabling centralized management and analysis without the need for extensive on-premise infrastructure. Privacy is another critical consideration, as EDR involves extensive monitoring of endpoint activities. Organizations must ensure compliance with data protection regulations, such as GDPR and HIPAA, by implementing measures such as data anonymization, encryption, and role-based access controls to safeguard sensitive information. Effective EDR implementation requires a combination of advanced technology and skilled personnel. Organizations must invest in training security teams to interpret EDR insights, conduct thorough investigations, and respond effectively to incidents. Automation can also play a significant role in enhancing the efficiency of EDR solutions, enabling rapid threat mitigation without human intervention. Future solutions may incorporate predictive analytics to anticipate potential threats before they manifest, as well as extended detection and response (XDR) platforms that integrate EDR with other security layers, such as network, cloud, and email security. The rise of IoT devices and remote work has expanded the attack surface, making EDR even more critical in securing diverse and dynamic environments. As organizations adopt hybrid and multicloud infrastructures, EDR solutions will need to adapt to protect endpoints across distributed architectures effectively. Endpoint Detection and Response solutions have become a cornerstone of modern cybersecurity. These tools continuously monitor endpoints such as computers, servers, and IoT devices for suspicious activity.

- Real-Time Monitoring: EDR tools track processes, file changes, and registry modifications in real time, enabling rapid detection of malware.
- Forensic Capabilities: When an incident occurs, EDR tools provide detailed insights into the timeline and scope of the attack, aiding in response and mitigation efforts.
- Automated Responses: Many EDR solutions incorporate automation to isolate compromised endpoints, block malicious processes, and notify security teams.

Deception Technology: It is a proactive cybersecurity approach designed to detect, divert, and neutralize cyberthreats by creating a virtual minefield of fake assets, traps, and decoys that mimic legitimate IT infrastructure. Unlike traditional defense mechanisms that focus solely on detection and blocking, deception technology adopts an offensive approach by actively engaging attackers and leading them into controlled environments where their activities can be monitored and neutralized. This innovative strategy leverages decoy systems, such as fake servers, databases, endpoints, applications, and credentials, strategically deployed across the network to appear as attractive targets to cyber adversaries. Once an attacker interacts with these deceptive elements, security teams are alerted to the presence of malicious activity, allowing for real-time threat detection and analysis. By relying on behavioral triggers rather than signatures or known attack patterns, deception technology is particularly effective against zero-day attacks, APTs, and insider threats. A key advantage of deception technology is its ability to reduce false positives, a common challenge in traditional security solutions. Since decoy systems are not accessed or used by legitimate users, any interaction with these traps is inherently suspicious, thereby reducing noise in alerts and enabling security teams to focus on genuine threats. Furthermore, deception technology enhances threat intelligence by capturing valuable information about an attacker's tactics, techniques, and procedures (TTPs) within the controlled decoy environment. This information can be used to strengthen existing security measures, improve incident response capabilities, and share actionable intelligence with the broader cybersecurity community. For instance, if an attacker deploys malware in a decoy system, security teams can analyze its behavior, signatures, and communication methods without risking the integrity of the real network.

The deployment of deception technology involves strategically placing decoy assets across different layers of the IT infrastructure, including endpoints, networks, applications, and cloud environments. These assets are designed to closely resemble real systems, complete with realistic operating systems, files, credentials, and user behaviors. Advanced deception solutions dynamically adapt to changes in the network, ensuring that decoys remain convincing and integrated into the organization's infrastructure. Some deception platforms use machine learning and artificial intelligence to refine and customize decoys, making them even harder for attackers to distinguish from genuine assets. Additionally, deception systems often include honeytokens—fake data elements like credentials or API keys that, when accessed or exfiltrated, provide immediate alerts to malicious activity.

One of the most significant benefits of deception technology is its ability to neutralize insider threats. Insiders, whether malicious or negligent, often have legitimate access to sensitive systems and data, making them difficult to detect using conventional security methods. Deception technology can identify unauthorized or unusual access patterns when insiders interact with decoy systems or attempt to misuse privileged credentials. Similarly, it helps mitigate the risks posed by compromised accounts, as attackers leveraging stolen credentials are likely to interact with decoy elements while navigating the network. Despite its numerous advantages, deception technology is not without challenges. The successful implementation of deception requires careful planning and customization to align with an organization's unique IT environment and threat landscape. Poorly configured or overly generic decoys may fail to attract attackers or, conversely, may be easily identified as fake, undermining their effectiveness. Furthermore, managing and maintaining a large-scale deception infrastructure can be resource-intensive, particularly in organizations with extensive and complex networks. Security teams must ensure that decoys remain indistinguishable from real systems, requiring ongoing updates and monitoring. Another potential challenge is integrating deception technology with existing security frameworks, such as SIEM, threat intelligence platforms, and EDR solutions, to create a cohesive and streamlined defense strategy.

Deception technology also raises ethical and legal questions, particularly when it involves engaging attackers in controlled environments. Organizations must ensure that their use of deception complies with data protection regulations and does not inadvertently expose sensitive information or violate privacy laws. Clear policies and guidelines are essential to avoid potential legal ramifications. Future solutions will likely become more sophisticated, capable of dynamically generating decoys tailored to specific attackers or attack vectors in real time. Integration with threat intelligence feeds, behavioral analytics, and predictive analytics will further enhance the effectiveness of deception strategies, enabling organizations to anticipate and counteract emerging threats proactively. Additionally, as cloud adoption and IoT ecosystems continue to grow, deception technology will play a critical role in securing distributed and hybrid environments. For instance, IoT-specific decoys can be deployed to lure attackers targeting connected devices, while cloud-based deception can protect virtualized resources and containerized applications. Deception technology uses traps and decoys to lure attackers into revealing themselves. These systems create realistic environments, such as fake servers or databases, that mimic legitimate assets.

- Honeypots and Honeynets: Deceptive assets are placed within the network to attract attackers. Once interacted with, these assets trigger alerts and provide insights into the attacker's methods.
- Lateral Movement Detection: Deception tools identify attackers who are moving laterally within the network, often before they reach their intended target.
- Threat Intelligence Gathering: By engaging with attackers, deception tools can collect information about their TTP.

Zero Trust Architecture: ZTA is a transformative security framework designed to address the evolving threat landscape of modern digital environments by shifting the focus from traditional perimeter-based defenses to a more granular, identity- and context-centric approach. Unlike traditional models that rely on a "trust but verify" principle, Zero Trust operates under the assumption that no user, device, or application should be inherently trusted, regardless of whether it is inside or outside the network perimeter. Instead, ZTA mandates continuous verification of access and strict enforcement of the principle of least privilege, ensuring that only authenticated, authorized, and contextually verified entities can access specific resources. This approach is particularly critical in today's dynamic environments, where organizations increasingly rely on cloud computing, remote work, and the IoT, all of which blur traditional network boundaries and expose systems to a wider range of attack vectors. A core tenet of ZTA is identity-based security, which emphasizes strong authentication mechanisms, such as MFA, to verify user identities before granting access to resources. This is often paired with device security checks to ensure that the requesting device meets organizational security standards, such as being free of malware or having the latest security patches installed. Access decisions are also informed by contextual factors, such as the user's location, device type, time of access, and behavior patterns. For instance, if a user attempts to access a sensitive resource from an unusual location or outside regular working hours, additional verification steps may be required, or access may be denied altogether. This continuous validation process minimizes the risk of unauthorized access, even in cases where credentials or devices are compromised.

Another critical aspect of ZTA is the segmentation of networks and resources to limit the lateral movement of attackers in the event of a breach. Micro-segmentation involves dividing the network into smaller zones, each with its own access controls and security policies, to ensure that even if one segment is compromised, the attacker cannot easily move to other parts of the network. For example, a breach in a low-risk segment, such as a guest Wi-Fi network, would not grant access to high-value resources like financial systems or sensitive customer data. Additionally, Zero Trust enforces fine-grained access control policies at the application and data levels, ensuring that users or devices can access only the resources they are explicitly authorized to use. This minimizes the attack surface and reduces the impact of potential breaches. ZTA also incorporates robust monitoring and analytics capabilities to detect and respond to threats in real time. SIEM systems, coupled with advanced behavioral analytics, continuously monitor user and device activity for signs of anomalies or malicious behavior. For instance, if a user who typically accesses a specific set of applications suddenly attempts to access an unrelated or highly sensitive system, the system can flag the activity for review or automatically block it. Similarly, integration with threat intelligence feeds allows ZTA to dynamically adapt to emerging threats by updating access policies or blocking known malicious IP addresses, domains, or devices. The implementation of ZTA often involves leveraging advanced technologies such as Software-Defined Perimeter (SDP) solutions, which create a "dark" network where resources are invisible to unauthorized users, reducing the likelihood of attacks. Zero Trust Network Access (ZTNA) solutions extend this concept by granting users access only to specific applications or resources based on their roles and contextual factors, rather than providing broad network access. This is particularly beneficial for remote and hybrid work environments, where employees and contractors may need to access resources from various locations and devices. Additionally, ZTA aligns closely with the principles of Secure Access Service Edge (SASE), which integrates security and networking services into a unified, cloud-delivered framework, further enhancing its scalability and applicability in distributed environments.

Transitioning from a traditional security model to Zero Trust requires significant investment in technology, process redesign, and workforce training. Organizations must conduct a thorough inventory of their assets, users, and devices, as well as map out access needs and interdependencies, to establish a baseline for Zero Trust policies. This process can be time-consuming and resource-intensive, particularly for large organizations with complex IT environments. Furthermore, achieving full Zero Trust compliance often necessitates the integration of multiple security tools and platforms, which can be challenging to manage without a centralized orchestration system. Another challenge is ensuring user productivity while maintaining security. Overly strict access controls or frequent verification steps can lead to frustration and hinder business operations. Striking the right balance between security and usability requires careful planning and the use of adaptive access mechanisms that adjust security requirements based on risk levels. For example, low-risk activities, such as accessing non-sensitive resources from a verified corporate device, may require fewer authentication steps than accessing sensitive data from a personal or unfamiliar device. The Zero Trust model operates on the principle of "never trust, always verify." This approach minimizes the attack surface by requiring strict verification for every user, device, and application attempting to access network resources.

- Micro-segmentation: Networks are divided into smaller segments, with access controls applied to each. This limits attackers' ability to move laterally.
- Continuous Authentication: Users and devices are re-verified at regular intervals, reducing the risk of compromised credentials being misused.
- Least Privilege Access: Users and devices are granted only the access they need to perform their roles, minimizing exposure to sensitive data and systems.

Threat Intelligence Platforms: TIPs are critical tools for modern cybersecurity strategies, designed to collect, aggregate, analyze, and disseminate actionable threat intelligence to enhance an organization's security posture. These platforms consolidate threat data from diverse sources, including open-source intelligence (OSINT), commercial feeds, internal telemetry, and community-shared intelligence, to provide a centralized repository of information about potential threats, vulnerabilities, and adversarial tactics. By leveraging automation, machine learning, and advanced analytics, TIPs enable organizations to process vast amounts of threat data in real time, extracting actionable insights that can be used to mitigate risks, improve incident response times, and strengthen defenses against sophisticated cyberthreats. In an era where cyberattacks are growing in scale and complexity, TIPs are indispensable for organizations aiming to stay ahead of evolving threats and enhance their overall resilience. One of the primary functions of a TIP is threat data aggregation. Organizations are inundated with information from multiple sources, including threat feeds, endpoint detection systems, IDS, and SIEM solutions. Manually correlating this information to identify relevant threats is time-consuming and prone to error. TIPs automate this process by ingesting data from various sources, normalizing it into a consistent format, and eliminating redundancies. This ensures that security teams have a unified and coherent view of the threat landscape, reducing the noise from irrelevant or duplicate alerts and enabling them to focus on high-priority risks. For example, a TIP might aggregate data on emerging malware variants from global feeds, correlate it with endpoint logs showing unusual activity, and highlight a potential attack targeting the organization.

Another crucial capability of TIPs is contextualization, which enhances raw threat data by adding information about the threat's relevance and potential impact. Contextualization involves mapping threat indicators— such as IP addresses, domains, file hashes, or email addresses—against known adversary TTP, frameworks like MITRE ATT&CK, or organizational assets. For instance, if a TIP identifies a malicious IP address linked to ransomware activity, it may also provide information about the ransomware family, its attack vectors, and its historical targets. This context allows security teams to prioritize their responses based on the potential severity and relevance of the threat to their specific environment, rather than treating all indicators as equally critical. TIPs also excel in enabling proactive threat hunting and prevention. By leveraging threat intelligence data, organizations can identify vulnerabilities or gaps in their security posture before adversaries exploit them. For instance, if a TIP highlights a surge in exploit activity targeting a particular software vulnerability, the security team can prioritize patching that vulnerability across their infrastructure. Similarly, TIPs support the development of IOC and automated rules for blocking malicious activity, such as blacklisting IPs or domains associated with phishing campaigns. This proactive approach reduces the likelihood of successful attacks and enhances an organization's ability to stay ahead of adversaries. Many platforms facilitate integration with industry-specific Information Sharing and Analysis Centers (ISACs), threat intelligence communities, and peer organizations to share threat data and insights. This collaborative approach enriches the threat intelligence ecosystem by enabling organizations to benefit from the collective knowledge and experiences of others facing similar challenges. For example, a financial institution might use its TIP to share information about a new type of banking trojan with other institutions, helping them prepare for or prevent potential attacks. At the same time, TIPs ensure that shared data is anonymized and managed securely, addressing privacy and compliance concerns. Automation is a defining feature of TIPs, streamlining processes such as threat detection, incident response, and mitigation. Many TIPs integrate with existing security tools, such as firewalls, SIEMs, and EDR solutions, to enable automated enforcement of threat intelligence. For example, if a TIP identifies a malicious domain linked to a phishing campaign, it can automatically update the firewall rules to block traffic to that domain, reducing response times and minimizing human intervention. This capability is particularly valuable in combating fast-moving threats, where delays in detection or response can lead to significant damage.

Moreover, TIPs contribute to strategic decision-making by providing insights into trends, adversarial behavior, and the evolving threat landscape. Through dashboards, reports, and analytics, TIPs help security leaders understand the organization's risk exposure and allocate resources more effectively. For example, if a TIP analysis reveals that the organization is frequently targeted by APT using spear-phishing techniques, security investments can be directed toward strengthening email security, employee training, and incident response capabilities. Additionally, TIPs support compliance efforts by documenting threat intelligence activities and providing evidence of due diligence in risk management. Despite their many advantages, implementing and managing a TIP is not without challenges. Organizations must ensure that the TIP is properly integrated with their existing security infrastructure and that staff are trained to use it effectively. Additionally, the quality of the intelligence ingested by the TIP is critical; low-quality or unverified data can lead to false positives, wasted resources, or missed threats. Therefore, organizations should carefully evaluate the sources of their threat intelligence feeds and consider using TIPs with built-in mechanisms for vetting and scoring the reliability of data. Threat intelligence platforms collect, analyze, and share information about emerging threats. These platforms provide organizations with actionable insights to improve their defenses.

- Real-Time Threat Feeds: Platforms aggregate data from multiple sources, including global security incidents, dark web forums, and malware analysis reports.
- Automated Integration: Threat intelligence is integrated into security tools such as firewalls and IDS to automate threat blocking.
- Collaborative Sharing: Organizations can share threat intelligence with peers and industry groups, strengthening collective defenses.

Secure Access Service Edge (SASE): It is an advanced cybersecurity framework that integrates networking and security services into a unified cloud-native architecture. Introduced as a response to the increasing complexity of modern IT environments, SASE addresses the challenges posed by the rapid adoption of cloud-based services, remote work, and the proliferation of mobile and IoT devices. It merges WAN capabilities with comprehensive security features such as ZTNA, Secure Web Gateway (SWG), Cloud Access Security Broker (CASB), and firewall-as-a-service (FWaaS). This convergence enables organizations to provide secure, efficient, and scalable access to their resources, regardless of where users, applications, or devices are located. Unlike traditional perimeter-based security models, which rely on fixed boundaries, SASE adopts a user-centric approach that extends security to the edge, ensuring consistent protection for a distributed workforce and decentralized infrastructure. The core principle of SASE is its cloud-native architecture, which provides flexibility, scalability, and reduced complexity. By delivering security and networking functions as cloud services, SASE eliminates the need for hardware appliances and reduces the maintenance burden on IT teams. This approach is particularly advantageous for organizations with geographically dispersed teams or hybrid environments, as it ensures consistent security policies across all locations. Additionally, SASE enables dynamic scaling to accommodate fluctuating workloads, making it an ideal solution for businesses undergoing digital transformation. For instance, organizations can seamlessly integrate new branches, remote workers, or cloud applications into their SASE framework without significant reconfiguration or capital expenditure.

A critical component of SASE is ZTNA, which enforces the principle of "never trust, always verify." Unlike traditional VPNs that provide broad access to the network once authenticated, ZTNA ensures that users and devices are granted access only to specific resources based on their identity, role, and context. This granular control reduces the attack surface and prevents lateral movement within the network, even if a user's credentials are compromised. For example, a remote worker accessing a corporate application through a SASE framework would need to undergo continuous authentication and context-based verification, ensuring that the access remains secure throughout the session. Another essential element of SASE is the Secure Web Gateway (SWG), which protects users from web-based threats such as phishing, malware, and malicious URLs. By inspecting and filtering web traffic, SWG enforces corporate policies and blocks access to unsafe content. When integrated into SASE, SWG provides real-time protection for all users, whether they are on-premises or working remotely. Similarly, the Cloud Access Security Broker (CASB) plays a vital role in monitoring and securing cloud application usage. CASB ensures compliance with organizational policies, prevents data leakage, and provides visibility into shadow IT activities, making it an indispensable component of SASE in the cloud-driven era.

Firewall-as-a-Service (FWaaS) is another cornerstone of SASE, delivering next-generation firewall capabilities from the cloud. FWaaS provides advanced threat prevention features such as intrusion detection and prevention (IDS/IPS), URL filtering, and application-level controls. By centralizing firewall functions in the cloud, FWaaS ensures consistent security across all endpoints and simplifies management. This is particularly useful for organizations managing hybrid environments with a mix of on-premises and cloud-based assets, as FWaaS eliminates the complexity of deploying and managing firewalls in multiple locations. SASE also enhances performance through its integration with Software-Defined SD-WAN. SD-WAN optimizes traffic routing based on real-time conditions, ensuring reliable and low-latency connectivity for critical applications. By combining SD-WAN with SASE, organizations can achieve both high-performance networking and robust security in a single solution. For instance, SASE ensures that a remote user accessing a cloud-based application experiences minimal latency while benefiting from comprehensive security policies, such as data encryption and threat detection.

One of the most significant advantages of SASE is its ability to support the modern workforce. With the rise of remote work, employees increasingly access corporate resources from diverse locations and devices. SASE addresses this challenge by providing secure and seamless access, regardless of the user's location. Furthermore, SASE supports device-agnostic security, ensuring that laptops, smartphones, and IoT devices are equally protected. This capability is particularly important in industries such as healthcare, finance, and manufacturing, where sensitive data and critical systems require stringent security measures. SASE also simplifies compliance with regulatory requirements by consolidating security and networking functions into a single framework. Organizations can leverage SASE to implement consistent policies for data protection, user access, and threat management, reducing the complexity of meeting compliance standards such as GDPR, HIPAA, or PCI DSS. Additionally, SASE's centralized logging and reporting features provide detailed visibility into security events and user activities, enabling organizations to demonstrate compliance more effectively. Organizations must carefully plan their migration to SASE to avoid disruptions and ensure compatibility with existing systems. A phased approach is often recommended, starting with the integration of core components such as ZTNA and SWG, followed by the gradual adoption of additional features such as CASB and FWaaS. Additionally, organizations must select a reliable SASE provider that offers robust service-level agreements (SLAs), scalability, and support for global deployments. SASE integrates networking and security functions into a single cloud-delivered service. This approach is ideal for modern organizations with distributed workforces and IoT ecosystems.

- Unified Security Policies: SASE ensures consistent security policies across all users and devices, regardless of location.
- Cloud-Native Scalability: As organizations grow, SASE scales to accommodate new devices and users without compromising performance.
- Improved Threat Detection: By analyzing all traffic through a centralized system, SASE identifies threats more effectively than fragmented solutions.

Blockchain for Cybersecurity: Blockchain technology has emerged as a transformative tool for enhancing cybersecurity in an increasingly interconnected and vulnerable digital ecosystem. At its core, blockchain operates as a decentralized and distributed ledger that records transactions across multiple nodes in a network, ensuring transparency, immutability, and tamper resistance. This unique architecture makes blockchain an ideal solution for addressing many cybersecurity challenges, such as data breaches, identity theft, and unauthorized access. Unlike centralized systems, where a single point of failure can compromise an entire network, blockchain's distributed nature eliminates this vulnerability, significantly reducing the risk of cyberattacks. Each transaction or data entry on a blockchain is encrypted and linked to the previous block through cryptographic hashes, making it nearly impossible to alter data retroactively without the consensus of the entire network. This immutable record-keeping is invaluable for industries such as finance, healthcare, and supply chain management, where data integrity and traceability are critical.

One of the most significant applications of blockchain in cybersecurity is in identity management. Traditional identity systems often rely on centralized databases that are susceptible to breaches, resulting in the exposure of sensitive personal information. Blockchain-based identity systems, on the other hand, provide users with control over their own data through a decentralized model. Users can store their identity credentials securely on the blockchain and share only the necessary information with third parties via cryptographic keys. This minimizes data exposure and enhances privacy, as no single entity has full access to an individual's information. For instance, self-sovereign identity solutions powered by blockchain allow individuals to prove their identity for services such as banking or healthcare without disclosing unnecessary personal details, thus reducing the attack surface for potential breaches. Blockchain also enhances cybersecurity in the realm of secure communication. Traditional communication systems, such as email and messaging platforms, are often vulnerable to interception and unauthorized access. By leveraging blockchain's decentralized nature, organizations can implement secure peer-to-peer communication channels that are resistant to tampering and eavesdropping. Messages or data shared between parties can be encrypted and stored on the blockchain, ensuring that only authorized recipients can access the information. This approach not only enhances confidentiality but also provides an auditable trail of communication, which can be invaluable for legal and compliance purposes.

Cybersecurity threats, such as counterfeit goods and data manipulation, are common in complex global supply chains. Blockchain addresses these issues by creating an immutable record of transactions and movements, enabling real-time tracking and verification of products. For example, in the pharmaceutical industry, blockchain can verify the authenticity of drugs by tracking their journey from manufacturer to consumer, ensuring that counterfeit products are identified and eliminated. Similarly, in cybersecurity contexts, blockchain can provide a secure and transparent method for tracking software updates and patches, ensuring that only verified updates are applied to systems. Another critical area where blockchain is proving its worth is in securing the IoT ecosystem. IoT devices, often characterized by weak security measures and centralized control systems, are a prime target for cyberattacks. Blockchain can enhance IoT security by providing a decentralized framework for device authentication, secure communication, and data integrity. For example, blockchain can establish a tamper-proof record of device identities, ensuring that only legitimate devices are allowed to connect to the network. Furthermore, smart contracts—self-executing programs stored on the blockchain—can automate security protocols, such as device updates and access controls, reducing human error and improving overall system resilience.

Blockchain's potential in combating DDoS attacks is also noteworthy. In traditional networks, DDoS attacks overwhelm a single server or system with a flood of traffic, rendering it unavailable. Blockchain's decentralized structure makes it highly resilient to such attacks, as there is no central point of failure. Additionally, blockchain-based solutions can implement distributed content delivery systems that mitigate the impact of DDoS attacks by distributing traffic across a network of nodes. This ensures that services remain available even during an attack, enhancing reliability and user trust. Despite its numerous advantages, the adoption of blockchain for cybersecurity is not without challenges. Scalability remains a critical concern, as the distributed nature of blockchain can lead to slower transaction speeds and higher energy consumption compared to centralized systems. Moreover, the integration of blockchain into existing infrastructures requires significant investment and technical expertise, which can be a barrier for smaller organizations. Interoperability is another challenge, as different blockchain platforms often use incompatible protocols, limiting their ability to work together seamlessly. Addressing these challenges will require ongoing innovation and collaboration among technology providers, policymakers, and industry stakeholders. Blockchain technology provides a decentralized and tamper-proof method for securing data and communications. Its applications in detection and prevention include:

- IoT Device Authentication: Blockchain can verify the identity of IoT devices, preventing unauthorized devices from joining the network.
- Secure Data Transmission: Blockchain ensures the integrity and confidentiality of data transmitted between devices.
- Attack Traceability: In the event of an attack, blockchain's transparent ledger provides a detailed record of events, aiding forensic investigations.

Advanced Encryption and Secure Communication Protocols: Advanced encryption and secure communication protocols are vital pillars of modern cybersecurity, ensuring the confidentiality, integrity, and authenticity of data in transit and at rest. As cyberthreats evolve in complexity and scale, the use of robust cryptographic techniques and communication frameworks has become essential for safeguarding sensitive information across networks, devices, and applications. Encryption, the process of converting plaintext into ciphertext using algorithms and cryptographic keys, provides a strong defense against unauthorized access. Algorithms such as AES-256 are widely adopted due to their high level of security and efficiency. These symmetric encryption algorithms ensure that data can only be decrypted by entities with the correct key, offering protection for sensitive transactions, emails, and stored information. Complementing symmetric encryption is public-key cryptography (asymmetric encryption), exemplified by algorithms such as RSA and ECC. These methods use a pair of keys—public and private—to enable secure key exchange and digital signatures, ensuring authenticity and non-repudiation in communications. Together, these encryption techniques form the backbone of secure communication protocols, which govern how data is exchanged over networks.

Secure communication protocols, such as TLS and Secure/Multipurpose Internet Mail Extensions (S/MIME), leverage encryption to protect data during transmission. TLS, widely used for securing web traffic and applications, establishes a secure channel between clients and servers by authenticating endpoints and encrypting data exchanges. It uses a combination of symmetric encryption for speed and asymmetric encryption for secure key exchange, ensuring that sensitive information such as login credentials and payment details remain protected from eavesdropping and man-in-the-middle attacks. Similarly, S/MIME secures email communication by encrypting messages and attaching digital signatures to verify sender authenticity, preventing unauthorized access and tampering. Another noteworthy protocol is IPsec (Internet Protocol Security), which secures data at the network layer by encrypting IP packets and authenticating communication sessions. This protocol is instrumental in creating secure VPNs that protect data traveling over public networks. For IoT ecosystems and constrained environments, lightweight encryption algorithms and protocols such as Datagram Transport Layer Security (DTLS) and CoAP are tailored to ensure security without overburdening resource-limited devices. DTLS, an adaptation of TLS for datagram-based communications, provides encryption and integrity for IoT applications that rely on UDP instead of TCP. CoAP, combined with DTLS, secures machine-to-machine communications by encrypting messages and ensuring authenticity through token-based mechanisms. These protocols address the unique challenges of IoT, where energy efficiency and low latency are paramount. Additionally, advanced techniques like quantum-resistant encryption are being developed to address the potential threat of quantum computing, which could break traditional encryption methods. Algorithms such as lattice-based cryptography and hash-based signatures aim to ensure future-proof security for sensitive communications.

Secure communication also involves key management and distribution, which are critical for maintaining encryption effectiveness. Protocols like the Diffie-Hellman key exchange and Kerberos authentication framework facilitate secure sharing of encryption keys between parties, ensuring that keys are not intercepted or compromised. Blockchain technology is also being explored for decentralized key management, offering tamper-resistant storage and distribution of cryptographic keys. Furthermore, advanced cryptographic techniques such as homomorphic encryption and zero-knowledge proofs (ZKPs) are emerging as innovative solutions for secure data sharing and computation. Homomorphic encryption allows computations to be performed on encrypted data without decryption, enabling privacy-preserving analytics in sensitive fields such as healthcare and finance. ZKPs enable one party to prove knowledge of a value to another without revealing the value itself, enhancing security in authentication and blockchain applications. Despite the strength of advanced encryption and secure communication protocols, their implementation requires careful consideration to avoid vulnerabilities. Weak or improperly managed keys, outdated algorithms, and poorly configured protocols can undermine encryption's effectiveness, leaving systems exposed to attacks. Therefore, adopting best practices such as regular updates, strong key management, and adherence to industry standards like FIPS 140-2 and NIST guidelines is crucial. Moreover, ongoing education and awareness are essential to ensure that developers, administrators, and users understand the importance of encryption and its correct application. Encryption remains a fundamental aspect of cybersecurity. Innovations in encryption focus on improving performance and addressing emerging threats.

- Post-quantum Cryptography: Researchers are developing algorithms resistant to quantum computing attacks.
- Homomorphic Encryption: This technology allows computations to be performed on encrypted data, enabling secure data processing.
- Encrypted DNS: Protocols like DNS over HTTPS (DoH) protect users' browsing activity from interception.

9.5 CONCLUSION

The rapid proliferation of the IoT has transformed industries, societies, and economies worldwide, yet it has also introduced unprecedented security challenges that require a global response. As IoT devices continue to grow in number and functionality, the risks associated with data breaches, cyberattacks, and privacy violations become more significant, necessitating a unified approach to security. Governments, regulatory bodies, industries, and cybersecurity professionals must collaborate to establish robust frameworks, enforce compliance, and develop cutting-edge security solutions to mitigate emerging threats. The global nature of IoT security concerns requires coordinated efforts across international borders, as cyberthreats do not adhere to geographic limitations. Nations must work together to create comprehensive policies, share threat intelligence, and establish interoperability standards that ensure the security and integrity of IoT ecosystems. The role of governments and regulatory agencies is crucial in defining and enforcing security standards that protect consumers and businesses while fostering innovation. Initiatives such as the European Union's GDPR, the US Cybersecurity Improvement Act, and global alliances like the IGF highlight the importance of establishing internationally recognized guidelines that promote security and trust in IoT environments. However, while regulations are essential, they must be complemented by industry-driven best practices and technological advancements that proactively address security vulnerabilities.

Industry leaders and IoT manufacturers play a vital role in enhancing security by adopting secure-by-design principles, implementing end-to-end encryption, and ensuring regular firmware updates to patch vulnerabilities.

Standardization efforts, such as the development of security certification programs and compliance frameworks, help create a baseline for securing IoT devices and networks, reducing the risk of exploitation. Additionally, organizations must prioritize cybersecurity awareness and user education to mitigate risks associated with weak passwords, default settings, and unpatched devices. Cyber resilience depends not only on technological solutions but also on human vigilance and informed decision-making. The advancement of AI and ML in cybersecurity is revolutionizing threat detection and response mechanisms. AI-driven security solutions enable real-time monitoring, anomaly detection, and automated incident response, strengthening IoT defense against sophisticated cyberthreats. As adversaries leverage AI for cyberattacks, security professionals must stay ahead by integrating AI-powered security measures that enhance predictive analytics and proactive threat mitigation. Another critical aspect of global IoT security is supply chain security. As IoT devices rely on complex global supply chains, ensuring the integrity of hardware and software components is essential. Governments and industries must implement stringent supply chain security measures, including secure hardware development, tamper-resistant manufacturing, and vendor risk assessments. Blockchain technology also offers promising solutions for enhancing supply chain transparency and data integrity in IoT security. The future of IoT security depends on continuous research, innovation, and collaboration among stakeholders. The emergence of quantum computing poses potential risks to traditional encryption methods, emphasizing the need for quantum-resistant cryptographic solutions. As IoT security evolves, organizations must embrace adaptive security architectures, zero-trust models, and decentralized identity management systems to strengthen defenses against cyberthreats. In conclusion, securing the global IoT ecosystem requires a multifaceted approach that combines regulatory frameworks, technological advancements, industry cooperation, and user awareness. By fostering international collaboration, promoting security best practices, and investing in emerging technologies, the global community can build a resilient IoT security infrastructure that safeguards digital assets, protects privacy, and ensures a secure and trustworthy connected future.

Summary

THE IMPORTANCE OF A PROACTIVE APPROACH TO IOT SECURITY

The rapid expansion of the IoT has revolutionized industries by enhancing connectivity, automation, and efficiency. However, this growing interconnectivity also introduces significant cybersecurity risks that threaten data integrity, privacy, and operational continuity. A proactive approach to IoT security is essential to prevent, mitigate, and respond to evolving cyberthreats effectively. Unlike reactive security measures that address vulnerabilities only after an attack has occurred, a proactive strategy focuses on anticipating threats, implementing preventive controls, and continuously monitoring security postures. Given the increasing sophistication of cyber adversaries, including nation-state actors, cybercriminal organizations, and opportunistic hackers, organizations must adopt a forward-thinking security framework that minimizes risks before they escalate into full-scale breaches. This involves integrating security by design, robust authentication mechanisms, real-time threat detection, and adaptive response strategies to create a resilient IoT ecosystem capable of withstanding emerging cybersecurity challenges.

One of the fundamental aspects of a proactive IoT security approach is security by design, which entails embedding security measures into devices, networks, and applications from the initial stages of development. This means manufacturers and developers must prioritize secure coding practices, vulnerability testing, and encryption protocols before IoT devices are deployed. Secure firmware and software development lifecycles should incorporate threat modeling, penetration testing, and regular security updates to prevent common vulnerabilities such as buffer overflows, hardcoded credentials, and insecure APIs. By enforcing rigorous security standards from the outset, organizations can significantly reduce the attack surface and minimize the likelihood of cyber intrusions. Additionally, a ZTA is a crucial component of a proactive security strategy, ensuring that all devices, users, and applications must be continuously verified before accessing resources. The zero-trust model eliminates the assumption of implicit trust and instead enforces strict access controls, MFA, and least privilege principles to prevent unauthorized access and lateral movement within IoT networks.

Another essential component of proactive IoT security is real-time threat intelligence and monitoring. Traditional security measures that rely on static rules and signature-based detection are no longer sufficient to combat APTs and zero-day vulnerabilities. Instead, organizations should deploy behavioral analytics, ML, and AI-driven security solutions to detect anomalies in IoT traffic patterns, device behaviors, and system activities. These technologies enable early threat detection by identifying deviations from baseline behaviors, flagging potential cyberthreats before they can cause significant damage. Advanced SIEM systems, combined with XDR platforms, can aggregate and analyze security logs, providing organizations with actionable insights to prevent breaches in real time. Furthermore, organizations should leverage threat intelligence sharing through cybersecurity alliances, government agencies, and industry consortia to stay ahead of emerging attack vectors and evolving threat landscapes.

Strong authentication and access control mechanisms are also pivotal in preventing unauthorized access to IoT devices and networks. Many IoT breaches occur due to weak passwords, default credentials, and inadequate authentication mechanisms that make it easy for attackers to exploit vulnerabilities. Implementing MFA, biometric verification, and certificate-based authentication can significantly enhance identity verification and reduce the risk of credential-based attacks such as brute-force attacks and credential stuffing. Organizations must also enforce RBAC and attribute-based access control (ABAC) to restrict device privileges based on user roles and contextual factors, ensuring that only authorized personnel can access critical systems and sensitive data. Another vital aspect of proactive IoT security is secure network architecture and segmentation. Many IoT environments suffer from flat network structures that allow attackers to move laterally across connected devices once a single-entry point is compromised. To counter this risk, organizations should implement network segmentation, micro-segmentation, and SDP to isolate IoT devices, OT, and enterprise networks from one another. By enforcing strict segmentation policies, organizations can limit the impact of potential breaches, preventing attackers from accessing critical assets and spreading malware across the entire infrastructure. Additionally, end-to-end encryption protocols such as TLS, Secure/Multipurpose Internet Mail Extensions (S/MIME), and IPsec should be employed to protect data in transit and at rest, ensuring that sensitive information remains confidential and tamper-proof.

Regular firmware updates, patch management, and vulnerability assessments are also crucial in maintaining a proactive IoT security posture. Many IoT devices operate on outdated firmware with known vulnerabilities that attackers can exploit to gain unauthorized access. Organizations must implement automated patch management solutions and enforce secure OTA updates to ensure that IoT devices receive timely security patches and feature enhancements. Additionally, regular vulnerability assessments, penetration testing, and red teaming exercises should be conducted to identify and remediate security gaps before cybercriminals can exploit them. Security researchers and ethical hackers play a vital role in proactive security efforts by identifying zero-day vulnerabilities, reporting them through responsible disclosure programs, and helping organizations fortify their IoT defenses.

Incident response and resilience planning are also integral components of a proactive IoT security strategy. Organizations must prepare for potential cyber incidents by developing comprehensive incident response plans (IRPs), disaster recovery plans (DRPs), and business continuity plans (BCPs). These plans should include predefined response protocols, escalation procedures, and communication frameworks to ensure a swift and coordinated response to security breaches. Establishing cybersecurity drills, tabletop exercises, and red team/blue team simulations can help organizations test their incident response capabilities and refine their mitigation strategies. Furthermore, cyber resilience frameworks such as the NIST Cybersecurity Framework and the Cybersecurity Maturity Model Certification (CMMC) provide valuable guidelines for organizations to enhance their security posture and minimize operational disruptions in the event of cyberattacks.

The role of regulatory compliance and industry standards cannot be overlooked in a proactive IoT security strategy. Governments and regulatory bodies worldwide are enforcing stricter cybersecurity laws and data protection regulations to ensure that IoT manufacturers and service providers adhere to security best practices. Regulations such as the GDPR, the CCPA, and the IoT Cybersecurity Improvement Act mandate stricter security controls, data privacy measures, and compliance requirements for IoT deployments. Organizations must stay up to date with evolving regulatory landscapes and align their security practices with industry standards such as ISO/IEC 27001, IEC 62443, and the OWASP IoT Top 10 to mitigate legal and financial risks associated with non-compliance.

Finally, collaboration and public–private partnerships are essential in strengthening IoT security on a global scale. Governments, cybersecurity researchers, academia, and private sector stakeholders must work together to establish cybersecurity best practices, share threat intelligence, and develop innovative security solutions. Cybersecurity alliances such as the Cyber Threat Alliance (CTA), the Forum of Incident Response and Security Teams (FIRST), and the IIC facilitate information sharing and coordinated responses to global cyberthreats. By fostering a culture of cybersecurity awareness, education, and cross-sector collaboration, the global community can enhance collective defense capabilities against IoT-related cyber risks. Organizations must move beyond traditional reactive security measures and embrace security by design, continuous threat monitoring, robust authentication, network segmentation, and regulatory compliance to safeguard their IoT ecosystems. As cyberthreats continue to evolve, the ability to anticipate, prevent, and respond to security incidents effectively will determine the resilience of IoT infrastructures. Through innovation, collaboration, and strategic security investments, organizations can build a secure, trustworthy, and sustainable IoT environment that protects data integrity, privacy, and operational stability in the digital age.

FINAL THOUGHTS ON THE EVOLVING IoT THREAT LANDSCAPE

The IoT has revolutionized connectivity by seamlessly integrating devices into everyday life, but its rapid expansion has also exposed an evolving and increasingly complex threat landscape. As billions of devices—from smart home systems and wearable health monitors to industrial sensors and autonomous vehicles—become interconnected, they create an immense attack surface for cyberthreats. One of the most concerning aspects is that many IoT devices are designed with limited computing resources and minimal security features, making them highly susceptible to exploitation. Attackers exploit these vulnerabilities to conduct a range of malicious activities, such as launching DDoS attacks, data breaches, device hijacking, and even leveraging compromised devices as entry points into larger networks. Furthermore, the diversity of IoT device manufacturers often leads to inconsistent security standards and infrequent firmware updates, compounding the risk. As threat actors evolve, so too do their tactics—ranging from traditional malware and phishing schemes to more advanced threats like botnets (e.g., Mirai), ransomware targeting critical infrastructure, and zero-day exploits aimed at industrial control systems. The integration of IoT with emerging technologies such as AI, 5G, and edge computing, while offering immense potential, also introduces new vulnerabilities, particularly around data integrity, privacy, and real-time decision-making. In sectors such as healthcare and transportation, the consequences of compromised IoT systems could be catastrophic, threatening not just data but human lives. Addressing these threats requires a multifaceted approach, including the development of standardized security protocols, robust encryption mechanisms, real-time anomaly detection systems, and secure-by-design principles embedded in device architecture. Collaborative efforts among governments, industry leaders, and researchers are essential to create global security frameworks and promote threat intelligence sharing. Additionally, user awareness and education play a critical role in ensuring the responsible use and maintenance of IoT devices. As the IoT ecosystem continues to grow, the threat landscape will undoubtedly become more sophisticated, necessitating continuous innovation in cybersecurity strategies. Ultimately, building a resilient IoT environment requires a proactive, layered defense strategy that balances innovation with security, ensuring that the benefits of IoT can be fully realized without compromising safety or trust.

Bibliography

1. A. W. Al-Dabbagh, Y. Li, and T. Chen, An intrusion detection system for cyber-attacks in wireless networked control systems, *IEEE Trans. Circuits Syst. II, Exp. Briefs*, vol. 65, no. 8, pp. 1049–1053, August 2018.
2. P. Amini, M. A. Araghizadeh, and R. Azmi, A survey on botnet: Classification, detection, and defense, *Proc. Int. Electron. Symp. (IES)*, 3, pp. 233–238, September 2015.
3. K. Ashton et al., That Internet of Things' thing, in the real-world things matter more than ideas, *RFID J.*, vol. 22, no. 7, pp. 97–114, 2009.
4. L. Da Xu, W. He, and S. Li, Internet of Things in industries: A survey, *IEEE Trans. Ind. Informat.*, vol. 10, no. 4, pp. 2233–2243, November 2014.
5. S. Khan, A. Gani, A. W. A. Wahab, M. Shiraz, and I. Ahmad, Network forensics: Review, taxonomy, and open challenges, *J. Network Computing Appl.*, vol. 66, pp. 214–235, May 2016.
6. M. Farhoumandi, Q. Zhou, and M. Shahidehpour, A review of machine learning applications in IoT-integrated modern power systems, *Electr. J.*, vol. 34, no. 1, p. 106879, 2021.
7. M. A. Al-Garadi, A. Mohamed, A. K. Al-Ali, X. Du, I. Ali, and M. Guizani, A survey of machine and deep learning methods for Internet of Things (IoT) security, *IEEE Commun. Surv. Tutorials*, vol. 22, no. 3, pp. 1646–1685, 2020, doi: 10.1109/COMST.2020.2988293
8. S. H. Mousavi, M. Khansari, and R. Rahmani, A fully scalable big data framework for Botnet detection based on network traffic analysis, *Inf. Sci. (Ny).*, vol. 512, pp. 629–640, 2020, doi: 10.1016/j.ins.2019.10.018
9. S. Dange and M. Chatterjee, IoT botnet: The largest threat to the IoT network, *Adv. Intell. Syst. Comput.*, vol. 1049, pp. 137–157, September 2020, doi: 10.1007/978-981-15-0132-6_10
10. E. Bertino and N. Islam, Botnets and Internet of Things security, *Computer (Long. Beach. Calif).*, vol. 50, no. 2, pp. 76–79, 2017, doi: 10.1109/MC.2017.62
11. F. A. Mikic, J. C. Burguillo, D. A. Rodríguez, E. Rodríguez, and M. Llamas, T-Bot and Q-Bot: A couple of AIML-based Bots for tutoring courses and evaluating students, *Proc. - Front. Educ. Conf. FIE*, pp. 7–12, 2008, doi: 10.1109/FIE.2008.4720469
12. C.-Y. Wu, T. Ban, S.-M. Cheng, T. Takahashi, and D. Inoue, IoT malware classification based on reinterpreted function-call graphs, *Comput. Secur.*, vol. 125, p. 103060, 2023, doi: 10.1016/j.cose.2022.103060

13. H. Alrubayyi, M. S. Alshareef, Z. Nadeem, A. M. Abdelmoniem, and M. Jaber, Security threats and promising solutions arising from the intersection of AI and IoT: A study of IoMT and IoET applications, *Future Internet*, vol. 16, no. 3, p. 85, February 29, 2024. doi: 10.3390/fi16030085

14. O. Habibi, M. Chemmakha, and M. Lazaar, Imbalanced tabular data modelization using CTGAN and machine learning to improve IoT Botnet attacks detection, *Eng. Appl. Artif. Intell.*, vol. 118, p. 105669, 2023, doi: 10.1016/j.engappai.2022.105669

15. H. S. Galal, Y. B. Mahdy, and M. A. Atiea, Behavior-based features model for malware detection, *J. Comput. Virol. Hacking Tech.*, vol. 12, no. 2, pp. 59–67, 2016, doi: 10.1007/s11416-015-0244-0

16. M. S. Abbasi, H. Al-Sahaf, M. Mansoori, and I. Welch, Behavior-based ransomware classification: A particle swarm optimization wrapper-based approach for feature selection, *Appl. Soft Comput.*, vol. 121, p. 108744, 2022, doi: 10.1016/j.asoc.2022.108744

17. N. Koroniotis, N. Moustafa, E. Sitnikova, and B. Turnbull, Towards the development of realistic botnet dataset in the Internet of Things for network forensic analytics: Bot-IoT dataset, *Futur. Gener. Comput. Syst.*, vol. 100, pp. 779–796, 2019, doi: 10.1016/j.future.2019.05.041

18. H. Hamid et al., IoT-based botnet attacks systematic mapping study of literature, *Scientometrics*, vol. 126, no. 4, pp. 2759–2800, 2021.

19. U. M. Khaire and R. Dhanalakshmi, Stability of feature selection algorithm: A review, *J. King Saud Univ. - Comput. Inf. Sci.*, vol. 34, no. 4, pp. 1060–1073, 2022, doi: 10.1016/j.jksuci.2019.06.012

20. H. Khazane, M. Ridouani, F. Salahdine, and N. Kaabouch, A holistic review of machine learning adversarial attacks in IoT networks, *Future Internet*, vol. 16, no. 1, p. 32, January 19, 2024. doi: 10.3390/fi16010032

21. A. Pozzebon, Edge and fog computing for the Internet of Things, *Future Internet*, vol. 16, no. 3, p. 101, March 16, 2024. doi: 10.3390/fi16030101

22. C. Wei, G. Xie, and Z. Diao, A lightweight deep learning framework for botnet detecting at the IoT edge, *Comput. Secur.*, vol. 129, p. 103195, June 2023, doi: 10.1016/j.cose.2023.103195

23. M. K. Hooshmand, M. D. Huchaiah, A. R. Alzighaibi, H. Hashim, E.-S. Atlam, and I. Gad, Robust network anomaly detection using ensemble learning approach and explainable artificial intelligence (XAI), *Alexandria Eng. J.*, vol. 94, pp. 120–130, May 2024, doi: 10.1016/j.aej.2024.03.041

24. M. Elattar, A. Younes, I. Gad, and I. Elkabani, Explainable AI model for PDFMal detection based on gradient boosting model, *Neural Comput. Appl.*, vol. 36, no. 34, pp. 21607–21622, September 2024, doi: 10.1007/s00521-024-10314-y

25. T. A. Al-Amiedy, M. Anbar, B. Belaton, A. A. Bahashwan, I. H. Hasbullah, M. A. Aladaileh, and G. A. Mukhaini, A systematic literature review on attacks defense mechanisms in RPL-based 6LoWPAN of Internet of Things, *Internet Things*, vol. 22, p. 100741, July 2023, doi: 10.1016/j.iot.2023.100741

26. S. D. A. Rihan, M. Anbar, and B. A. Alabsi, Approach for detecting attacks on IoT networks based on ensemble feature selection and deep learning models, *Sensors*, vol. 23, no. 17, p. 7342, August 2023, doi: 10.3390/s23177342

27. K. Shinan, K. Alsubhi, A. Alzahrani et al. Machine learning-based botnet detection in software-defined network: A systematic review, *Symmetry*, vol. 13, no. 5, p. 866, 2021.

Index

Pages in *italics* refer to figures and pages in **bold** refer to tables.

Access Control Lists (ACLs), 90, 130
actuators, 2, 8, 21, 108, 138, 140
adaptive defenses, 182
Address Space Layout Randomization
    (ASLR), 38–39
Advanced Encryption Standard (AES),
    3, 23, 32, 127
  AES-128, 26–27
  AES-256, 139, 148, 149, 196
Advanced Message Queuing Protocol
    (AMQP), 29
antivirus software, 49, 51, 58, 61, 79,
    83, 93
application and API security, 71–72
application layer, 24–25
Application Programming Interface
    (API), 25, 71–72, 88, 104,
    122, 140, 187
Artificial Intelligence (AI), 19, 135, 166,
    171, 187
  and cybersecurity, 68, 73–74, 150,
    168, 170, 172, 174, 180–184,
    199
  and ethical practices, 163, 181
  and evasion tactics, 84–85
  and industry standards and
    certifications, 156
  and IoT botnets, 90–91, 95, 100,
    119–120, 166, 174–178
  and threat intelligence, 67–68, 70,
    96, 178
  and user education, 153; *see
    also* Explainable Artificial
    Intelligence (XAI)
Asia-Pacific Economic Cooperation
    (APEC), 167, 169

attack chain disruption, 184
Attribute-based Access Control
    (ABAC), 201
Augmented Reality/Virtual Reality (AR/
    VR), 173–174
authentication, authorization and
    encryption mechanisms,
    126–128, 148–149
automated threat hunting, 181–182

behavioral analysis, 65, 73–74, 85,
    90, 118, 132, 135, 174, 180,
    182–184
blockchain technology, 90–91, 128,
    168, 170–171, 179–180,
    194–197, 199
Bluetooth, 1–2, 23, 27
Bluetooth Low Energy (BLE), 7–8, 27,
    155
bootkits, 48, 85
Bothunter, 101, **110**
botnet anatomy, 47–49, *48*
botnet attacks, recent, 96–99, **97**
Botnets-as-a-Service (BaaS), 18
botnet types, **55**
Bro, 101, **103**
brute force attacks, 25, 40, 47, 79, 81,
    92, 96, 128, 201
buffer overflows, 37, 39, 77, 138, 140,
    147, 149, 200
Business Continuity Plans (BCPs), 202

California Consumer Privacy Act
    (CCPA), 9–10, 155, 160, 162,
    202
Chirp Spectrum (CSS), 27

Cisco, **103**, 165
Cloud Access Security Broker (CASB), 192–194
cloud-based botnets, 54
cloud computing, 2, 2, 4, 54, 57, 80, 188
command-and-control (C&C) infrastructure, 59, 59–60, 113, 175
    mitigation of threats, 64–76, 150
    types of, 62–64
command-and-control (C&C) servers, 47–49, 52–53, 59, 87, 113
confidentiality, 3, 26, 31, 69, 122, 126, 128, 196
    loss of, 21, 25, 61, 81, 135; *see also* data protection and privacy; data theft
Constrained Application Protocol (CoAP), 1, 4, 7, 26, 29, 137–138, 141, 161, 197
continuous authentication, 169, 190, 193
Control Objectives for Information and Related Technologies (COBIT), 155
credential stuffing, 55, 58, 99, 139, 152, 201
Cross-Site Scripting (XSS), 25, 71, 138
cryptojacking, 54, **55**, 57–58, 86, 98, 152, 165
cyberattacks, 6, 13, 59, 70, 121, 130, 145, 163, 165
    and blockchain technology, 194–195
    future, 169, 172–173, 177–180
    phases of, 60–61
cybercriminals, 18, 68, 70, 73, 77–78, 82, 135–136
    and botnets, 47, 49, 51, 53, 87, 98, 177
    investigation of, 134
    raising awareness of, 17, 134, 152
Cyber Resilience Act, 169
Cybersecurity and Infrastructure Security Agency (CISA), 164, 166
Cybersecurity Maturity Model Certification (CMMC), 202
Cyber Threat Alliance (CTA), 167, 202

Dark Nexus botnet, **16**, 50, **97**
Data Execution Prevention (DEP), 39

Datagram Transport Layers (DTLs), 3
Datagram Transport Layer Security (DTLS), 29–30, 138, 141, 149, 197
data management, 3–4, 8–9, 13, 19, 146
data protection and privacy, 10, 41–44, 115, 141, 143–144, 146, 153, 172, 183–184, 202
data theft, 16, 35–36, 51–54, **55**, 57, 59, 81, **97**, 126
deception technology, 186–188
Deep Packet Inspection (DPI), 66, 68, 90, 96, **103**
Denial of Service (DoS) attacks, 6, 23, 25, 31–36, 55, 71, 102–103, 141
device anomaly detection, 184
device-to-cloud (D2C) communication, 138
device-to-device (D2D) communication, 138
Diffie-Hellman key exchange, 197
Directed Acyclic Graph (DAG), 28
Disaster Recovery Plans (DRPs), 202
Discontinuous Reception (eDRX), 30
Distributed Denial of Service (DDOS) attacks, 6, 14, 72, 172, 178, 203
    and AI, 176
    and blockchain technology, 195–196
    and IOT botnets, **16**, 17, 47–56, 59, 87–88, 93–95, **97**
DNS over HTTPS (DoH), 73, **114**, 198
domain fronting, 64, 84
Domain Generation Algorithms (DGAs), 62, 94, 113, **114**, 115
Domain Name System (DNS) security, 72–73
drive-by downloads, 50, 77, 80–81, 98
Dynamic Application Security Testing (DAST), 71, 140
Dynamic Link Libraries (DLLs), 83

edge computing, 3–4, 7–9, 11, 13, 146, 172, 177, 203
Emotet botnet, **16**
end-of-life (EOL) management, 44, 126, 144–145, 157
Endpoint Detection and Response (EDR), 67, 70, 74, 85, 98, 132, 184–187

endpoint protection, 69–71, 85
Endpoint Protection Platforms, 70, 168
endpoint telemetry, 184–185
energy efficiency, 4–5, 7–8, 13, 26–27,
    135, 170, 197
End-to-end Encryption (E2EE), 14, 32,
    121, 127, 149, 198, 201
Espoo finland botnet, 16
ethical hacking, 148, 155, 202
ethical practices, 9–10, 12, 43, 82, 156,
    158, 162–164, 170, 181, 187
European Data Protection Board
    (EDPB), 164
European Telecommunications
    Standard Institute (ETSI), 137,
    154, 159–160
European Union Agency for
    Cybersecurity (ENISA), 162,
    165
European Union's Cybersecurity Act,
    90, 162
European Union's Network and
    Information Systems (NIS)
    Directive, 163
evasion tactics, 61, 83–86, 93, 97, 114,
    175
Explainable Artificial Intelligence (XAI),
    115–117, 117

fast-flux-based detection, 111, 150
fast-flux domains, 50, 53, 113, 114
fast-flux networks, 48, 63
Federal Trade Commission (FTC), 164
federated learning, 181, 184
Firewall-as-a-Service (FWaaS), 192–194
firewalls, 33, 58, 71–73, 79, 90, 96,
    122, 130, 139, 191
firmware and software, 32, 37, 82, 85,
    150, 157
    updates, 125–126
    vulnerabilities of, 36–39, 44, 77–78,
        80, 98, 151

General Data Protection Regulation
    (GDPR), 10, 69, 75, 155, 162,
    180, 185, 198, 202
Global Cyber Alliance (GCA), 167
Global Forum on Cyber Expertise
    (GFCE), 165, 169
Governance, Risk, and Compliance
    (GRC), 75
Graphical Convolutional Neural
    Network (GCNN), 118
G20 Digital Economy Task Force, 164

Hajime botnet, 91–93, 97, 99
Hardware Security Modules (HSMs),
    122, 127, 139, 148, 170
Health Insurance Portability and
    Accountability Act (HIPAA),
    69, 141, 146, 155, 180, 185
hidden channels, 66
Hidden Markov Model (HMM), 107
homomorphic encryption, 128,
    197–198
honeypots and honeynets, 53, 90, 96,
    109, 114, 188
hybrid botnets, 53

Improved Deep Belief Network (IDBN),
    118
incident response and recovery,
    132–134
incident response plans (IRPs), 86,
    132–133, 151, 179, 202
Incident Response Team (IRT), 132
Indicators of Compromise (IOC), 67,
    90, 183, 185, 191
industry standards and certifications,
    see regulatory compliance and
    standards
infection vectors, 76, 92, 98
    common types of, 76–78
    impacts of, 81–82
Information Sharing and Analysis
    Centers (ISACs), 67, 191
Information Technology Infrastructure
    Library (ITIL), 155
insider threat detection, 184
Institute of Electrical and Electronic
    Engineers (IEEE), 159–160, 163, 166
    and IEEE 802.15.4, 23, 26, 28, 160
International IoT Council, 164
International Organization for
    Standardization (ISO), 159,
    166
international standards and
    frameworks, 159–161
International Telecommunication Union
    (ITU), 159–160, 163, 165
Internet Engineering Task Force (IETF),
    111, 161
Internet of Things Architecture (IoT-A),
    166
Internet of Things Cybersecurity
    Improvement Act, the, 45, 91,
    169, 202
Internet of Things (IoT) botnets, 15,
    15–19, 16, 51–52, 55

challenges in detecting, 119–120
findings of case studies on, 99–100;
    see also Dark Nexus botnet;
    Hajime botnet; Mirai botnet;
    Mozi botnet; Murdoc botnet;
    Phorpiex botnet; Reaper
    botnet; Torii botnet
Internet of Things (IoT), the
    challenges associated with, 3–13, 5,
        19–20
    components and architecture of,
        1–3, 21–25, 22
    definition of, 1
    device security, 121–125, 149
    protocols, 25–30
    security issues in, 13–14, 30–36,
        39–46; see also firmware and
        software
Internet of Things Security Foundation
    (IOTSF), 166
Internet Protocol Security (IPSEC), 197,
    201
Internet Society (ISOC), 166
Intrusion Detection Conditional
    Variational Autoencoder
    (ID-CVAE), 105–106
Intrusion Detection Systems (IDSs), 3,
    14, 34, 49, 52, 100, 168, 178
    anomaly and behaviour-based, 36,
        104, *104*, **110**, 150
    DNS-based, 111–115, *112*, **114**
    and explainable AI (XAI)
        approaches, 115–117, **117**
    programmed behavior-based,
        107–110
    self-intelligence-based, 105–107
    signature-based, 101–103, *102*, **103**
IPv6 over Low-power Wireless Personal
    Area Networks (6LoWPAN),
    23, 28, 102, **110**

Jha, Paras, 87

Kalis, 106–107
Kaspersky, 165
Kerberos authentication framework,
    197
Krebs, Brian, 88
KV botnet, **16**

lateral movement detection, 188
Least Privilege Access, 91, 190

Lightweight M2M (LwM2M), 29–30
Local Interpretable Model-agnostic
    Explanations (LIME),
    115–116, **117**
Long Range Wide Area Network
    (LoRaWAN), 2, 8, 11, 23, 27,
    155
Long-Term Evolution (LTE), 6–7, 11, 30
Low-Power Wide-Area Network
    (LPWAN), 30, 160
Lua-based script, 94, 96

Machine Learning (ML), 4, 14, 19
    and anomaly detection, 105–106,
        110, 114
    and cybersecurity, 65, 68, 70, 74,
        108, 122, 150, 168, 180–184,
        190, 199
    and evasion tactics, 84–85
    and IoT botnets, 90, 96, 99–100,
        114, 118, 166, 174–178
malicious attachments, 50, 55, 56,
    77–79, 98, 151, 181
Man-in-the-Middle (MITM), 23, 73,
    78, 145, 197
Message Queuing Telemetry Transport
    (MQTT), 1, 7, *26*, 28–29, 137,
    155
metamorphic malware, 61, 84
micro-segmentation, 130, 151, 169,
    189–190, 201
middleware layer, 23–24
Mirai botnet, 15, **16**, 25, 40–41, **97**
    case study of, 87–91, *89*, 98–99
    detection of, **103, 110, 114, 117,**
        167
mobile botnets, 51
Mozi botnet, 51, **55, 97, 103**
Multi-factor Authentication, 31, 40, 44,
    121, 149, 151, 201
Murdoc botnet, 97–99

Narrowband Internet of Things
    (NB-IoT), 11, 30
National Institute of Standards and
    Technology (NIST), 35, 75,
    161, 163, 202
Near-Field Communication (NFC),
    27–28
Netscout botnet, **16**
network/adoptive layer, 21, 23–24, 27,
    197

network segmentation, 14, 19, 33, 79,
85, 122, 139, 150, 201
and botnet threats, 90, 95–96, 98
and isolation, 129–131; *see also*
micro-segmentation
Network Traffic Analysis (NTA),
68–69, 117–118
Norman, Dalton, 87
NotPetya malware, 76

Open Connectivity Foundation (OCF),
161, 163
Open Mobile Alliance (OMA), 29
Open-Source Intelligence (OSINT), 190
Open Worldwide Application Security
Project (OWASP) IoT Top Ten,
72, 138, 153–154, 202
Organization for Economic
Cooperation and Development
(OECD), 166
over-the-air (OTA) updates, 32, 37, 42,
128, 139–140, 143, 148, 150,
201

Palo Alto Networks, 165
patch management, 14, 80, 88, 96,
125–126, 148–150, 201
Payment Card Industry Data Security
Standard (PCI DSS), 69, 72,
129, 137, 155
PC-based botnets, 49–50
peer-to-peer botnets, 52–53, 92–93
penetration testing, 45, 86, 123–124,
139–140, 148, 151, 179, 200,
202
perception layer, 21–23
persistence tactics, 48–49, 60–61,
83–86, 94, 99–100
Personally Identifiable Information
(PII), 129, 145
phishing, 47, 50–51, 55, 60, 63, 76–78,
81, 176
mitigation of, 67, 69, 79, 82, 149,
151–153, 178, 181, 191, 193
raising user awareness of, 53, 57–58,
179
Phorpiex botnet, 98
polymorphic malware, 74, 84, 175–176,
180
Post-quantum Cryptography (PQC), 91,
128, 169, 198
Power Saving Mode (PSM), 30

Process for Attack Simulation and
Threat Analysis (PASTA), 147,
155
Product Security and
Telecommunications
Infrastructure (PSTI) Act, 162
propagation of malware, 49, 76, 92,
94–96, 175
impacts of, 81–83
techniques, 78–80, 96
public-key cryptography, 196
Public Key Cryptography Standards
(PKCS), 139
Public Key Infrastructure (PKI), 41, 127
Public-Private Partnerships (PPPs), 9,
11, 167, 169, 171, 202

quantum computing, 91, 128, 168–170,
181, 184, 197–199
quantum key distribution (QKD), 169

ransomware, 6, 17, 59, 65, 78, 81–82,
93, 172
distribution of, 82, 95, 98–99, 111
mitigation of, 178–181, 184, 191,
203
Ransomware-as-a-Service (RaaS), 98
Reaper botnet, 93–96, 99
regulatory compliance and standards,
74–76, 135, 146, 149,
154–157, 180; *see also*
international standards and
frameworks
Remote Administration Tools (RATs), 83
Remote Desktop Protocol (RDP), 61,
78, 81
removable media, 77, 79
replay attacks, 23, 31
Role-based Access Control (RBAC), 31,
41, 121, 139, 148, 201
rootkits, 33, 48, 83, 85, 93, 108
Routing Protocol for Low-Power and
Lossy Networks (RPL), 28,
103, 108, **110**
RSA encryption, 3, 139, 148, 196

Secure Access Service Edge (SASE), 189,
192–194
Secure and Trustworthy Cyberspace
(SaTC), 166
Secure/Multipurpose Internet Mail
Extensions (S/MIME), 197, 201

Secure Software Development Life
    Cycle (SDLC), 137–138
challenges of, 145–146
deployment phase of, 142–143, 179
implementation phase of, 138–139
maintenance and monitoring phase
    of, 143–144
testing phase of, 140–142; *see also*
    end-of-life (EOL) management
Secure Web Gateway (SWG), 192–194
security audits, 43, 45, 123–124, 135,
    151
security-by-design, 86, 128, 146–151,
    157, 200, 202
Security Information and Event
    Management (SIEM), 67, 74,
    132, 185, 187, 189, 201
Security Operations Center (SOC), 75,
    116, 154
sensors, 1–2, 7–8, 21, 27, 30, 42, 138,
    140–141
industrial, 1, 14, 41, 51, 203
Service-level Agreements (SLAs), 194
server-based botnets, 50–51
SHapley Additive exPlanations (SHAP),
    115–116, **117**
sinkholing, 53, 91, 95
Small and Medium-sized Enterprises
    (SMEs), 9, 156
smart homes, 2, 6, 11, 40, 121, 172
Snort, 101, **103**
social engineering tactics, 77–79, 173,
    176
raising awareness of, 82, 149, 152,
    179
Software-Defined Networking (SDN),
    7, 91, 109, 130–131
SolarWinds attack, 78, 80
spam campaigns, 47, 50–51, **55**, 56–57,
    59, 65, 86, 165
spoofing, 23, 72
Spoofing, Tampering, Repudiation,
    Information Disclosure,
    Denial of Service, Elevation of
    Privilege (STRIDE), 147, 149
SQL injection, 25, 77, 140, 149
stealthy communication, 64–65
steganography, 66, 84, 175
Stuxnet worm, 77, 79

supply chain security, 78, 80, 95, 168,
    173–174, 195, 199
Suricata, 102, **103**

Temporal Convolution Networks
    (TCNs), 118
threat intelligence, 66–68, 85, 90, 95,
    100, 125, 178–179, 188, 201
Threat Intelligence Platforms (TIPs), 96,
    150, 179, 185, 187, 190–192
threat modeling, 71, 137, 147, 149, 200
Torii botnet, 99, **110**
traffic filtering, 90, 96, 150
Trusted Platform Modules (TPMs), 33,
    41, 45, 122, 127, 139, 149, 170

Uniform Resource Identifier (URI), 29,
    111
Universal Plug and Play (UPnP), 33, 96
user behavior analytics (UEBA), 74
user education, 41, 51, 55, 57, 82, 131,
    149, 151–153, 170, 179, 199

Virtual LANs (VLANs), 129, 139, 150
Virtual Private Networks (VPNs), **16**,
    49, 70, 78, 96, 142, 193, 197

WannaCry ransomware, 76, 79, 81
Waste Electrical and Electronic
    Equipment (WEEE), 144
wearable technology, 6–7, 15, 203
White, Josiah, 87
Wi-Fi, 2, 11, 23, 26, 78
Windows Management Instrumentation
    (WMI), 83
World Economic Forum's (WEF) Centre
    for Cybersecurity, 169
World Wide Web Consortium (W3C),
    161

zero-day attacks, 67, 73, 77, 186
Zero-knowledge Proofs (ZKPs), 197
Zero Trust Architecture (ZTA), 81, 91,
    131, 151, 168–170, 188–190
zero-trust models, 81, 151, 169,
    199–200
Zero Trust Network Access (ZTNA),
    189, 192–194
Zigbee, 2, 4, 8, 23, 26, 155, 160

.

For Product Safety Concerns and Information please contact our EU
representative GPSR@taylorandfrancis.com
Taylor & Francis Verlag GmbH, Kaufingerstraße 24, 80331 München, Germany

www.ingramcontent.com/pod-product-compliance
Lightning Source LLC
Chambersburg PA
CBHW060551220326
41598CB00024B/3072